STUDIES IN THEOLOGY

STUDIES IN THEOLOGY

LECTURES DELIVERED IN
CHICAGO THEOLOGICAL
SEMINARY: BY THE REV.
JAMES DENNEY, D.D.

BAKER BOOK HOUSE
Grand Rapids, Michigan

*Reprinted from the 1895 edition
published by Hodder and Stoughton.
Paperback edition issued 1976
by Baker Book House
ISBN: 0-8010-2850-7*

*Introduction by David Wells
copyrighted 1976 by
Baker Book House Company*

PHOTOLITHOPRINTED BY CUSHING - MALLOY, INC.
ANN ARBOR, MICHIGAN, UNITED STATES OF AMERICA
1976

INTRODUCTION

James Denney, "supreme alike as scholar, teacher, administrator, and man of God, to whom many owed their souls,"[1] was remarkable for the way in which he reforged the links between thought and practice in the ministry. He was a pastor-theologian who found that elusive blend of simplicity and profundity that characterized Jesus' teaching. In a style that was terse and pungent, he reaffirmed the abiding truth of New Testament faith so memorably that it would be a significant loss to a new generation of evangelical Christians if these studies were not republished.

The difficulty of forging this link between thought and practice must be great because it is so rare. Across our land today are to be found innumerable preachers whose boast it is to be orthodox but whose ministries are infected by a superficiality that, however popular and comforting it may be, is also cheap, worldly, loud, and miserably unedifying. Profound preaching is a scarce commodity today, as scarce, indeed, as profound preachers. And, on the other hand, rare is the contemporary theologian who has not confused scholarly objectivity with personal detachment. Those who believe least and who believe least passionately are theologians.[2] Denney's conquest of both errors—sermons without thought and theology without commitment—single him out as a man

[1] These words appear on a plaque beside the Denney stained-glass window in the chapel of Trinity College, Glasgow.

[2] See, for example, Van A. Harvey, "The Alienated Theologian," *McCormick Quarterly* 23 (1970): 234-65.

whose contribution to our own day might conceivably be more needed than it was even in his.

Denney was born in 1856 in Paisley, Scotland, of parents who were Reformed Presbyterians (or "Cameronians," as they were nicknamed). After his initial schooling, during which his brilliance was already evident, he went to Glasgow University, finally graduating with "double firsts" in classics and philosophy. After an interlude of five years he began his theological training at the Free Church College and then, in 1886, succeeded the eminent Christian apologist A. B. Bruce as minister of East Free Church, Broughty Ferry.[3]

Denney's earlier Presbyterianism, which tended to be rather severe and strict, began to change during the years that followed. Marriage to Mary Brown in 1886 brought him into contact with lively evangelical faith. It was largely through her influence that he began to read Charles Spurgeon, the great London preacher, and there is no mistaking the warmth, evangelistic concern, and spiritual perception that came to characterize his ministry.[4]

[3]Broughty Ferry in the late nineteenth century served as a refuge for the affluent (especially those in the financially rewarding jute business) from the uncongenial atmosphere of Dundee, even then a large industrial city. Shortly after the conclusion of Denney's ministry, in 1913 in fact, Broughty Ferry became an official suburb of Dundee. It is, however, still indiscreet to refer to "Ferry folk" as Dundonians.

[4]Two series of sermons from this period were published, *The Epistles to the Thessalonians* (1892) and *The Second Epistle to the Corinthians* (1894). Glasgow University, in recognition of their academic and spiritual merit, awarded him, at the age of thirty-nine, his first honorary Doctorate of Divinity. These works had been preceded by Denney's critique of Henry Drummond in 1885, entitled *On "Natural Law in the Spiritual World," by a Brother of the Natural Man*, and were followed by *Gospel Questions and Answers* (1896).

The influence of this young pastor soon came to be felt not only outside the confines of his church but also outside the boundaries of Scotland. In May 1894 he delivered at Chicago Theological Seminary a series of lectures that were soon published as *Studies in Theology*. With these studies, W. P. Patterson asserted, "he made a brilliant *debut* in his academic vocation,"[5] and T. H. Walker, his first biographer, judged that "few books have exercised a more potent influence throughout the religious world."[6] Here, J. Laidlaw said, were lectures of "real power" in which the major themes of Christian faith were given "admirable treatment."[7] More recently A. M. Hunter described the volume as "the best short book on Christian Doctrine that I know," and he added that he would not exchange it for the entire works of Barth.[8]

In view of this striking accomplishment, it was no surprise that in 1897 the General Assembly of the Free Church of Scotland appointed him to succeed James Candlish as professor of systematic and pastoral theology at Glasgow College. Among his colleagues were James Orr, whose statements of Christian doctrine have had an enduring effect on American evangelicalism; Thomas Lindsay, the noted historian of the Reformation; and George Adam Smith, exegete and scholar of the Old Testament. Despite his extraordinary theological acumen, however, Denney was not to occupy this chair for long. In 1900, following the vacancy left by Bruce, it was felt that Denney should once again follow his old mentor, and

[5]"Dr. Denney's Theology," *Constructive Quarterly* 7 (1919): 75.

[6]*Principal James Denney, D.D.: A Memoir and a Tribute* (New York: Marshall, 1918), p. 59.

[7]"Denney's *Studies in Theology*," *Church Quarterly Review* 40, no. 93 (1895): 479.

[8]"The Theological Wisdom of James Denney," *The Expository Times* 60 (1949): 240.

so he became professor of New Testament language and literature.

For the next fifteen years Denney taught and lived in the world that is disclosed by Scripture, but especially as it centers upon the person and work of Christ. To trace the lines of Biblical teaching, to lay bare its principles and axioms, and to apply its sharp demands became his chief occupation and joy. His last two years, however, took him away from the work he loved so well to assume larger responsibilities in the church and to become principal of the college. It was in this capacity that he died in 1917.[9] At the time of his death he was, H. R. Mackintosh said, "at the summit of his power," and, Mackintosh added sadly, "evangelical religion throughout English-speaking lands has suffered a loss greater, we may say with sober truth, than would have been inflicted by the withdrawal of any other mind."[10]

[9]During the years in which Denney was professor and principal, the following books were published: *St. Paul's Epistle to the Romans* (1902); *The Death of Christ: Its Place and Interpretation in the New Testament* (1902), which was subsequently revised and edited by R. V. G. Tasker for Inter-Varsity Press, 1951; *The Atonement and the Modern Mind* (1903); *Jesus and the Gospel* (1908); *The Church and the Kingdom* (1910); *Factors of Faith in Immortality* (1911); *The Way Everlasting* (1911); *War and the Fear of God* (1916); and *The Christian Doctrine of Reconciliation* (1917), which was republished in 1959 by James Clarke. In addition to these works were essays that he contributed to several volumes; substantial contributions to such works as Hastings, *A Dictionary of the Bible;* journal articles that appeared mostly in *The Expositor* and in *The Union Magazine*, which he jointly edited with Orr; and newspaper articles, almost all of which were published by *The British Weekly.* Two volumes of letters were published posthumously, entitled *Letters of Principal James Denney to W. Robertson Nicoll, 1893-1917* (1920) and *Letters of Principal James Denney to His Family and Friends* (1921).

[10]"Principal James Denney as a Theologian," *The Expository Times* 28 (1917): 488.

The details of the invitation to lecture at Chicago Theological Seminary in 1894 are somewhat obscure. Denney himself had no idea that he was to be awarded an honorary doctorate, for he wrote to his friend J. P. Struthers that "the first intimation I had of it was in a crowded church in Chicago, where at the annual meeting of the supporters of the seminary the President [Franklin Woodbury Fisk] announced from the platform that the directors. at the request of the Faculty (Senatus), had conferred this degree on me."[11] From the surviving archival records it is not clear whether this was the reason for the invitation or the result. All that can be ascertained is that the seminary was without a theology teacher for the academic year of 1894.[12] At the very least, then, Denney provided a badly needed theology course in the seminary, which at that time had a student body of 175. And judging from the few comments he made during this time, the seminary made the most of his visit.[13]

On the eve of his departure to Chicago, Denney disclaimed any intention of producing an imposing system

[11]James Moffatt, ed., *Letters of Principal James Denney to His Family and Friends* (London: Hodder and Stoughton, 1922), p. 58.

[12]In October 1893 the faculty secretary entered into a correspondence with Professor Foster of California about the possibility of teaching some courses in the early months of 1894. See Publicity Scrapbooks: Correspondence (archives, Chicago Theological Seminary).

[13]To J. P. Struthers he wrote humorously: "Here we have gone on with existence with a vengeance. We arrived in Chicago on a Tuesday, and I started to lecture on the Wednesday, and lectured every lawful day except Saturday and Sabbath. The way they go at it here, morning, noon, and night, without so much as a comma between, is too much for a lazy man like me. It makes me long for lotus-eating or any human way of improving time. They don't improve it here at all, but spend it with terrific diligence." *Letters to Family and Friends*, p. 55.

of theology. To William Robertson Nicoll, his intimate
friend, he wrote: "What I mean to do, though the subject is systematic theology, is not anything very systematic: rather a review of the chief *loci communes theo-
logici* with reference to current ideas, especially those of
Ritschl, and also ideas not so current as they should be,
especially those of the Epistles of the New Testament."[14]
His refusal to spin a fine, interconnected web of theological truths offered potential critics an opening. Not
surprisingly, one of the first reviewers of the published
lectures complained that the difficulty with them "is that
they contain no root idea, and therefore have no vital
unity. They do not suggest a system of theology;
they only contain a number of theological thoughts of
varying degrees of excellence and suggestiveness."[15] That
may be, but Denney's respect for the Bible was sufficient to preclude his imposing an alien system on its
teaching. What system our Christian thoughts derive
must reflect the contours and accents of the Bible itself;
no man is at liberty to arrange its truths as he pleases.

Theology, according to Denney, is the systematic
organization of our knowledge of God and His world.
It thus includes both vertical and horizontal dimensions,
but the latter arises from the former, and the former
derives from Jesus Christ. The unique relationship of the
Son to the Father issued in a unique knowledge; it is
this knowledge that is the birthright of the Son's follow-
ers. It is with this knowledge that theology is concerned,
and to think of theology as anything other than this is
to think of it in a manner that is less than Christian.

The relationship of Christ to Christianity, then, is

[14]*Letters of Principal James Denney to W. Robertson Nicoll,
1893-1917* (London: Hodder and Stoughton, 1920), p. 3.
[15]"Review of *Studies in Theology*," *Outlook* 52 (1895): 511.

different from that of other religious leaders to the faiths they initiated. To their disciples, they left behind ideals and teachings; to His, He gives not merely ideals and teachings but also Himself. They are dead; He lives forever, both within and also beyond the confines of the spatio-temporal world. The New Testament, therefore, disallows any merely religious appreciation of Jesus. He came to do a work, to be the climax of the ages, and to occupy the throne of God's glory, as no other could do. He is the Lord or He is nothing, and Scripture will accept no patronizing compliments from those who comfort themselves on middle territory by speaking of Him as a great religious leader. If He is great, it is because He is whom He claimed to be; if He lied or was deceived, He is neither great nor a religious leader worthy of a following.

That He was unique and set apart from other men, even those with the loftiest visions and highest ideals, was clear from the start. He taught with authority, and what He taught arose from His unique self-consciousness. As Son of God, He shared a unity of being, will, and purpose with the Father; as Son of Man, He made common cause with us in our sin and shame. It is these unique elements of identity that joined together in His self-consciousness. Thus, He constantly called attention to Himself, though He was the humblest of men. He identified the universal interests of religion with Himself, even though He was meek and lowly in heart. To this Nazarene carpenter there was nothing incongruous either with picturing Himself on the throne of glory or with ministering to those broken in body or spirit. In Him history reaches its climax and grace its termination.

And it is the unimpaired consciousness of this that reaches serene maturity by the time of the Cross.

It is impossible to explain the figure of Christ, to make sense out of this element of transcendence, unless His preexistence is assumed. This toiling and ill-received carpenter was none other than the second Person of the Godhead who forfeited His glory for love's descent to time and death. Because He was Son of God His Cross-work is effective, being universal in scope, perfect in completion, and eternal in duration.

The birth, death, and resurrection of Christ was, of course, made necessary by both the corruption of man and the wrath of God. Theologians have tended to see the atonement as being directed toward man alone. It was not merely man's distrust of God that sent Christ to the Cross, but God's condemnation of man. Christ bore that wrath, wrath which was as real as a bad conscience, as enduring as the difference between right and wrong, and which could neither be evaded nor overlooked.

At the same time, the corruption of man remains a stubborn fact of existence; it is a contradiction that is daily touched off by the variance between man's *nature*—what he was made to be—and his *state*—what he has become. With respect to man's nature, there are both physical and spiritual components. On the one hand, he is anchored in the material universe, grows out of it, and is conditioned by it. On the other hand, he is related to God and has an ineradicable capacity for Him. In virtue of this capacity, he accepts his intellectual superiority over the physical world with equanimity, rightfully sees himself as its pinnacle, and, as a part of his relationship to God, subdues it to his own ends. It is nevertheless clear, however, that man does not discharge his obligations either to God or to the rest of the creation as he ought; his nature is contradicted by his sinful state.

Sin is not primarily an incident or a moment of disobedience that can be treated by itself. It refers not so much to actions as to people; it describes what a man is rather than what he does. What he is inwardly may be far more offensive to God than anything he does outwardly. People are sinful not merely because they fail to make God's revealed will their guide and end but because they deliberately and persistently resist that will. The consequences of this sustained hostility are guilt, condemnation, disintegration, and finally death. While it is tempting to think of physical death as a "natural" event, an essential lever in the mechanism of the world that must be pulled each day, Denney argued that it is actually quite unnatural. Man was born to live, not to die. Death is an intrusion into the plan of God, not its intended outcome.

The atonement of Christ, then, becomes clear both in its Godward and manward aspects. He bore our sin and the death that God's condemnation required, making them both His own. In the Bible, Denney insisted, there is no ambiguity surrounding these key terms. To say that Christ bore our sins is to say that He died for our sins; He could not bear them without dying for them. He assumed the full responsibility for these sins and suffered the unmitigated consequence of divine wrath. His Crosswork, therefore, is wrought in one fabric from both judgment and mercy. Christ, by forfeiting His free life and doing for man what man could never have done and will never have to do for himself, frees man's forfeited life.

Although in His death Christ finished the work of atonement, His work was nevertheless not finished. Christian faith depends not merely on who He was but on who He is, and His presence in the church is made known through His *alter ego*, the Holy Spirit.

If the kingdom of God was the fundamental model in the Gospels for those who were the object of God's saving love and who obeyed His revealed will, in the epistles this has become the church. The former is the notion as it was conceived in the mind of Jesus, the latter is its expression as it was wrought out in the lives of the early disciples. It is in this church, as age succeeds age, that God's variegated wisdom is declared, not merely to sinful people but also to principalities and powers. Here creation and redemption are consummated and God's providence is concentrated.

It is to the church that God gives the means of grace, the principal one being Holy Scripture. In viewing Scripture in this way, Denney broke with the conventional view that in turn derived from the Westminster Confession. It was his contention that a mistake had been made in first treating the nature of Scripture, especially its inspiration, and then moving on to consider its place in Christian life. To define inspiration apart from an experience of Scripture's power and authority is merely to play with empty words. Instead he argued that in Scripture, and through Scripture, God communicates His will, makes known His desires, and informs Christian thought and practice. Once this has been felt, the reader is left with no option but to affirm its inspiration.

The volume concludes with eschatology, a subject about which, Denney admitted, it is perilous to speak. And it is obvious that he was rather less interested in this topic than his audience was. Privately he complained about the unhealthy interest he had observed in America in "the millennium, premillennial notions, and in general the fads of the uneducated and half-educated man."[16] Those who knew rather more about these subjects than he (and who, he observed caustically, "spoke as boldly as if they had been initiated into the secrets of God") must have found his ideas rather thin and sketchy.

The Old Testament, Denney said, looked forward not only to a kingdom of God on earth, but one decisively consummated on the day of the Lord, that day when God will interpose to prosecute His cause and destroy His enemies. Although the New Testament carries over this teaching and pictures Christ returning before the millennial reign, Denney believed it was trifling to expect a literal realization of this teaching. At the most, it indicates an intensified struggle between good and evil as the end approaches; that is what the Christian should learn from it. Yet eschatology is of paramount importance to those who take an ethical view of life. The final judgment of all things that will demolish the notion of good and evil being equally durable and ultimate, is what allows us now to put a moral construction on life. And whatever are the details of the intermediate state, the precise nature of the resurrection body, and the perfection of nature, the final environment of the blessed will match their new existence. The bondage into which all has fallen by sin will be overthrown, and heaven will ring with worship at the feet of the Lamb.

These lectures were, of course, forged in the general context of Protestant liberalism, to which they were in-

16*Letters to Family and Friends*, p. 56.

tended to be a sharp rebuke, especially on the Ritschlian side. For Denney found the German theologian not only "brusque, peremptory, and occasionally insolent"[17] but also disastrous as a guide in matters of Christian faith. Ritschl, he charged, had sundered theology from any relationship to the world, either physical or metaphysical, turning it into an unrelated compartment of knowledge. In so doing, he undercut belief in theism and because of his distaste for the transcendent did away with the divinity of Christ. He conveniently ignored the Biblical teaching on the resurrection, excised Jesus' eschatological teaching, confused and emptied of any significance Jesus' roles as prophet, priest, and king, minimized the doctrine of sin, and undermined that of the church.[18] It is a scathing indictment that Denney issued, although in later years his attitude toward Ritschl softened a little.

The publication of these lectures provoked considerable interest. Within two years the American edition was already into its fifth printing, having sold over ten thousand copies.[19] The key to its success undoubtedly was its firm grasp on those matters central to Biblical and evangelical faith, especially the person and work of Christ. It was here that Denney's perception was keenest. His doctrine may indeed have been as he "learnt it at his mother's knee,"[20] but it was expounded so lucidly and

[17]Ibid., p. 179.

[18]Cf.: Oliphant Smeaton, "Recent Scots Theology," *Westminster Review* 148 (1897): 654-64; D. Macmillan, "The German View of Scots Theology," *Scots Magazine* 7 (1890-91): 174-83.

[19]Unfortunately a German bombing raid during the Second World War destroyed all of Hodder and Stoughton's records and correspondence about Denney's works, including *Studies in Theology*, so it is now impossible to secure the precise figures on sales. The original records of the American publisher, A. C. Armstrong, I have been unable to locate.

[20]Walker, *James Denney*, p. 88.

trenchantly, it abounded in so many memorable and
epigrammatic expressions, that it made and makes an
indelible impression on the reader's mind. Here already
conceived are those ideas on the Cross that Denney
was to make his life's work and that were to issue in his
later classic works on this theme. "The *Studies*," Walker
said rightly, "constitute an essentially conservative volume, in many of its chapters pleasing even the ultra-
conservative section of his own Free Church, but not
all." To those, however, who leaned toward an orthodoxy
that was "too sensitive," Walker conceded, Denney caused
"some soreness."[21] And Nicoll was to say of him later
that "there is a singular vein of scepticism in him, for
all his apparent orthodoxy."[22]

There is no question that Denney combined a staunch
conservatism on soteriology with an almost careless, and
certainly fearless, independence on less central matters.
He saw little merit in the Chalcedonian definition,
treated predestination brusquely, dismissed Biblical inerrancy, showed little interest in the problem of Adam,
believed too little in eschatology, was sometimes less
than fully trinitarian, and in christology wobbled between
Nestorianism and Monophysitism. With his developed
knack for blurring those fine distinctions that it was the
delight of some theologians to make, he showed rough
edges to those who were not completely sympathetic to
him. It is difficult to anticipate which of these matters
will provoke similar "soreness" today, but two questions
in particular seem to require some further comment.

First, Denney's christology, despite the extraordinarily

[21]Ibid.
[22]Quoted in Thomas Herbert Darlow, *William Robertson
Nicoll: Life and Letters* (London: Hodder and Stoughton, 1925),
p. 364.

powerful and orthodox expression given to it, also contained some elements that some have felt are discordant and jarring. The most interesting, but hardly the most noticeable, omission in Denney's treatment is any flat statement that Jesus is God. Jesus' preexistence is asserted; His titles such as "Son of God" are acknowledged; His divine prerogatives, such as that of judgment, are recognized; but Denney is unwilling to use the phrase "Jesus is God." It was this lacuna, in this and other writings, that led his old friend Nicoll to wonder whether Denney was not a trifle more sympathetic to Arianism than he ought to have been. Denney replied, however, that his hesitation was merely linguistic and not theological at all. "As for your remark that you missed an unequivocal statement that Jesus is God, I feel inclined to say that such a statement seems unattractive to me just because it is impossible to make it unequivocal. It is not the true way to say a true thing. I think I have made it plain that for me to worship Jesus as God is worshipped, to trust Him as God is trusted, to owe to Him what we can owe to God alone, is the essence of Christianity. I have said in so many words that no one means what a Christian means by God, unless he includes in that all that a Christian means by 'Father, Son, and Spirit.' This I hold to be the Catholic doctrine of the Trinity, but I dread ways of putting it which do nothing but challenge contradiction. 'Jesus is God' seems to me one of those provocative ways, and therefore I avoid it. It has the same objectionableness in my mind as calling Mary the Mother of God."[23]

Denney must have known that a quibble such as this, whose theological effects are negligible, could easily be

[23]Ibid.

misunderstood. For it is natural to conclude that anyone who is chary of the expression "Jesus is God" must have some reservations about His full divinity. In Denney's case, however, this was not so; he did believe, in an unqualified way, that the undiminished Godhead was enfleshed in Jesus. Following Lightfoot, he rejected the efforts of Kenoticists to truncate the divine nature as the necessary price of a full incarnation, and against the Ritschlian school he vigorously argued that Jesus does not merely have the value of God for the *believer*. And against the Arians of all shades of opinion, but especially the unitarians, he postulated that the Son's preexistence and relationship of coequality with the Father is eternal. Only if this is so do we have a way of conceiving of Christ that answers His greatness. Denney affirmed all of the essential elements of an orthodox view of Christ's divinity and omitted none; his quibble really was, as he said, linguistic and not theological at all. Since that is the case, it is appropriate to wonder why he flirted with such serious misunderstandings for such small gains, if they are gains at all. The only explanation that is feasible is that Denney reasoned this was the way the apostles had stated the matter, so this was the way he would have to state it, too, regardless of the cost.

On the same theme, Denney also provoked some concern by his rather light rejection of the Chalcedonian definition, especially as it was transmitted through the Westminster Confession, "that two whole, perfect, and distinct natures, the Godhead and the Manhood, were inseparably joined together in one person, without conversion, composition, or confusion." Perhaps, Denney conceded, this formula may have seemed helpful once, but at most it now has the power only of excluding error. It no longer has the power of reconstituting for the mind the person of Christ.

Denney's complaint, however, was not so much directed against the orthodox christology as against the business of doing theology in general. The manner in which the Evangelists treated the person of Christ was quite different from that of later theologians. In the writings of the former a portrait of Jesus emerges that is compelling and winsome; in those of the latter, he has been reduced to legal terminology. To Denney, at least, this had as little religious attraction as did a chemical formula or a table of logarithms. It could, of course, be replied that no one would be foolish enough to think that the historical figure of Christ is identical with the protective theological casing in which the church has enveloped Him; theologians must always return to Him, as Denney said, "not by deducing the consequences of an arbitrary definition of God-manhood, but by actually looking at Him and listening to Him." The question, however, is whether this Biblical Christ would have survived the acids of criticism and the perversity of theological scholarship without the buttresses of Chalcedon.

Second, Denney's doctrine of Scripture as expounded in these lectures deserves some comment, not least because by his own admission it "excited considerable discussion" among his audience.[24] Not only did he outline a

---

[24]Denney himself left no explanation as to what precisely excited his audience. Speaking of these Chicago lectures, Walker said that they "attracted crowded audiences, and evoked keen discussion. It was the one on Holy Scripture that mainly, perhaps entirely, caused the 'fluttering' in the ecclesiastical dovecots. The reason we may never know, for when in the autumn of that year the lectures were published under the title of *Studies in Theology*, it was found that this particular lecture had been written over again by the author. . . ." *James Denney*, pp. 85-86.

different role for Scripture in a Christian's life, but he also set himself partly against the Hodge-Warfield view of inspiration, especially in the matter of inerrancy, although he could also appeal to them, too. For though Denney affirmed the full authority of the Biblical word as they did, he did allow that there might be a few errors in incidental details, which they refused to do.

Nicoll voiced the dissatisfaction that some evangelicals had felt with this aspect of *Studies in Theology*. He found it rather "disingenuous" that Denney had omitted, as he claimed, any discussion of Christ's attitude to the Bible, for not only did the Princeton theology rest its case upon this but so, Nicoll added, do "99 Christians out of 100." "On the lowest view of Christ, His appreciation of the Old Testament is a signal fact."[25] Moreover, Nicoll felt that Denney had not given enough weight to the way in which Christ's biographers were guided and "kept from blurring and staining the Image" as they actually utilized their sources. There is, in the relationship of the natural and supernatural, unquestioned mystery, but more should have been made of the facts with which the writers had to work. The future of the Bible, moreover, should not have been left so open. "People are tired of being told that they must give up this, that, and the other thing," Nicoll concluded.[26]

On most of these charges, however, Denney could justifiably claim to be innocent. Contrary to Nicoll's accusation, he did not omit the discussion of Christ's attitude to Scripture, although he did not draw as many inferences from it as he might have. It would, he declared, be "extraordinary rashness and presumption" for us to assert

[25]Quoted in Darlow, *William Robertson Nicoll*, p. 341.
[26]Ibid., p. 342.

that Scripture cannot have the same place in our life as in His and that we cannot use it as He did. Whether Denney really was as "open" on the future of the Bible as Nicoll feared is disputable. What apparently caused some apprehension was Denney's propensity to utilize the means and methods of Biblical criticism. Yet it is clear, too, that he had no intention of running with the hares in church and hunting with the hounds in the classroom. For him, these were always and only matters of truth, and for that reason he disliked the terms *moderate* and *extreme criticism.* "The answers to the critic's questions are not moderate or extreme," he said, "but true or false; and of all men a Christian ought to be willing to go any length with truth." What this meant, then, was that Denney saw more matters of truth in the findings of the Biblical scholars than did Nicoll. On the other hand, Denney's general argument that what is inspired is the *message* of the Bible, not the details of which it was composed, potentially opened a pandora's box, the likes of which he probably could not conceive and certainly did not see. He died a year before Barth's *Commentary on the Epistle to the Romans* was published and several decades before Bultmann and Tillich rose to prominence. In them we see both the tendency and the results of separating the Biblical "message" from the Biblical text, the Christ of faith from the Jesus of history. Denney doubtless would have repudiated their views as sharply as he did those of Protestant liberalism, but it remains to be said that the relation of the inspired message to the text in his thought was not as clearly worked out as it ought to have been.

What Nicoll did not criticize and which, in terms of the standard evangelical theology, was quite as serious was Denney's apologetic method. He argued that inspiration is not a logical a priori but rather an experiential conclusion. "We do not use the Bible," he declared, "because of an antecedent conviction that it is inspired; we are convinced it is inspired because it so asserts its authority over us, as we read, that we cannot but use it in that way." What the young Scottish theologian did not grasp is that the subjective grounding of this argument empties it of much of its apologetic usefulness. It is conceivable that an adherent of Islam, for example, could argue that the Qur'an so asserts its authority over him experientially that he has no alternative but to view it as uniquely inspired. And the Therada Buddhist could argue similarly for the Three Pitakas. Indeed, any religious writing important to any faith, sect, or cult can be justified by this means. Why, then, did Denney pursue this line of argument?

It will be recalled that in the previous year, 1893, William Sanday had delivered the Bampton lectures.[27] In these lectures he began with the premise that critical study had shown the text of Scripture to be errant. How, then, should inspiration be conceived? Sanday argued that it ought to be related not to the text of Scripture but to the writers of it. The writers were inspired and thus the Bible is the record of God's education of mankind. What is important is not so much what an author said, but what he had experienced. Later generations should therefore concern themselves with finding that awareness of God that had first moved the Biblical writers. And this category of religious experience, it will be found, does

[27]Published as *Inspiration: Eight Lectures on the Early History and Origin of the Doctrine of Biblical Inspiration: Being the Bampton Lectures of 1893* (New York: Longmans, Green, 1896).

not cut across the grain of evolution; on the contrary it is a very remarkable illustration of it.

Sanday was not without his critics, probably the most caustic of whom was Ronald Knox,[28] but by and large his view was readily accepted. It relieved the church of the burden of proving a thesis that was languishing for supporters and seemed doomed to an ignominious conclusion. It would either suffer from studied neglect or die the death of a thousand qualifications.

Denney was not one to shy away from controversial issues, nor was he ever a temporizer. But he clearly believed that the evangelical phalanx that had been duly drawn up in battle array against Sanday and others had not chosen its ground carefully. Even if the argument for inspiration were won, the practical consequences might be minimal, for it is entirely possible for one to affirm inerrancy with a loud voice but never be submissive to the actual teaching of Scripture.

However flawed and shortsighted Denney's argument might have been, then, it ought to be considered on its positive side, too. For Christian orthodoxy can be undermined by its defenders quite as much as by its detractors. Few doctrines are quite so vulnerable to the deathly effect of formalism as this. The church then had those who would fight to the death for the right doctrine of Scripture but who were, nevertheless, often strangers to its power in reforming their lives, and all too seldom did they see its liberating capacities in the pulpit. It is to these people in particular that Denney directed his remarks.

[28]See Knox's *Reunion All Round: or, Jael's Hammer Laid Aside, and the Milk of Human Kindness Beaten up into Butter and Serv'd in a Lordy Dish, By the Author of "Absolute and Abitofhell"* (London: Society of Ss. Peter and Paul, 1914).

It is a sobering and melancholy fact that the numerical growth of evangelicalism in recent years has not always been matched by a significant intellectual growth; in theology particularly there is a dearth of serious work by evangelicals. If the republication of *Studies in Theology* is seen to be a substitute for the hard work we ourselves ought to be doing, then the project will have misfired badly. The justification for this volume, rather, is to be found, first, in the new generation of evangelical pastors and scholars who are largely unacquainted with Denney at first hand; and, second, in the abiding significance of much of what he had to say.[29]

In his own day Denney exercised a powerful influence on the formation of evangelical thought and practice, and we would be richer for it if his influence could also be extended to ours. He made theology religious and he

[29]The lengthiest attempt in recent years at rediscovering Denney's abiding theological significance is John Randolph Taylor, *God Loves Like That! The Theology of James Denney* (Richmond: John Knox, 1962). Despite its overall merit, the volume is flawed by some omissions from its supposedly full and complete bibliography of Denney's works. Examples are his essay "Can Sin Be Forgiven" in *Questions of Faith* (New York: A. C. Armstrong, 1904), pp. 151-76; an unentitled chapter in John Watson, *A Series of Letters to Ministers* (New York: Dodd Mead, 1898); the preface to James Candlish, *The Christian Salvation: Lectures on the Work of Christ: Its Appropriation and Its Issues* (Edinburgh: T. and T. Clark, 1899); journal essays such as "Constructive Task of Protestantism," *Constructive Quarterly* 1 (1913): 213-26; and of course his translation of Franz Delitzsch, *Biblical Commentary on the Prophecies of Isaiah* (New York: Funk and Wagnalls, 1889). A substantial secondary source literature was missed by Taylor, too. See also S. J. Mikolaski, "The Theology of Principal James Denney," *The Evangelical Quarterly* 35 (1963): 89-96, 144-68, 209-22; Philip Edgcumbe Hughes, "Evangelist-Theologian: Appreciation of James Denney," *Christianity Today* 1 (1956): 3-4, 30-31; I. Howard Marshall, "James Denney," in Philip Edgcumbe Hughes, ed., *Creative Minds in Contemporary Theology* (Grand Rapids: Eerdmans, 1966), pp. 203-38.

made pastoral practice theological. It was his view that an ideal church would be nearer to realization when "evangelists were our theologians or theologians our evangelists," for the work of theology and that of evangelism should not be separate spheres of activity, as they are so often today. "The simplest truth of the Gospel and the profoundest truth of theology," he declared, "must be put in the same words—He bore our sins." And to the exposition of this truth he brought to bear a mind that was penetrating and creative, a heart that was warm and beat in every word he wrote, and a style—so unlike that of many theologians—that was lucid and incisive. Denney no doubt made mistakes, but it would be hard to disagree with Mackintosh's estimate of him: "As theologian and as man, there was no one like him. I have known many theologians both scholarly and devout; but I have never known his equal for making the New Testament intelligible as the record and deposit of an overwhelming experience of redemption, and for generating in those who listened to him the conviction that the gospel incarnate in Jesus is the only thing that matters."[30]

DAVID WELLS
*Professor and Chairman
Department of Church History
and the History of Christian Thought
Trinity Evangelical Divinity School*

[30]"Principal James Denney," pp. 493-94.

PREFACE

THE lectures which compose this volume were delivered in April 1894 to the Chicago Theological Seminary, and are published at the request of the Faculty of that Institution. They do not amount to a system of theology, but the writer believes they are consistent with each other, and would find their place in a system. They are printed as they were delivered, with one exception. The ninth lecture, which excited considerable discussion in the circles to which it was first addressed, has been re-written ; not with the view of retracting or qualifying anything, but in order, as far as possible, to obviate misconception, and secure a readier acceptance for what the writer thinks true ideas on the authority of Scripture. The notes have been added, partly to justify the statements made in the lectures as to the opinions of various theologians and schools, partly to acknowledge the writer's obligations to others.

CONTENTS

CONTENTS

LECTURE I

THE IDEA OF THEOLOGY

A TREATISE on systematic theology usually begins
with a definition, the analysis and defence of which
may show all that the theologian has to teach us.
For the purpose which I have in view, it is not
necessary that I should aim here at excessive precision; but it is necessary to indicate what I conceive the subject to be, what can be made of it, and
what a fair treatment of it requires. If this lecture
seems too abstract or indefinite, I can only hope that
this appearance will be removed when we come to
consider the various special topics.

Theology is the doctrine of God: systematic
theology is the presentation in a systematic form of
that doctrine. But the doctrine of God, in the very
nature of the case, is related to everything that
enters into our knowledge; all our world depends
upon Him; and hence it follows that a systematic
presentation of the doctrine of God involves a
general view of the world through God. It must
contain the ideas and the principles which enable us
to look at our life and our world as a whole, and to
take them into our religion, instead of leaving them
outside. What, however, we have specially to deal
with is not theology, but Christian theology—that
knowledge of God which belongs to us as Christians,
and which is traced back to Christ. We know that

Christ claimed to possess a unique and perfect knowledge of God, and to impart that knowledge to His
disciples; if we are really Christians, we must be
sharers in it; we must know God; and our task,
when we theologise, is to define our knowledge; to
put it in scientific and systematic form, and to show,
at least in outline, that general view of the world
which it involves. The Christian Religion, it has
been said truly enough, is not a revealed metaphysic; still less is it a revealed natural science;
nevertheless, the Christian mind which would understand the truth which it possesses—which would not
keep its religious convictions in one compartment
of the intelligence, and all its other operations in
others—must not be afraid of as much metaphysics
as is implied in this general view of the subject.

I put this in the foreground, because by far the
most influential, most interesting, and in some ways
most inspiring, of modern theologians virtually
makes the denial of it a great principle of his theology—I refer to the late Professor Ritschl. Religion,
according to Ritschl, is one thing; metaphysic is
another: theology has to do only with religion;
of metaphysics it must be carefully kept clear. The
Christian knowledge of God is not scientific; it is
not a 'natural theology,' derived from principles of
reason; it has not even a relation to such a natural
theology; it depends simply and solely on the revelation made of God in Christ. The certainty we
have of this revelation, the knowledge of God which
we have through it, are not scientific, but religious;
our judgment upon these things is not a theoretic
one, which can be made good to anybody indiffer-

ently; it is what Ritschl calls a Werthurtheil—a value-judgment; it has validity only for those who happen to be impressed as we are by the revelation on which it rests; and it must not be carried out in its consequences into other spheres than the strictly religious one. In other words, it has no scientific validity. Theology, instead of involving such a general view of the world and life as I have spoken of—instead of standing in direct and vital connection with the whole framework of our knowledge—is shut up into itself, and, doctrine of God though it be, neither affects, nor is affected by, any independent scientific interpretation of God's world.[1]

It is easy to see the superficial attractions of this conception. I presume you are as familiar in America as we are in Scotland with the idea that religion and science can never come into conflict, because each has a sphere of its own. Let the theologian confine himself to religion, people say, and the scientific man to nature, and they will never meet, and therefore never come into collision. But it is a superficial platitude all the same. The theologian cannot think of God and leave out of sight the fact that the nature with which the scientific man is busy is constituted by God and dependent on Him; and one would hope that the scientific man also, living not only in nature but above it, and as its interpreter, would feel the need of defining the relation of nature as a whole to the spiritual power which can be recognised both in it and in himself. The religious man has to live his religious life in nature, and to maintain his faith in God there; the

[1] See Note A.

scientific man, if he be religious, has precisely the same task ; and they are bound, by the very nature of intelligence, to come to an understanding. They cannot agree to differ ; they cannot agree to ignore each other. *All* that man knows—of God and of the world—must be capable of being constructed into one coherent intellectual whole. All that any one of us knows, as a Christian, or as a student of science, physical, historical, anthropological, archæological, must be capable of such a construction ; and our doctrine of God, instead of being defiantly indifferent here, must involve the principles on which this construction shall proceed. We deceive ourselves, and try to evade the difficulties of the task which is laid on us, when we deny the essential relation in which theology must stand to all the contents and problems of our mind and life.

The world is all of a piece ; man's mind is all of a piece ; and those easy and tempting solutions of our hardest problems, which either arrange the world or the activities of the mind in compartments having no communication with each other, are simply to be rejected. It is quite true that a man may be a very good Christian without being either a physicist or a metaphysician ; but the moment one begins to reflect on the contents of his intelligence, he must be able to bring them all—religious, physical, or metaphysical—to harmony among themselves. In particular, he must be able to bring everything else into subordination to his idea of God : it must not be a separate thing, but the explanation and interpretation of all his science, physical, historical, and moral.

These generalities, I fear, may not be very impressive, and I will try by one or two examples to show the results to which this separation of the religious and the scientific leads. Made avowedly, at least by theologians, in the interest of religion, it ends, as a rule, in leaving religion without its indispensable supports.

1. As a first example, take the fundamental doctrine of the being of God itself. It is granted, of course, that we owe to Christ our specifically Christian thoughts of God. But for the revelation in the Son, we should not have known the Father. We call God the God and Father of our Lord Jesus Christ: that is the very soul of our knowledge of Him, the most intimate and adequate expression we can give to it. But is it a wise or right thing, on the strength of this fact, to discredit the arguments by which the human mind has sought to explain and vindicate its belief in God on other grounds, and to deny them either place or consideration in theology? Granted that we could never attain, simply along the line of these arguments, to that idea of God which is given in the Christian revelation, does it follow that the Christian idea of God stands in no relation to them, that it does not need their support, that all that labour of the human mind on its religious convictions and instincts is simply an irrelevance to the pure and perfect religion? I do not believe it; and I am sure the result which follows from the contempt with which these philosophical arguments are treated by most of Ritschl's school, is not that theology is kept more purely Christian, but that it loses in solidity and in objective value. The Chris-

tian thoughts of God are not wrought into a piece
with the instinctive movement of intelligence toward
its author; the mind is, as it were, discredited by
revelation, and divided against itself.   This is an
intellectual condition which cannot be permanent.
Even before Christ came, God did not leave Himself
without a witness in man; there was that which
testified of Him not only in the chosen people of the
Old Testament, but in every race, and under every
sky; there is still a witness, wider than the proclama-
tion of the gospel; and it is surely the business of the
theologian, not to flout it as superfluous, now that
Christ has come, but to understand it, to interpret it,
to set it in its proper relation to Christ; and in so
doing to reconcile all revelation with that in which
the Christian rejoices   For the essential point to
notice in all the arguments, as they are called, for the
being of God, is this: they are not mere fantasies;
they are attempts to construe to intelligence the
impression which we have received, directly or in-
directly, of something divine in nature, or in man,
or in the relations of nature and man to each other.
They are not meant to create, but to interpret,
impressions; and impressions just as real, if not as
important, as the impression produced by the
revelation of God in Christ.   The interpretation
may be mistaken or inadequate, but so it may be
also where the Christian revelation is concerned:
the point is, that justice must be done to it in the
one case as well as the other, and that the revelation
which is consummated in Christ must not be divorced
from, but shown in its real connection with, those
obscurer revelations which have been interpreted

in the well-known and much-criticised arguments for the being of God. Christian theology is not a separate department of intelligence, having no connection with others; just because it is a doctrine of *God*, it must have a place and recognition for all those impressions and convictions about God which have exerted their power in man's mind, even apart from the perfect historical revelation. It is not meant at all that no one can be a Christian unless he understands the arguments called cosmological, teleological, or ontological; still less, that he is not a Christian unless he understands these names; but this is meant, that after all criticism, these arguments do interpret, more or less adequately, impressions made on the human mind by God and His works—in other words, revelations; and that for that reason they ought not to be summarily ruled out of court, but treated seriously, and shown in their true connection with the full Christian truth. To pooh-pooh them because they never made anybody religious is unintelligent; what is really claimed for them is that there is a truth of God *in* them, especially in their combination, a truth which Christianity presupposes, a truth without which it could not stand; a truth, therefore, which must have an organic place in a true Christian theology. It is not safe to say that in Christ we have *everything* we can know of God or need to know, and that when we say 'God,' as Christian people, we mean nothing but the Personal Character revealed in Christ; the idea of God must be essentially related to *all* we know; *all* our knowledge must have something of revelation in it, and must contribute to our theology.

An extreme result of the tendency I have been combating is seen in the view expressed by Herrmann, one of the chief adherents of Ritschl, that as far as maintaining the impulse to religious faith is concerned, it does not matter whether our conception of the world is theistic, pantheistic, or materialistic; its general religious character is unaffected. Ritschl himself, with the same surrender of science, and indeed of reason, in theology, had even spoken of God, not as the most real of realities, but as a Hülfsvorstellung—a help-conception—for the attainment of the believer's practical ends.[1] God, in other words, is a necessary assumption of the Christian view of man's chief end; but scientifically—in its bearing on the interpretation of nature and history, for example—it may be left an open question whether there is a God or not. In principle, this attempt to distinguish between the religious and the theoretic, to assign separate spheres to reason and faith— for that is what it comes to—amounts to a betrayal of the truth; it is really an attempt to build religious certainty on indifference to reason, or scepticism of it; and reason always avenges itself by keeping in its own power something which is essential to faith.

2. Another example, which seems at first to be on a smaller scale, yet in its consequences reaches very far, may be found in the treatment, by this same school, of the idea of the supernatural. Here also the avowed intention is to exclude the metaphysical, and to do justice to the religious. It is carefully pointed out, for instance, that the Bible

[1] See Note B.

never defines miracle as the apologists or dogmatists
of a scholastic theology try to define it. Peter and
John knew nothing about laws of nature; they
could not have understood such an expression, to
say nothing of defining it as it would be defined by
Herschell or Mill; hence it is absurd to define what
they called miracles by any relation to laws of
nature, whether as the violation of them, their
suspension, their modification, combination, or what
not. Instead of aiming at such pseudo-scientific
precision we should seek for a purely religious
definition, and say that anything is a miracle in
which the religious man recognises that God has
powerfully interposed in the interests of His
kingdom. What the relation of such interposition
may be to what the scientific man calls laws of
nature is not a religious, and therefore not a
theological, question. The scientific man may have
his own explanation ot what the religious man calls
a miracle; but with that the religious man has
nothing to do. It does not concern him at all. He
has no more right to interfere with the man of
science in his merely mechanical explanation of
what has happened, than the man of science has
to interfere with him in his religious explanation.

Here again, we are compelled to remark, the
solution is too easy. I agree entirely that we ought
to keep in the forefront the religious conception of
a miracle; the main thing in it is that it is a great
interposition of God, in furtherance of the interests
of His kingdom and people; not that it is related
in this or that way to the order of nature. But the
mind cannot have two *unrelated* explanations of the

same thing; it cannot interpret it, in the first place religiously, and in the second scientifically, without being compelled to define the connection of the two interpretations with each other. If they are both true, it will not be impossible to do so; but if we cannot do so, the impression will be irresistible that one or other of them is not true. And the true, we may be sure, or the one which is regarded as true, will simply displace the other.

It is doing no injustice to the whole school of writers, which has magnified the religious at the expense of the scientific conception of miracle, and declined to acknowledge any obligation to be scientific in the matter, to say that in point of fact they reject miracle altogether, in any sense which gives it a hold on man's intelligence or a place in his creed. Thus Ritschl himself says frankly that if certain narratives of miracles in the Bible seem to conflict with the rule that the whole world is bound together by inviolable physical laws, it is neither a scientific problem to explain away that seeming conflict, nor to establish it as a matter of fact; nor is it a religious problem to recognise the events in question as effects produced by God counter to natural laws. In plain English, it does not matter whether the Bible miracles happened as they are recorded or not. Every believing man, Ritschl goes on, will have miracles in his own life; he will be able to point to occasions on which God has wonderfully interposed for him; and in comparison with this nothing could be more superfluous than that he should grope and grub over those that are said to have been experienced by others.[1] There are those, perhaps, to whom this will seem fascinatingly religious; those also to whom it will seem brusque, peremptory, and possibly insolent; but surely every one will feel on reflection that the division which it establishes between the religious and the scientific interpretation of events is one to which the very nature of intelligence must refuse its consent. In point of fact, the scientific interpretation is regarded as the only objectively true one by those who write in this strain; the religious one is a mere pious opinion which the pious man may hold for himself, but which he has no right to impose, and no means of imposing, on others.

Now, if the Christian religion, when it referred to the supernatural, had in view only what could plausibly be considered a number of lucky chances or coincidences, in which pious people had seen God's special favour to them, there might be something to say for this way of looking at the subject. But this is far from the case. Take the supreme miracle of the Resurrection, on which, according to the New Testament itself, the whole Christian system—with its belief in a life triumphant over death—depends. Granted the fact, and the religious interpretation of it is clear. It is a supreme interposition of God in vindication of His Son, and in pursuance of the work of Redemption. Those who believed in it could only say, God hath raised Him up. But writers of this modern school, knowing that science, in its incapacity to explain the fact in accordance with natural laws, does not hesitate to reject it, follow suit. Thus Harnack, a leading representa-

[1] See Note C.

tive of the tendency, writes: 'The historian is not in a position to reckon with a miracle as a certainly given historical event; for in doing so he destroys that very method of looking at things on which all historical investigation rests. Every single miracle remains, historically, entirely dubious; and no summation of the dubious can ever amount to a certainty. If, in spite of this, the historian convinces himself that Jesus Christ has done what is extraordinary, and even in the strict sense miraculous, he argues from an ethico-religious impression which he has received of this person to a supernatural power belonging to him. This inference belongs itself to the domain of religious faith.'[1] The underlying assumption is, that because it belongs to the domain of religious faith it cannot belong to the domain of assured fact. But surely it is the grossest of inconsistencies to lay immense stress, as writers of this school with their anti-metaphysical bias do, on the historical character of Christianity, and especially of the revelation of God in Christ; and then to maintain that the historicity of many of the most characteristic of the facts through which the revelation is made, is entirely and permanently dubious. Surely also we must feel that the mind will inevitably revolt against this schism in its life—this clean cut division between its action in religious faith and its action in historical investigation. It is the same living being who has to live in all the characters of historian, physicist, and, if we say it without scorn, pious theologian; and there must be a way in which

[1] See Note D.

he can bring them all to a unity. It is his task as a theologian not to deny, but to define, their relations to each other; not to cast the shadow of subjectivity and unreality on the religious interpretation of life, and leave objective truth only to an interpretation which dispenses with God; but rather to vindicate the reality of the religious, and show, through the true idea of God, that both nature and history may really be made his instruments, and that both in nature and in history there may be events and facts the whole character of which is this, that they are embodiments of divine truth, or manifestations of divine love and power. When we define the supernatural only in a religious way, and refuse to form a conception of it in relation to nature or history, the practical result is that we surrender it altogether.

3. Perhaps the most important subject to which these considerations can be applied is that central one in Christian theology—the divinity or Godhead of Christ. There is nothing to which theologians of the school of Ritschl have given greater attention; nothing on which they express themselves with greater amplitude and fervour. But they make their very devotion a plea for refusing to be more than devout in the matter. Christ has, they say, for the Christian consciousness the religious value of God. Our highest thought of God is that which is revealed in Him; our truest fellowship with God is that which is mediated through Him; He not only speaks about God, but in Him God Himself comes to us. All this, of course, the

[1] See Note E.

Christian will say; but it is not possible for him to stop here. He cannot suppress the instinctive motion of the mind to seek an explanation of this extraordinary Person. He cannot say, in the long-run, No man knoweth the Son save the Father, and it is idle for me to seek any other explanation than the purely religious one—He came from God. We have no choice in the matter but to seek an explanation. We must, as rational beings, try to clear up to our own minds what is necessarily involved in the existence among men of a Person who has the religious value of God. Theologians who refuse to go beyond this are invariably found to cover, under the guise of a religious indifference to metaphysics, a positive disbelief of everything which gives Christ's Godhead an objective character. They do not admit the supernatural birth, they do not admit the pre-existence taught by St. Paul, they do not admit the doctrine of the Incarnation of the Logos, at least as taught by St. John; in short, though Jesus has for the Christian consciousness the religious value of God, he has for the scientific consciousness only the common real value of man. He is, in truth and reality, to the neutral consideration of science, mere man like any other; it is only the Werthurtheil, the subjective estimate of the pious Christian, that gives him the value of God. But it can hardly be necessary to say that this is a position in which the human mind must sooner or later—and it will be sooner rather than later—refuse to rest. Again and again in the course of history this idea of two kinds of truth has flitted before men as a way of railing-in religion, and securing for it a province of its own where science cannot assail it; but we ought to have discovered by this time that it is a way which never ends in good. Our religious convictions, if they do not have an objective value which is as real as that of our scientific convictions, and quite capable of being wrought into one intelligible whole with them, will simply pass away. The separation of the religious and the scientific means in the end the separation of the religious and the true; and this means that religion dies among true men.

But, you will naturally ask, if the case be as you have represented it, why should the idea of such a separation have the fascination which it undoubtedly possesses for many minds? Why should people snatch at it as a thing which at least promises mental relief? What is the element of truth in it by which it appeals to them?

I think it is this, that the apprehension of religious truth *is conditioned* in a way in which the apprehension, say, of the truths of physical science is not. 'The natural man discerneth not the things of the Spirit.' It needs a certain condition of the heart, the conscience, and even the will, to see the truth of the Godhead of Christ, and there is such a thing here as resisting the evidence. In physics, again, nothing is needed but open eyes and a sound understanding; the evidence cannot be resisted. Nevertheless, the knowledge of Christ's Godhead, when we attain to it in the way in which it can be attained, is no more to be qualified as subjective, than our knowledge of the law of gravitation. And if it is true knowledge, then it is a problem which will press upon us, to relate it to all our other knowledge, to show what it presupposes, and what will flow from it. Take, again, a truth like that of man's immortality. It is not easy, it is not possible, to demonstrate it to every man. The facts which can be urged against it are so omnipresent, so importunate, so insurmountable; those which can be urged in favour of it, though far deeper and more significant, are certainly much less obtrusive. It needs a moral effort to keep the higher conviction in our grasp; we require, as St. Paul says, to fight the good fight, and so to lay hold on eternal life. No truth by which a man is to lift himself to a higher moral level will ever be won or kept without unceasing effort. Nevertheless, the conviction we have of immortality is not to be described as religious, in a sense which implies that we may dispense with treating it as objective, or scientifically valid; it *is* objectively valid, though there are spiritual conditions under which alone it can be gained and held; if it were not so, it could have no interest for us whatever. But granted its objective value, it follows immediately that we must relate it to all our other knowledge; we must have, and be able to vindicate, a doctrine of human nature to which immortality is not alien but akin. This remark applies to the whole field of theology, and to every subject within it. *Pectus facit theologum:* there can be no theologian without religious experience. But religious experience is not a fancy subjective thing, of which there can be no science, or only a science which declines relations with other departments in which the human spirit is at work; all knowledge is one, all intelligence is one; and it belongs to theology, above every science, not to dissolve, but in the very name of God, to maintain and interpret that unity.

In giving a short course of lectures on systematic theology, this is the principle on which I shall proceed. It is granted that the material with which the theologian deals can only be certified to him through religious experience; in other words, only a living Christian is competent to look at the subject. But it is not granted—it is on principle denied—that theology can do its work without involving any question either of physics or of metaphysics. The theologian himself is a creature of body as well as spirit; his roots are in nature; it is to be hoped, if not presumed, that he has some kind of acquaintance with the science of his time, physical and mental; and if he is not to stultify his reason by living two or three separate lives, he must combine and harmonise in his theology all his knowledge and experience, physical, metaphysical, historical, and religious.

The starting-point, of course, in Christian theology must be the revelation of God in Christ. Christ has, to use the form of words already quoted, for the Christian consciousness the religious value of God. In a sense, then, it is Christ who is the great problem of the Christian theologian; our first task is to answer His own question, 'Whom say ye that I am?' It accords with this, that from the very beginning the mind of the Church busied itself with Christology. In the apostolic writings we find a theology, so to speak, involved; but a Christology fully and explicitly developed. It did not content

the New Testament writers to recognise that Christ
had for their hearts the religious value of God; they
were impelled, or rather, let us say, were constrained,
under the teaching and guidance of the Spirit, to
set Christ in such a relation, objective and real, to
God and the world, as justified that judgment of the
heart.   This is a fact of great significance; and it
is characteristic that Harnack, a prominent representative of the theological tendency I have
described, expresses his disappointment with it.[1]
To him, it was the first step on the down-grade,
when the Church, forgetting the purely religious
and ethical aims of Jesus, was misled by its faith in
the Resurrection to concentrate all its thoughts on
the Person of Christ Himself.   This is an opinion
which need not here be discussed: it only shows
that in the sharp line of division that he draws
between the religious and the 'metaphysical' view
of Christ, Harnack is conscious of having the
apostles against him.   We may be content, meanwhile, to be on their side.

In starting with Christ, however, it will be
necessary to make a distinction; and so I shall
speak, in one lecture, of Christ's testimony to Himself, and in another, of the testimony of the
apostles to Christ.   In this last, it will be in place
to examine the grounds on which the apostolic interpretations of Christ's person have been questioned,
and attempts made to do justice to His own claims,
and especially to His own consciousness of what He
was, and was doing, while rejecting the apostolic
interpretations as 'theologoumena' without binding

[1] See Note F.

authority. After saying what I have time to say
on these subjects, I purpose speaking of man, and
especially of man's condition as related to the
coming of Christ. In other words, I shall lecture
on the nature of man, and especially on sin. In
doing so, I hope to keep in view the state of the
question at the present time, and the bearing upon
Bible doctrine and Christian experience of recent
discussions on evolution, heredity, the solidarity of
the race, and so forth. Then I shall take up the
work of Christ in relation to man as sinful—that is,
the doctrine of reconciliation. This is the most
urgent, in a religious sense, of all doctrines; it is
the one in which most is revealed of God, and the
one of which man has most need to hear. It is, I
believe, the doctrine in which the offence of the
gospel is concentrated, as well as its divine power
to save; and for this very reason, I also believe, it
is more apt to be manipulated and tampered with
than any other, both within the Church and without. I shall try in one lecture to make as clear as
I can what I conceive the New Testament teaching
on reconciliation to be—I believe, for my own part,
that it is not ambiguous; and in another I shall
speak of those attempts to construe Christ's work as
a reconciler, which have been so numerous in all
the churches, but which seem to me, for various
reasons, unequal to the problem; and while capable
enough of being incorporated in the apostolic
doctrine, yet in no sense capable either of displacing
or of replacing it. After that, I hope to speak of
Christ in His exaltation—the Giver of the Holy
Ghost, the Heavenly Intercessor, the King of Grace.

That movement in theology which has for its watch-word Back to Christ, and which has done so much for the vivification of the gospel record, making us see Jesus again as they saw Him who walked by His side in the fields and villages of Galilee, has had its drawbacks as well as its advantages. One of them is that it has thrust into the background the living Christ. But the Church lives, not by what Christ was, but by what He is; not by what He did only, but supremely by what He does. It is His own word, Because I live, ye shall live also; and though the original application of that word may have been to a promise of immortality, it is not forcing it to give it an application to the continued existence of the Church in the world as dependent on the continued life of the Lord. After that I shall speak of the Church, as conceived by Christ and His apostles; of its relation to the great New Testament idea of the Kingdom of God; and of the bearing which these regulative conceptions have upon the functions of the Church in our own time, the claims made on her, and perhaps the charges laid against her. The next lecture will be on the Bible and its place in the Church. This has been a burning question in Scotland, and is so, I understand, in some of the American churches; it is bound to become so, sooner or later, in them all. What has God given us in the Bible? is a question to which the right answer has not yet been found; but we are in process of finding it. I assume in all the lectures, as the whole Christian Church does, that we have in it a supreme gift of God, however it may be defined; and meanwhile I can only hope

that the use which I make of it in passing will be
such as to justify itself. In the Westminster Confession, which is acknowledged by the Scottish
churches, the doctrine of Holy Scripture occupies,
as you will be aware, the very first chapter; but in
the original Confession of the Reformed Church in
Scotland, drawn up by John Knox in 1560, it stood
very much later: it came in, indeed, in subordination to the doctrine of the Church, under the
heading of the means of grace. That, I think, is
its true place, and ought to secure for it a treatment
which, while rigorously scientific, will always be
controlled by recognition of the avowedly practical
end which the Scripture has to serve. The last
lecture will be on eschatology. Schools which so
insist upon the religious and the historical as to
deny the transcendent in every sense, and make
Christ's resurrection itself permanently dubious,
have, of course, no eschatology at all; it is one of
the most remarkable features in the system of
Ritschl that it simply eliminates this whole department of theology. Of course it cannot be historically treated, but there are real relations between
what now is, and what is to be—there are words
of Christ and Christian convictions—which claim,
as decidedly as any others, systematic exposition.
If we are only humble enough, we may depend on
being shown our way.

It will be seen that this programme, though it
contains only a limited number of lectures, covers a
very wide field. When the authorities of this
seminary did me the honour of asking me to address
their students, they left it perfectly free to me to

choose the subject. I have thought it better, on consideration, to survey as wide an area as possible, with reference to present movements and tendencies in theology, than to devote more minute attention to one or two leading doctrines. This last work could only be profitably done by a teacher with whose general ideas and principles students were familiar; and I believe I shall best consult your interest by following the other plan, as I have announced. It will sometimes be necessary to be summary, but never, I hope, in a bad sense superficial. It may have struck you that the subjects, as I indicated them, came, at least at the beginning, in the order in which they have emerged historically in the theology of the Church. Christology comes first. This was the great subject in the primitive Church—the Church before the decisive disruption in Christendom had declared itself: this, and the doctrine of the Trinity as involved in it. Then came, in the Latin and especially in the African Church, anthropology. Augustine occupies a place here as significant historically as that of Athanasius for the doctrine of the Person of Christ. When the Reformation came, the great interest was soteriology. Men were seeking an answer to the question, How shall a sinner be justified before God? and they found what they sought in the work of Christ. Justification by faith is the correlate of Christ's work as reconciler; and Christ's work as reconciler is the great theme of the Protestant theology— Lutheran and Reformed. This sequence probably indicates that the order in question has something natural and unforced in it, and I hope this will come out as we proceed. The other subjects, important as they are, have never occupied the attention of the Church to the same extent; one is less guided, but at the same time less overawed in the discussion of them. But even in the earlier ones it must be our endeavour to come to convictions, to an insight, and, as far as we can, to a system of our own. Recognising the importance of great historical decisions and formulations of the faith, we shall feel that the ground on which these were made must be as accessible to us as to those who have gone before; and that the mind's mastery of itself and of the world around it may have given us instruments of precision which in earlier times were wanting. Our intellectual environment, at all events, whatever be said of our intellectual equipment, is not that of the Nicene Age, or the Augustinian, or even of the Reformation; our religious experience with all that it presupposes and involves has to be read in new light, and set in relation to a new world. It will be the utmost I aim at if I can assist any of you in any degree in your work as theologians; if I can help you to be true to all you know, and at the same time to keep a complete and joyful faith as Christian men.

LECTURE II

THE WITNESS OF JESUS TO HIMSELF

1. CHRIST occupies, in the faith of Christians, a position quite distinct from that which is occupied, in the minds of their adherents, by the founders of other religions. He is more to us who believe in him than Moses to the Jew, Sakya Muni to the Buddhist, or Mohammed to the Moslem. The importance of these great men, whose ideas dominate to this day the minds of millions, is mainly historical. They stood at the head of movements which have had a grand fortune in history; they communicated to them the initial impulse, stamped upon them, to a certain extent, their own individuality; but that was all. It is not so with Christ. The Christian religion depends not only upon what He was, but upon what He is. It involves in the individual believer a direct relation to Him, not simply an appropriation of His ideas, but a devotion to His person. It involves an interpretation of human life, and of nature as the background and palæstra of humanity, in which everything is referred to Him both as Originator and as End. This present, permanent, and all-embracing significance of Christ is the mark of the Christian religion in all

24

its historical forms; it is thoroughly defined in the earliest Christian writings, the epistles of the New Testament; and it is the purpose of this lecture to inquire how far it is based upon Christ's witness to Himself; in other words, how far our way of thinking about Christ answers to His own; how far our conception of what faith in Christ involves is supported by the demand for faith made by the Master Himself.

2. We may remark, by way of introduction, that Jesus, in all the accounts we have, speaks much about Himself. He knows that He is a problem to those by whom He is surrounded, and that on the true solution of the problem everything depends. When His death has come within a measurable distance, and He wishes to be assured that the disciples to whom His work will be left are fit to undertake it, the testing question He asks is, 'Whom say ye that I am?' If they have found out *that*, they have found out the great open secret, and are equipped for the future.   But though this discovery of what Christ is is the one thing needful—and therefore must be of cardinal and comprehensive importance—though Christ pronounces the man blessed to whom the secret has been revealed, He does not, as a rule, tell it Himself in so many words. No religious truth, no spiritual truth, can be communicated in this way.   On the one side there must be revelation, or unveiling; on the other, intuition, or perceiving at first-hand; mere telling is nothing. Not direct dogmatic assertions of Jesus about Himself led up to the first Christian confession—Thou art the Christ, the Son of the living God—but the

sum-total of all His words and works, the united and accumulated impression of all He was and did, upon a sincere and receptive soul. It is in this way also that we must approach the subject, for it is in this way only that we can appreciate and appropriate those apostolic words.

3. What, I think, strikes every reader of the gospels, and what must have been immensely more striking to those who heard Him speak, is the moral authority claimed and exercised by Jesus. The first evangelist, after giving a specimen of His teaching in the Sermon on the Mount, adds that the multitudes were astonished at it, for He taught them as one having authority, and not as their scribes. That was the dominating impression which remained. In olden times there had been authoritative teaching in Israel, when prophets introduced their oracles with Thus saith the Lord; but the claims of Jesus surpassed even that high measure; His solemn asseveration is, Verily, *I* say unto you. He once confessed ignorance, but he never betrayed doubt. This is, of course, a commonplace, but it is a fundamental one; the whole of Christianity goes back to it; and it is, I believe, far oftener than anything else, the starting-point of a living Christian faith. For these reasons, it will repay us to examine it more closely.

(*a.*) Christ claimed, authoritatively, to be the consummator of the old religion. He recognised in it, as we should expect, a real revelation of God. He called the temple His Father's house. He said salvation was of the Jews. He was familiar with the scriptures of the Old Testament—the law and the prophets, as they were usually called—and did not dispute their value. But He said in every kind of way, expressly and by implication, that that whole dispensation had a forward look which terminated on Him. He traced in the loftiest passages of ancient prophecy the outline of His own features—the dim shadow cast before by Him who should come. He applied the most sacred oracles to Himself; in the synagogue at Nazareth that gracious one in the 61st of Isaiah—'The Spirit of the Lord is upon me, because He hath anointed me to preach glad tidings to the poor;' in the upper room that far-reaching one in the 31st of Jeremiah —the new covenant based on the forgiveness of sins. In the one case as in the other He says, This day is this scripture fulfilled in your ears. And these are only illustrations of the consciousness which underlies all His words, that the Law and the Prophets—which means not merely the words of the Bible, but the Old Testament religion as a whole—were consummated, and because consummated, superseded, in Him. Consider now how great this person was, at least in His own consciousness, who felt that He was the end aimed at in the very existence of the true religion in the world. It was for me, He virtually said, that God called Abraham, Isaac, and Jacob; for me that he led Israel out of Egypt and gave them laws by Moses, and read the lessons of history, and adumbrated the future, by the prophets; it is for Me that the whole course of God's providence and redemption has been working through the ages; all these laws, prophecies, institutions, catastrophes, deliverances, revelations, are justified—they are shown to have a divine right to exist—because they end in Me. Consider, I say, how great a claim is involved here, and how unique. We sometimes feel that it means little or nothing now to say that Jesus is the Christ. This is what it means, this at the very least, when the claim is made by Him; and if the claim is justified, which here is taken for granted, it puts Jesus in a place which no one can share with Him.

(*b.*) Again, it was part of the moral authority exercised by Jesus that He criticised, and where He thought fit, abrogated, even what had hitherto possessed divine authority. 'Ye have heard that it was said to them of old time . . . but *I* say unto *you*.' He compared Himself, to their disadvantage, with the most venerated persons and institutions in the sacred history. A greater than Jonas—or rather, more than Jonas—more than Solomon, more than the Temple, was there. By a word he made all meats clean, virtually abolishing the Levitical law; by another word, he replaced the Jewish law of the Sabbath by its divine intention; and by yet another displaced the Jewish law of marriage to introduce its divine ideal. These, indeed, are but consequences of what has been said under the last head; but in the naturalness and decision with which Jesus speaks and acts, we see how deep and untroubled was His consciousness of being a spiritual authority to which every other is subordinate. He is not a critic, but a judge; his sentence is not the expression of a private opinion, but carries the weight of law; it is at once annihilating and creative. The more fully we appreciate this side of His work, the more we shall feel that here also He stands alone.

(c.) But Christ's authority is principally exercised, in the first instance, in the demand for personal obedience and personal confidence. *Follow me* is a summary of all He has to say to men. We attenuate its meaning when we take it, as we almost instinctively do, metaphorically; those to whom it was first addressed had to take it literally as well. So taken, it meant a complete abandonment of life to Christ. When we regard the gospel as an order of grace, we are apt unconsciously to cheapen it; but Jesus never does this. The salvation which is in Him is not merely a gift, but a vocation; it is a high calling, meant for all who are ready to count the cost and to pay it; and there is no sacrifice which He hesitates to ask from men. 'If any man come to me, and hate not his father and mother, and wife and children, and brethren and sisters, yea, and his own life also, he cannot be my disciple. . . . Whosoever he be of you that forsaketh not all that he hath, he cannot be my disciple.' A truly noble man is overwhelmed with the responsibility of asking others to make sacrifices like these even in a public cause: it pierced the great heart of Mazzini with the sharpest pain to think that young Italy had been roused by his voice to shed its blood, even for freedom, and in vain. But Christ never betrays the faintest hesitation in asking the most stupendous sacrifices for His own sake, in demanding the most unhesitating trust and obedience for Himself. It is true that He combines with Himself sometimes the gospel, sometimes the Kingdom of God, as when He says, 'Whosoever

shall lose his life for *My* sake and the *gospel's*;' but
the very simplicity with which He identifies these
universal interests with Himself is only another
aspect of His unique position and unique authority.
Now to give ourselves up entirely to another, as
Jesus requires men to give themselves up to Him, is
the very essence of religious faith. 'The believer,'
as Didon has finely said, 'no longer belongs to
himself; he renounces his own thoughts, his own
interests, his own initiative; everything, in short;
and belongs without reserve to Him in whom he
believes. He dies to himself in order to live morally
in another: he exchanges his own life for the life of
another. No one but God has the right to demand
absolute faith; for every man has his errors, his
faults, his imperfections, and in abdicating before a
man, one would become the slave of this man's
weaknesses. Jesus claimed this complete faith, a
sign that He claimed the prerogative of God.' [1]

4. But to draw this inference at this point is to
anticipate the conclusion of an argument, the force
of which is really cumulative. It is enough if we say
that the facts just adduced—Christ's claim to be the
consummator of the Old Testament religion, and
therefore to occupy a place which no other could
share in the working out of God's redemptive purpose;
His claim to criticise, and where necessary to abrogate,
the old revelation; His claim to implicit confidence
and obedience from His disciples—it is enough if
we say that these facts imply in Jesus a unique
knowledge of God and of His will, and a unique
relation to God. Even if such a knowledge and
such a relation were never expressly asserted, we

[1] See Note A.

should be justified in assuming them on the ground
of the facts. Such a dignity, we should feel certain,
and such a practical sovereignty over man's conscience, will, and affections, as Christ not only
exercised, but felt entitled to exercise as a right,
could never be treated as accidental; they must
have a real basis and background in the nature of
the Person to whom they belong. This inference
is put beyond doubt when we find that it is supported by the explicit testimony of Jesus to Himself: it is an anticipation of our own minds, but it
is verified by *His* self-consciousness. If there is
one thing which the gospels make more indubitable
than another, it is that He claimed a unique knowledge of God, and claimed it on the basis of a
unique relation to Him. He revealed God as the
Father, and He was able to do so because He
knew Himself as the Son. Even if we leave the
fourth gospel out of account, this is one of the
certainties of the case. It is true that in Matthew,
Mark, and Luke, Jesus never calls Himself in so
many words 'the Son of God'; but again and
again He calls God his Father. Recent theology
has magnified the idea of the divine Fatherhood,
and spent much of its best strength in trying to
define it in relation to mankind in general; but
our interest in this question should not blind us
to the truth that the relation claimed by Jesus to
the Father was something quite other than that
in which all men stand to God as the author of
their being. He was not *a* son among others, but
the Son through whom alone the Father was interpreted to the world. His Sonship was as much

a mystery in the world as the divine Fatherhood; the two were in necessary and indissoluble relation. 'No man,' He said, 'knoweth the Son save the Father; neither knoweth any man the Father save the Son, and he to whomsoever the Son willeth to reveal Him.' This incomparable relation to God —this relation to God which was His and His only —was part of the consciousness of Christ; He knew Himself only in it, and not apart from it. He knew Himself, in virtue of it, as the only source from which the knowledge of the Father could flow to men; the only luminary from which that great light could shine out on those who were sitting in darkness and the shadow of death. How He came to this knowledge of Himself—what, in other words, was the growth of the filial consciousness in Christ—is an interesting question, but one which need not detain us here. It is sufficient to say that it had attained to complete serenity and certainty by the time He entered on His public ministry, and that it was attested by specially impressive revelations at the great crises of His life. At His baptism, when He deliberately committed Himself to His work—at His transfiguration, when He turned His back on the heavenly glory, and with the Cross now full in view, set His face steadfastly to go to Jerusalem,—a heavenly voice was heard, 'This is My beloved Son, in whom I am well pleased.' On these high occasions, on which He gave Himself obediently to His Father's will, taking from His hand our bitter cup, the consciousness of His Sonship was, as it were, intensified in Jesus; He had a triumphant heavenly assurance of it. This reminds us that, with all its uniqueness, it was not something quite alien and incomprehensible to us. We can understand, in a measure, what it means that in solemn acts of self-dedication and self-devotion the Son received from the Father such attestations of His Sonship as the gospels record. With such acts the Father was well pleased; they were worthy of the Son of His love (Col. i. 13). They warn us that the relation of Father and Son is not to be conceived abstractly, or without spiritual contents; it may involve metaphysical presuppositions, but these alone do not constitute it; we miss the mark altogether if we do not see that it is constituted out of love, confidence, obedience, fellowship in a work for men. On the other hand, express words of Jesus warn us against reducing it to a relation which can be paralleled in every man. No man knoweth the Father save the Son. Jesus makes common cause with us in every-thing, as far as possible, but He does not identify Himself with men here. Candid Unitarians have admitted that it is a striking fact, that while Jesus often speaks of God as *the* Father, *My* Father, *your* Father, He never associates Himself even with His disciples to say *Our* Father. ' My Father and your Father,' He says, after the Resurrection, ' My God and your God '—keeping up the distinction to the very last.

Jesus, then, was the Son of God in a peculiar and unique sense: this was how He conceived Himself, and this is, fundamentally, how we have to conceive Him. The Jews sometimes used this ex-pression—Son of God—in a kind of official way, which we must be careful to exclude. Prophets had spoken of Israel as God's son, His firstborn;[1] and Psalmists had applied these titles to the hoped-for Messianic king.[2] It is probably in this quasi-official sense that Son of God is used in the gospels by other speakers than Jesus. Thus when Nathanael exclaims 'Rabbi, thou art the Son of God, thou art the King of Israel,' Son of God and King of Israel are convertible terms.[3] So when the high priest asks Him at his trial, 'Art thou the Christ, the Son of the Blessed?' the Son of the Blessed means no more than the Christ.[4] It is an official title, not a personal name: it denotes dignity, not nature. But Jesus is in no sense an official, and He has no titles which are not real names. When He calls Himself the Son, it is because He is conscious of being the peculiar object of the Father's love, the peculiar possessor of the Father's mind, the peculiar organ of the Father's will, for the salvation of men. The name is personal, not official; its content is spiritual, not legal. We cannot define it apart from Christ, and then see whether He answers to the definition; the only definition of it must be sought *in Him.* Its content is revealed to us in a religious experience in which the Father draws us to the Son, and the Son interprets to us the Father; it is on such a religious experience alone that our theology can be built. It is revealed to us, as it was to His disciples, in actual intercourse with Jesus; it must impress itself on our hearts before we can make a confession of Christ that shall answer to

[1] Ex. iv. 22; Hos. xi. 1; Jer. xxxi. 9.
[2] Psalms ii. 7; lxxxix. 27.
[3] John i. 49.
[4] Mark xiv. 61.

what He really is. And the Christ in whom the
Son of God has to be discerned is He with whom
men associated from His Baptism to His Crucifixion;
it is the man Christ Jesus, as He lived and moved
among men, in whom the unique relation to God
is to be discovered. If we cannot find it there,
we will not find the true import of it through
anything that went before or anything that came
after. Neither the miraculous conception nor the
Resurrection from the dead can reveal what the
divine Sonship of Jesus means to one who is blind
to the witness to it in His life. What they do
mean and teach I will consider further on; meanwhile, let us remember that the Son of God has to
be found, confessed, and believed in, in one who
lived a truly human life, and in that truly human
life itself. Not apart from but in our human
nature, did Jesus know Himself to be in this unique,
this for all other men mediatorial sense, the Son
of God. In other words, we have to find, confess,
and believe in the Son of God, in one who was
a son of man.

5. This name—the Son of Man—brings us to another important element in the self-consciousness of
Christ—one of unsurpassed importance, to judge by
the frequency with which it rose to His lips. It has
the rare distinction, also, of being used in His lifetime by Himself alone. It has been the subject of
infinite discussion, and it lends itself so readily to
all sorts of philosophical, dogmatic, and pious uses,
that the discussion has been even less limited by
reference to the facts than such discussions usually
are. But some points are very generally accepted

now.   One is the original dependence of the name
on the Book of Daniel.   This is put beyond doubt
by the solemn answer of Jesus to the high priest
on the occasion of His trial.   To the query already
referred to, 'Art thou the Christ, the Son of the
Blessed?' He answers : 'I am, and ye shall see the
Son of Man sitting on the right hand of power, and
coming with the clouds of heaven.'   This description
of His majesty is borrowed from Dan. vii. 13 f., and
it is hardly open to doubt that this passage is the
basis on which the conception of 'the Son of
Man' rests.   Daniel's vision contains, in the briefest
outline, a religious philosophy of history—a sketch
of the rise and fall of powers in the world till the
final sovereignty comes.   The prophet sees four great
beasts come up from the sea and reign in succession.
What they have in common is that they *are* beasts—
brutal, rapacious, destructive.   But they have their
day; the dominion they exercised is taken away
from them; it is transferred—and here the vision
culminates—to one like a son of man.   The brute
kingdoms are succeeded by a human kingdom, the
dominion of selfishness and violence by the dominion
of reason and goodness; and this last is universal
and everlasting.   This is the historical antecedent of
that name, at once so intimate and so mysterious,
which Jesus appropriated to Himself—the Son of
Man.   It had an apocalyptic side, which, as we
shall see, He did not disclaim; but what primarily
determined its significance was its contrast to the
lion, the bear, the leopard, and the terrible beast with
iron teeth.   When Jesus defined it and made it His
own—when he turned 'one like unto a son of man'

into 'the Son of Man,' and used the name almost
as a periphrasis for 'I'—He intimated to those
who were able to understand it His consciousness
of being head of a new, universal, and everlasting
kingdom, in which all that was truly and characteristically human should have authority.   The wild
beasts had had their time; now the hour had come
for the dominion of the human; *man claimed his
sovereignty in Jesus.*   This is the root idea in
the name—the Son of Man—and it covers and
explains all that has been legitimately connected
with it.   For instance, many have interpreted the
words as if they meant 'the *ideal* man,' he who is
all that God designed man should be.   This is
included in the true meaning, for as head and
founder of the coming human kingdom the Son
of Man is the true representative of the race; but
as an explanation it is inadequate, for its presuppositions are philosophical, not religious, and it
stands in no relation to the historical purpose of
God, in carrying out which Jesus felt the appro-
priateness of the name to Himself.   Others, again,
have interpreted it as a symbol of Christ's tenderness, compassion, and condescension to human
weakness, and have felt something inappropriate
in associating 'the Son of Man' closely with the
idea of sovereignty.   But we lose the very graciousness of our Lord Jesus Christ if we shut out this.
It is one great part of His work, in this very
character of the Son of Man, to revolutionise the
current idea of sovereignty by exhibiting the true
and everlasting one.   'Ye know,' He said to His
ambitious disciples, 'that they who are accounted

to rule the nations—accounted only, for it is no real sovereignty they wield—they who are accounted to rule the, nations lord it over them, and their great ones deal arbitrarily with them. But it shall not be so among you. Whosoever is minded to be great—to be a ruler—among you, shall be your servant; and whosoever is minded to be first among you—to be actually sovereign—shall be your slave; for even the Son of Man—the Head and Founder of the one everlasting universal dominion, in whom humanity really comes to its sovereignty—even the Son of Man came not to be ministered unto but to minister, and to give His life a ransom for many.' [1] It is not, then, simply nearness to us, brotherly tenderness and sympathy, that the name ' the Son of Man' expresses; it is nearness, brotherly tenderness and sympathy, ministering life and ransoming death, as the essential marks and attributes of the one true King of our race. The brute kingdoms of violence and selfishness pass, and the kingdom of God comes, where sovereignty is exercised in the spirit of Jesus, and inspires its subjects with its own truly human character.

No doubt these names—the Son of God and the Son of Man—in some sense correspond to each other. As the first expresses a unique relation to God, so does the other a unique relation to our race. Each of us is a son of man; each of us is, or may be, a son of God; but there is one only who is at once *the* Son of God and *the* Son of Man. The first name expresses, at the very lowest, an entire oneness with God in love, in will, and in purpose; the second an

[1] See Mark x. 42 ff.

entire oneness with man in sympathy, in experience, and in interest. When Christ calls Himself the Son of God He means that He is to God, and for God's work in the world, what no other could be; and when He calls Himself the Son of Man He means that He is to our race and to its hopes what no other can be. He makes common cause with us in our actual life, taking to Himself, and feeling as His own, all that is ours, of pain and sickness, of shame, defeat, sin and death; but He is at the same time the bearer of victory to our beaten company, the Sovereign Man who overcomes all that has overcome us, and makes us partakers of His triumph. It is for this reason, I think, that what Christ does for our race, especially in the way of deliverance or redemption, is regularly associated with this name. 'The Son of Man came to seek and to save that which was lost.' 'The Son of Man came, not to be ministered unto but to minister, and to give His life a ransom for many.' 'The Son of Man is Lord of the Sabbath,' and entitled to see that the mode of its observance makes it a boon and not a burden to the race. 'The Son of Man hath power on earth to forgive sins'—to lift the weight from the conscience, to liberate the enslaved will or the paralysed limbs, and enable those who have defeated and destroyed themselves to become free men again. In all these passages, and in many more, the point of the name lies in its combination of two things in one person—an entire identification with men, which makes all that is theirs His; and a sovereignty exercised in purest humanity which makes this true brother the Redeemer of His kind.

6. This last idea leads me to notice another which is related to it: with all His identification of Himself with our interests—making common cause with us as men to the very uttermost—Jesus, it is plain on every page of the gospel, was conscious of the immense interval which separated Him from us. This comes out in many distinct ways. Earlier messengers of God to Israel were only servants; He is the Son, only and well beloved. Other men are lost sheep; He is the good shepherd who has come to gather them into the fold. Other men are stricken with disease; He is the physician who has come to heal. Other men have consciences laden with guilt; He is the sacrifice whose blood is to be shed for the remission of sins. The lives of other men are forfeited; His is the one free life which is to be given a ransom for them. At the present time, I imagine, there are few elements in the self-consciousness of Jesus which have less justice done to them than this. Yet this is a true and an essential element in it. This it was which was formulated in the apostolic doctrine of the sinlessness of Jesus, and which is a presupposition of every Christian creed. This doctrine of the sinlessness of Jesus has been criticised as meagre and misleading, and so it would be if it were supposed to exhaust the character of Jesus. It does not suggest the fulness of His love, the overflowing communicative goodness and purity of His spirit; but it is not meant to do so. It is negative merely, but intentionally so. It maintains a distinction between Jesus and all others, in spite of the perfection of His nature and His sympathy; He was *not* one thing which we all are; He was *not* a sinner. It

was part of His consciousness that He was not; it would have been the worst insincerity if, when He challenged others, or rather defied them, to convict Him of sin, He had been able to convict Himself. When we consider His knowledge of the human heart, and how His words are able to wake the sleeping conscience and make it tell over to us all things that ever we did; when we consider how our knowledge of Him is the very standard by which we measure ourselves, and develop whatever tenderness of conscience in regard to sin we have, we feel how absolutely alone Christ stands in the world, and by how deep—and from our side how impassable—a gulf He is separated, as sinless, from all men. This separateness from sinners is not a little, but a stupendous, thing; it is the presupposition of redemption; it is that very virtue in Christ without which He would not be qualified to be a Saviour, but would, like us, need to be saved. Few doctrines have greater apologetic interest and value than this. If the impression can once be made upon the mind —and an open unbiassed mind is very accessible to it —that Jesus, to His own self-consciousness, stood solitary among men, alone untainted by the universal disease, alone unburdened in conscience, alone with unimpaired vigour of will, a great step has been taken toward complete Christian faith. A moral miracle has been admitted—a new beginning found for a new course of human life and history. It is comparatively easy, then, to acknowledge Christ's other claims; He has begun to take possession of the soul, and will carry His work through.

7. But there is one character of supreme import-

ance in which Jesus often puts Himself forward and
to which I have not yet referred—I mean the
character of a Judge.   He is a supreme moral
authority, legislating without misgiving, and demanding implicit obedience; He is the Son of God,
uniquely related to the Father; He is the Son of
Man, uniquely related to the race as its ministering
and redeeming King; he is separate from sinners,
that He may be able to save.   Beyond all this, He
is the Judge of men.   In a later lecture I will have
occasion to inquire what is meant by such statements
as that all men are judged by their relation to Him;
here, what I wish to insist upon is not the principle
of the judgment, but the fact.   Man's life is not a
natural, but a moral concern; it is subject not only
to physical, but to divine laws.   The meaning and
worth of it may be obscure here, but a day is coming
when they will be made plain; and on that day
Jesus Christ will be the revealer and the Judge.
He judged men while He lived; He read hearts and
pronounced sentences.   But especially He spoke of
His coming again as Judge at the end of the world.
This is an extraordinarily important conception when
we remember the history of the Jewish religion.
Until He came, inspired men had always looked
onward to something that was to come, something
that was not yet there.   The future was filled for
them by a Coming One.   Jesus also looked into the
future, but what He saw there was not the coming
of another, but His own coming again.   In other
words, He was no prophet, but the subject of all
prophecy.   To His own consciousness, He was the
last as well as the first.   In His own consciousness,

the revelation which He brought had the character of finality; there was no more grace to come than was there already in Him; no more perfect knowledge of God to come than that which He was there to impart; what the future would disclose would only be the relation which men had assumed to Him, and this He Himself would declare when He came in glory as Judge. I said a little while ago that Jesus made a stupendous claim when He claimed to be the Christ, and asserted that all earlier revelation, all earlier providence of God in Israel, had its chief end and its consummation in Him; but even that stupendous claim fades before this. For He asserts here the absolute finality of the revelation of God made in His Person, and tells us that not only all the history of Israel, but all human history, terminates in Him. To be acknowledged by Him at His coming is final blessedness; to be disowned by Him is final shame. The consummation of the ages is the manifestation of His glory, the submission of all that is to His sentence. It baffles imagination to enter into the consciousness of one who, we know, was meek and lowly in heart, yet who thus put the worlds under His feet, and did not feel that He did anything presumptuous or incongruous in picturing Himself on the throne of glory, judging all nations. Consider how great this man was—this carpenter of Nazareth —for whom the world, time, history, providence, and grace ended, or at least terminated upon His own coming in glory as Judge of all. There is nothing in man's life to compare with this anywhere. Christ as Universal Judge, representing and vindicating the finality of the religion and life He inaugurated, is as much alone as Christ the Supreme Lawgiver, Christ the Son of God, the Son of Man, the Sinless One. He lived, to Himself, in all these characters; they all entered into His consciousness of Himself. They must all enter into our conception of Him—that conception which is the fundamental thing in Christian religion and in Christian theology. I have taken it for granted that Jesus did know the secret of His own being, that He spoke of Himself the words of truth and soberness, and that the record which we have of these words—and I have confined myself practically to the synoptic gospels— is a reliable record. I am certain of this, that if we do not know concerning Christ those things which have just been passed in review, we do not know anything as He would have us know. And if we know these, how much they come to! What a problem for the theologian they present! What a task is set to us when we have to explain the appearance of such a One in the world, and look at God and man, at life and death and the future, in the light which His presence throws!

Before concluding this lecture, I should like to insist again upon one point which has been already touched in passing—this, namely, that it is the historical Christ to whom we have to go back as the true fountain of our theology. What He knew God to be in relation to Himself,—what He knew Himself to be in relation to God,—what that consciousness involved for the relations of God and man in general— this must be our starting-point as Christian students. Of course we are members of the Church; we are partakers of the one Spirit which is the life of all

who have a place in it; and as such we have a
witness in ourselves, and might conceivably make a
theology by simply thinking out what is involved in
our consciousness as Christian men.   Distinguished
theologians like Dr. Dale in England,[1] and the
lamented Dr. Stearns[2] among yourselves, have tried
to make an apologetic use of Christian experience,
and to argue back from it to what Christ must have
been.   Whatever the value of such an argument
may be for the apologist, it is not of a nature to be
of much service to the dogmatist.   No doubt Christ's
testimony to Himself must assert itself in our hearts
before we can understand it, or see what it involves;
the claims He makes must vindicate themselves, and
subdue us; but all that is creative and normative
in the Christian consciousness depends upon Him;
and with Him, therefore, we must start.   It is the
great merit of the Ritschlian theology, though a
merit qualified by much inconsistency, that it has
thoroughly understood this.   It takes us back to the
Person of the Founder, to His mind and His life;
and it finds there all the great determining ideas by
the aid of which God and man, sin and redemption,
life and death, are to be interpreted.   It cannot be
repeated too often, or with too great emphasis, that
this is the right way.   Mere conceptions soon
become barren; definitions the most curious and
precise become curiously unreal; nothing but
personality and life is infinitely inspiring.   There
is a tendency in theology, manifested in every age,
to become scholastic.   The theology of the Greek

[1] In *The Living Christ and the Four Gospels.*
[2] In his Ely Lecture : *The Evidence of Christian Experience.*

Church became scholastic in the fifth century; the theology of the Latin Church in the later middle age; the Protestant theology in the seventeenth century. We are only recovering from the last scholastic epoch now; and we are recovering by a return to Christ. Not the Christ of any creed, not even the Christ of any single apostolic conception; but Christ as He lived and moved among men, full of grace and truth. The Bible is our text-book because it puts us in communication with Him; but He is our authority. We must always fail more or less decidedly unless our whole thoughts are inspired and controlled by Him who says, *I* am the Truth.

LECTURE III

THE APOSTOLIC DOCTRINE OF CHRIST

THE fundamental thing in Christology is Christ's testimony to Himself—a testimony which we find not only in His consciousness of Himself as Son of God, Son of Man, Christ and Judge, but in all His works and words, and even in His sufferings and death. To come in contact with this we go back to the gospels, and put ourselves as directly as possible in communication with Christ Himself. The impression that *He* makes upon us, as He lives and moves before our faces, must certainly be our starting-point: if we are *not* impressed, if we do not discover in some sense His unique and even His divine dignity, we need not try to approach Him in any other way. But having started here, and received a certain impression of His solitary greatness, the question arises whether the mind can simply rest in it without seeking further explanation. This is the attitude which is not only assumed, but asserted to be the sole legitimate one, by Ritschl and his school. Christ, they say, has for the Christian consciousness the religious value of God ; all that we really mean when we say *God* is to be seen in its purity in His human life. To ask for explanations is a complete mistake. It is to put the spirit at fault, and divert it from religion, and even from theology, to metaphysics. It is to carry it from the region of ethical and spiritual certainties to the region of the transcendent, where no certainty can be attained. To those who have been vexed with barren unethical speculations in theology, there is something in this plea both plausible and fascinating, but it is one which the mind cannot permanently concede. We must seek for the explanation of a phenomenon so stupendous as a man who has the religious value of God. We must try to define the relations in which a man who occupies a place so exclusively His own stands to God on the one hand, and to men on the other. We must, especially when we consider the immense historical importance of Christ—His own claim to sum up the previous history of the world, and at its consummation to judge the ages that are yet to be—we must, in view of these things, try to work our religious estimate of His human personality into the framework of all our thoughts about God and man, the world and history.

This is what the various New Testament writers have done, and it is with their interpretation of Christ that this lecture is concerned. The starting-point with all is the resurrection and exaltation of Jesus. This is the grand illuminative fact from which they all proceed. Not a single New Testament writer, unless he is engaged in simply recording Christ's earthly life, thinks of Him as He lived on earth. They all think of Him as He lives now, on the throne of the universe, with angels and principalities and powers put under Him. His sovereignty in glory is not a thing which may or may not, as one pleases, be added to the religious appreciation of His life on earth as having the value of a revelation of God; it is the first and last and dominating element in the Christian consciousness of the New Testament. It depends, of course, on the belief in the resurrection; if the disciples had not believed that Jesus rose from the dead on the third day, the Christian religion, as the New Testament exhibits it, would never have existed. But belief in the resurrection introduces decisively, at least at one point, that transcendent element into the Christian faith which so many wish to exclude. Hence it is explicitly or tacitly rejected by the school to which I have referred. Writers like Ritschl, Harnack, and Wendt, not only ignore it, but, on the ground that on such points we cannot separate the authoritative words of Jesus from the Jewish commonplaces put into His mouth by the apostles, reject along with it all the eschatological elements in the teaching of Christ Himself.[1] The one step is as arbitrary and as unjustifiable as the other; and to take both is simply to land ourselves in a position in which the Christology of the New Testament is irrelevant to the Christian religion—is, in short, an irrationality, which it is our business, as good Christians, not to explain, understand, or accept, but merely to explain away. I do not propose to assail or defend anything, but, starting from the point from which the New Testament writers started, to explain their conceptions of the Person whom they worshipped as Lord of all. [1] See Note A.

To them, as to us, Jesus was uniquely related to God even on earth : the well-beloved Son of the Father, who alone could reveal the Father to other men. To them, as to us, He was uniquely vindicated by God after the crucifixion—uniquely exalted at His right hand. When they put these two things together, and let them tell upon their minds, they felt instinctively that more was involved. He who was so exclusively related to God in those years of human life, so exclusively exalted by God after that terrible death, must have been in an exclusive way *from* God. Of course there is a religious or pious acknowledgment of this which falls short of what I mean. A man may say of Christ's life : There is only one explanation of this : it is of God ; but that is not enough. Every good life is of God ; and the thing to be explained here is not that which Christ has in common with others, but that in which He stands by Himself, with a consciousness of Himself which is exclusively His own, doing a work which no other can do, anticipating a future in which He is the goal of all things, and exalted, as in the Resurrection He was, to the throne of the world. The apostolic writers are agreed in the idea that there is a transcendent element in what is now called the Godhead of Christ : in other words, they not only believe that the man Christ Jesus has the religious value of God for those who know Him ; but that behind His manifestation on earth, in the fulness of that grace and truth which were revealed to Moses as the grand attributes of God, there is an essential and transcendent relation to God. They are agreed that His appearance on earth is of the nature of an

Incarnation. He is not a saint offered by humanity
to God; He is the Son who has come from the
Father into the world.[1] I speak of this as if the
apostles had merely thought out, or fought out,
unassisted, the presuppositions of their faith in the
Risen Lord; but I do not believe this was the case.
However we are to conceive it, there surely was a
special guidance given by the Spirit of God to the
men who at that critical epoch had the duty given
to them of shaping the mind of Christ's church to
all generations. What Paul says of himself re-
peatedly, that he received his gospel—which surely
included his conception of Christ—*by revelation,*
gives his Christology an authority above that of
mere intellectual construction. The spirit of the
new religion was in it: the Spirit of the Father and
of the Son; and it goes back, in essential points, to
words of Christ Himself.

The very simplest expression that can be given
to the ideas of incarnation, and of a transcendent
element in Christ's Godhead, is given in the idea of
His pre-existence. This is assumed by Paul, as an
element in the Christian faith, in his first Epistle to
the Corinthians, which, next to the Epistles to the
Thessalonians, is the earliest of his letters. 'To us
there is one God, the Father, of whom are all things,
and we unto Him; and one Lord Jesus Christ,
through whom are all things, and we through Him.'[2]
The pre-existence is nowhere expressly defined. The
attempt of Baur and others, on the basis of 1 Cor.
xv. 47—the second man is from heaven—to make
out that for Paul Christ existed as man before the

[1] See Note B.   [2] 1 Cor. viii. 6.

Incarnation, is not to be treated seriously. More important than this is the attempt to discredit the Pauline thought of Christ's pre-existence by the assertion that it was a Jewish commonplace, applied to all that was supposed to be peculiarly valuable to God. Not only important persons, like Adam and Moses, but even things, like the tabernacle and the tables of the law, were supposed to have heavenly archetypes, *i.e.* to be pre-existent. The conception of pre-existence would thus be due to a speculative incapacity in the Jewish mind : the Jew speaking of a pre-existent archetype where the Greek would have spoken of ideal as opposed to actual existence. In any case, this notion of pre-existence was applied, it is asserted, *inter alia*, to the Messiah ; and Paul, in speaking of Christ as pre-existent, was merely doing as his countrymen did, but not doing what has any authority, or even any precise significance for us. His utterances on this point may be disregarded as private theologoumena, or idols of the time.

This is very summary, and not very intelligent criticism, though it is covered by great names. Not to speak of the fact that the evidence of a Jewish belief in the pre-existence of Messiah is scanty in the extreme, and that the New Testament in particular shows no trace of it except among Christians, it overlooks all that body of facts, religious and historical, included in Christ's life, death, and resurrection, which forced the minds of Christian men to seek a transcendent background for Christ's appearance ; it overlooks express and well-authenticated words of Christ Himself—we may call them

such though they only appear in the Fourth Gospel;[1]
it overlooks the fact that whereas pre-existence
with the Jews is merely a doubling of the thing
which exists—a heavenly counterpart, which may
be the model of, but is not otherwise related to, the
earthly reality—with Paul it is quite different; the
pre-existent One has a life and functions in that
pre-existent state; He comes to exist among men,
and He returns to His original glory.   It is simply
trifling with a word to set aside all this as insignifi-
cant and unauthoritative, because the Jews, forsooth,
believed that the tables of the law existed two
thousand years before the creation of the world.[2]

Accepting, then, this Pauline thought of Christ's
pre-existence, as covering an essential truth, how,
let us ask, does the apostle unfold its contents?
The amplest and most deliberate statement is that
of Col. i. 15 ff.   It has been asserted, indeed, that
the subject of this statement is not the pre-existent
One, but the Risen Lord, Jesus Christ: it is enough
to say that the contrast implied in the objection is
false.   Paul believed that Jesus Christ the Risen
Lord had pre-existed; and it is of Him not only as
exalted, but as pre-existent, that he is speaking.   I
cannot do better here than quote Lightfoot's
paraphrase of this important passage: 'He is the
perfect image, the visible representation, of the
unseen God.   He is the Firstborn, the absolute
Heir of the Father, begotten before the ages; the
Lord of the Universe by virtue of primogeniture,
and by virtue also of creative agency.   For in and
through Him the whole world was created, things

[1] John viii. 58 ; xvii. 5.   [2] See Note C.

in heaven and things on earth, things visible to the
outward eye, and things cognisable by the inward
perception. His supremacy is absolute and universal.
All powers in heaven and earth are subject to Him.
This subjection extends even to the most exalted
and most potent of angelic beings, whether they
be called Thrones or Dominations or Princedoms or
Powers, or whatever title of dignity men may confer
upon them. Yes, He is first and He is last. Through
Him, as the mediatorial word, the universe has been
created; and unto Him, as the final goal, it is
tending. In Him is no before or after. He is
pre-existent and self-existent before all the worlds.
And in Him as the binding and sustaining power,
universal nature coheres and consists.'—(P. 144.)
' And not only does He hold this position of absolute
priority and sovereignty over the Universe—the
natural creation. He stands also in the same
relation to the Church—the new spiritual creation.
He is its head, and it is His body. This is His
prerogative, because He is the source and the
beginning of its life, being the Firstborn from the
dead. Thus in all things—in the spiritual order
as in the natural—in the Church as in the world—
He is found to have the pre-eminence.'—(P. 156.)
This summary which, with all its fulness, does no
more than justice to the text, shows how far the
idea of Christ's pre-existence is from being an
accidental or alien thing to the Christianity of St.
Paul. It enabled him to put Christ—the Lord
whom he knew—in relations to God, to the world,
and to the Church, which satisfied at once his
intelligence, and his religious consciousness. At an

earlier stage in his life St. Paul had thought of Christ, as Dr. Fairbairn points out,[1] mainly in his work as the saviour of sinners; he had defined the gospel in relation to the law; he had thought out the significance of Christ as the counterpart of Adam; his Christology had been mainly historical. Even then, as we can see from 1 Cor. viii. 6, xv. 47, the pre-existence was in his mind; but it was under new conditions, under the constraint of a new environment, that he was led into all the truth which it involved, and advanced, to use Dr. Fairbairn's terms, from the historical to the cosmical Christology. This would be a mistaken expression if it suggested that in his advance he left the historical behind; but it is true if it means that the longer St. Paul lived, the more he appreciated the universal bearings of the revelation made in Christ. The pre-existent Christ is demanded by the historical; the work the historical redeemer does cannot be understood unless all that is involved in the pre-existence lies behind it. A work universal in its scope, eternal in its duration, perfect in its manifestation of wisdom and of reconciling love, requires that He who works it should be eternally and essentially related to God, to man, and to all that is. Nothing less than this is involved in the Pauline doctrine of the pre-existence of Christ.

It is difficult for us to state this without giving it the aspect of a speculation, which may more or less have power to persuade, according to the mind to which it is addressed, but which can hardly be put forward as essential to the Christian religion. To

[1] *Christ in Modern Theology*, pp. 302-318.

discuss what is essential to the Christian religion is
not usually very profitable, and it may be agreed at
once that no one would use the doctrine of Christ's
pre-existence to introduce an unbeliever or any outsider to the Christian faith.   We must make Christ's
acquaintance where He offers it—in the common
human life depicted in the gospels ; we must become
persuaded of what He is, even in His manifestation
in the flesh, before we raise the question of what is
presupposed in it.   But to forbid us to raise the
question is to deny a right and a duty which the
mind will not forego ; and to maintain that there is
no question to be raised is simply to show that we
have not been impressed by Christ at all as *they*
were who first were saved and regenerated by Him.
An apostolic sense of the debt man owes to Christ,
an apostolic acceptance of the reign of Christ
now, an apostolic belief that He is one day to be
the judge of the living and the dead, relieve the
faith in his pre-existence of its speculative cast, and
give it a natural aspect and a secure grasp of the
mind.   It fits in with the whole scale of Christ's
Person and work, and though we cannot know it
directly, as we know His earthly life, or even His
Resurrection, it may become as profoundly sure and
true.

That it was so to St. Paul is evident from the manner
in which he appeals to it in 2 Cor. viii. and Phil. ii.
He frankly takes it for granted, as a truth which no
Christian would think of questioning, and he appeals
to it to enforce the moral duties of charity, humility,
and consideration for others.   He urges the Corinthians to contribute liberally to the collection for

the poor; such liberality is only what you owe, he says, for ye know the grace of our Lord Jesus Christ, that though He was rich yet for your sakes He became poor, that ye through His poverty might be made rich.   It was the pre-existent One who was rich; the poverty which He assumed was that to which the Incarnation brought Him.   So in the passage in Philippians, with even greater distinctness.   St. Paul is urging on the Christians in Philippi the duties of lowliness, and of regard to others' interests as well as their own, and he turns instinctively to the supreme example.   'Let that mind—that moral temper—be in you which was also in Christ Jesus: who, being originally in the form of God, counted it not a prize to be on an equality with God, but emptied Himself, taking the form of a servant, being made in the likeness of men.'   Here, again, it is the pre-existent One who is originally in the form of God; the form of a servant is that which the Incarnation brings with it.   These passages are extremely interesting for various reasons.   They both contain the idea of an exchange of states, or modes of being; wealth is given up for poverty; fulness and the form of God for emptiness and the form of a servant.   This idea impresses the imagination and touches the heart rather than aids the intelligence; the attempts that have been made in what are known as the Kenotic Christologies to interpret it metaphysically hardly take us much further on.[1]   Another point of interest in both passages is this.   They construe the Incarnation ethically.   Mr. Gore has laid just emphasis on this

[1] See Note D.

in his Bampton Lectures.[1] St. Paul is sure that he
knows the motive of it; he is sure that he knows
more or less the nature of it, even if he can but
dimly guess at the method of it. If he has not a
metaphysical, he has a moral key to it. It was an
act of condescension, inconceivably great, but of a
quality that we can both understand and imitate.
The pre-existent One did not think only of His own
things, but of the things of others; He looked on us
in our low and poor estate; and for us men and
for our salvation He gave up His heavenly for the
earthly life. If we can know nothing else here,
at least we know *the grace* of our Lord Jesus Christ;
we appreciate the spirit of the incarnation, and that
is the main thing. And it is to be remembered
that, if this conception is rejected, there disappears
along with it one of the most subduing aspects of
the divine nature as it is revealed in the Bible. We
can no longer feel that God Himself has bowed down
to bless us in and by His Son. Yet this, it is safe
to say, is one of the most characteristic features
of the whole New Testament religion; and it
makes a great difference when men consent to
do without it.[2]

The doctrine of Christ's pre-existence, thus interpreted, is specially Pauline : we have a more finished
form of it, so to speak, in the gospel according to
John. Of course I assume here that the gospel
has John's authority—that it is to all intents and
purposes the work of one who knew Jesus in His
human life more intimately than any other person.
There is a considerable consensus of opinion now

[1] See Note E.　　　　　　　[2] See Note F.

as to its historical value : even those who discredit
the discourses cannot avoid the impression that the
incidental notices of time, place, and event are
peculiarly like truth. It used to be said that it was
not a history at all, but an idealising of tradition in
the interest of a speculative idea : now, theologians
are agreed that if John is the most speculative, he
is at the same time the most personal, of New
Testament writers.[1] Christ may conceivably be
more or less lost in ideas for those who, like St.
Paul or the writer to the Hebrews, never knew
Him ; to St. John He never ceases to be strictly
personal and historical. It is from an intimate
acquaintance with Him that he proceeds in all his
theological interpretation ; and the impression Christ
made on him was so deep, so incomparable, that no
mere idea could ever compete with it, or even
modify it. It remained with him to the end, vivid,
overpowering, dominating everything. It might
use as its instruments any ideas that suited it ; it
might find access for itself to men's minds by
attaching itself in this way or that to their ordinary
modes of thought ; but it is simply shutting our
eyes to the necessary proportions of things—mis-
conceiving the efficiency of forces—to suppose that
any speculative idea should have overpowered in
the mind of John the actual impression made by
Christ. The force that created Christianity could
not be deflected or transformed, where it was
working in all its pure intensity, by any abstraction
of the brain.

This consideration alone should enable us to

[1] See Note G.

appreciate rightly John's use of the term and idea
'Logos' in his doctrine of Christ. He does not
start with the Logos, but, like the other New
Testament writers, with Jesus. Indeed the term
is not used in the gospel at all, but only in the
prologue, so careful is he, when on historical
ground, to be strictly historical. But John felt, as
all the New Testament writers did, that the
historical Christ, in His solitary greatness, called for
explanation. All through the gospel Christ is the
Son—the Son in a unique and exclusive sense ; one
with the Father, in the bosom of the Father, the
only way to the Father, the Revealer of the Father.
Under the impulse of the same need—or may we not
say under the guidance of the same Spirit ?—which
prompted Paul, John sought and found the transcendent element which this unique relation to God
presupposed in the idea of the Word, or Logos.
There has been much discussion about the genealogy
of this idea, and especially about its relation to
Philo.   It is generally acknowledged now that
much of it has been beside the mark.   'John and
Philo,' says Harnack, 'have little more in common
than the name.'[1]   The antecedents of that Logos
doctrine which we find in John's prologue—the
prologue to a book which every one now admits to
be as intensely Jewish in its mental and historical
characteristics as anything in the New Testament—
are surely to be sought, not in the Platonic or the
Stoic philosophy, but in the earlier revelation of
God to Israel.   There, too, they are to be found.
It is not denied that in Platonic and Stoic specula-

[1] See Note H.

tion, and in the combination of them with the
Jewish faith in Philo, there was a providential preparation for a book like the Fourth Gospel, but that
book was not produced by them. It does not come
in the line of these philosophies, abstract and
rationalising; it stands on the ground of historical
fact, and in the line of God's revealing activity. To
the writer, on the basis of his full and intimate
knowledge, the historical Christ, the well-beloved
Son, was the perfect revelation of God; revelation
could not conceivably go further; the very principle
of it was identical with this Person; the Word had
become flesh. This great sentence not only puts
Christ in an essential relation to God, it puts Him
in essential relation to all through which God is
revealed—to creation, to human reason, to prophecy
and providence in Israel. He is the light through
which the meaning of all is discovered; they have
all been made *for* Him, and they were not made
without Him. He has significance, primarily for
man, in the order of knowledge; but for all that is,
in the order of being. He was in the beginning,
He was with God, He was God. The first sentence
in John's preface is the last conclusion to which the
place of Christ in his life leads him, but it is the
only one in which his mind can rest. He who is
the Omega must also be the Alpha; He who is the
chief end of the world must also be the mediator
through whom it came into being.

To John, then, as to Paul, the pre-existence of
Christ is an essential element in Christianity. His
eternal relation to God is the only way of conceiving
Him which answers to His real greatness. It is the

only way of conceiving Him which puts the final and perfect revelation made in *Him* in proper relation to inferior and preparatory revelations. It is the only way of conceiving Him, the Absolute Revealer of the Father, which gives coherence and intelligibility to God's general manifestation of Himself to men. But it is not simply a way of conceiving Christ to which the mind is driven by inner necessities of its own; it is not simply the mind's solution of the problems raised by the historical Christ. It is a solution directed and authorised by Christ Himself. Those who believe that He spoke of a glory which He had with the Father before the world was will not hesitate to admit this. No *a priori* assumptions about the necessity of a purely human consciousness, to which such a reminiscence were inconceivable, and no exegetical bewilderments, like those of Wendt, can be pleaded against words so plain.[1] They fall in exactly with that passage in Philippians to which reference has been already made. John, like Paul, conceived the pre-existent One 'in glory.' Anything more definite it is out of our power to say. It is true that he says 'We *beheld* His glory, when He dwelt among us,' and this, no doubt, Paul also would have said; but to both the life on earth has the character of a limitation, a condescension, a renunciation; and Christ returns from it *to* His glory. There is not in John, any more than in Paul, a hint as to the *mode* of the incarnation. The Word became flesh; the fact, in its stupendous simplicity, is stated, and that is all. It is as futile here, as in

[1] See Note I.

Philippians, to try to extract a scientific system from the words. Taken by themselves, they suggest the same idea of an exchange of modes of being which makes up St. Paul's idea of the Incarnation, and they guarantee, as his language does, a real condescension on the part of God to man. Taken in their connection with the rest of the gospel, they suggest the same ethical key to the incarnation which St. Paul also used; the Word became flesh that, as the Incarnate Son, He might give eternal life to a perishing world. Writers of a school which ignores or denies any transcendent element in what it acknowledges to be the Godhead of Christ—Bornemann, for instance—are fond of asserting that the Pauline doctrine of pre-existence and the Johannine doctrine of the Logos are disparate; that is, they are on different planes of thought, have no relation to each other, and cannot, in point of fact, be combined. It is plain, I think, from what has been said, that this is a mistake. In their contents, in their motive, in the ethical impression they produce, they are identical; and the mere fact that the form in which they are stated is not precisely the same, gives all the greater weight to the sameness in substance.[1]

In all this, as has once or twice been remarked, an important point remains unexplained. Nothing at all has been said of the manner of the incarnation; of the process by which the Word became flesh, of the transition made by the pre-existent One from wealth to poverty, from the form of God to the form of a servant. The transition must have

[1] See Note K.

been made somehow. Granting without the least
reserve that men recognised in Christ, and may still
recognise in Him, the Son of God and Saviour of
their souls, without having any ideas on this ulterior
subject, it remains a matter on which a believing
mind is certain, sooner or later, to seek enlightenment.
Christ is unique as He exists in history—unique,
according to His own consciousness, in His relation
both to God and man : is it possible that there can
be nothing unique in His origin ? He came from
God, all the apostles believed, in a *sense* in which
no other came : does it not follow that He came in
a *way* in which no other came ? The precise
matters of fact involved in His origin, whether
historical or physical, may not be of immediate
religious importance ; but if the doctrines of the
pre-existence and of the incarnation of the Word
are true, *some* matters of fact are involved which
the mind cannot but seek to apprehend.

The only light which Scripture throws upon this
subject is contained in the narratives of the miraculous birth of Christ. This, we are to understand,
is the point and the mode of transition between
the heavenly and the earthly life : ' He was conceived of the Holy Ghost, in the womb of the
Virgin Mary.' At the present moment a violent
controversy is raging in Germany over these words
of the apostles' creed. Professor Harnack heads
the assault on this venerable symbol, treats the
narratives in the early chapters of Matthew and
Luke as discredited by criticism, and maintains that
the conception of the virgin birth has no real
authority, and no value for the Christian religion.

When we consider the place that the Virgin and
the virgin birth have held in historical Christianity,
these seem daring assertions, and one is not sur-
prised to hear that a Prussian Synod has pronounced
that the miraculous conception is the essential basis
of the Christian faith. Opinion on this question
will turn, I feel sure, not on the results of un-
christian criticism of the gospel of the infancy, but
on the conception previously formed of the Person,
power, and claims of Christ. Those who are not
compelled to recognise anything transcendent *in*
Him—who reject the idea that He came from God
in a sense in which others do not—who ignore the
resurrection, exclude from their world all Christ's
eschatological revelations, and deny the pre-existence—they, of course, find these stories incredible.
They have a man to deal with, like other men, who
is only God in the sense that He is as full of grace
and truth as God could be in His place—but they
do not really put Him in a *solitary* place; His
eminence, and it is nothing but eminence, is, so far
as one can see, purely accidental. He might *not*
have been what He was, or some other might have
filled His place and done His work. We feel how
inconsistent with the New Testament conception
of Christ such ideas are, and the inconsistency does
not escape the notice of those whose system compels
them to defend it. Thus Ritschl, after defining
Christ's oneness with God as having reference to the
whole scope of His vocation, and consisting in this,
that Christ in His vocation was perfectly obedient to
the Father, and as such the object of the Father's
love, proceeds as follows :—' Hence Jesus, inasmuch

as He is the first to realise the aim of the Kingdom
of God in His personal life, is unique in His kind
for this reason, that every one who would solve
the same problem with the same perfection as He,
would yet, in depending upon Him, be unequal to
Him.'[1]   I cannot see that this is consistent, in the
long-run, with any form of Christianity whatever.
Christ has a casual pre-eminence, that is all.   The
person of whom we can speak in this fashion is not
He who said to John : 'I am Alpha and Omega, the
beginning and the end, the first and the last.'[2]   I
should make the same criticism upon Nitzsch, who
has written the last complete *Dogmatik* of this
school, and who sums up his doctrine of the Person
of Christ by saying that a holy manhood, and a
representation of God, are united in Him in a
degree to which there is not even an approximation
at any other point in the religious life of man.[3]
This is not a Christian conception of Christ at all ;
it makes Him no more than *primus inter pares*, and
even that only by chance.   It is easy to understand
why those who appreciate the historical Christ
in this way should reject or ignore the Scripture
account of his supernatural origin : it stands in no
relation to anything which they wish to explain.
But when we accept that view of the necessary,
eternal, incomparable significance of Christ, which
is the only view represented in the New Testament,
we approach this account with a different bias, and
are prepared to find it more than a childish attempt
to utter the greatness of Jesus.   It supplies a real

[1] *Unterricht in der christlichen Religion,* § 22.
[2] Rev. xxii. 13.   [3] See Note L.

link in the chain of Christian thought, and when we take it, not alone, but in its place in the chain, its inherent credibility is greatly increased. Of course no one would start with it in introducing a stranger to the Christian faith. Even a Roman Catholic writer like Didon says : 'The miracle of the origin of Jesus is not a motive of faith for unbelievers, it is one of those that confirm faith in the souls of believers, and believers alone are able to accept it.' [1] This may be considered tantamount to giving it up, as indifferent to faith, but it is not really so. Faith inevitably raises questions as it comes to a consciousness more adequate to its object, and the miracle of the origin of Jesus is the answer to one of the questions which it inevitably raises. It is not necessary at the beginning, but a time comes at which it is ; and any one who, reaching the need which it is meant to satisfy, notices how the story is told in Matthew from the point of view of Joseph and his interests, and in Luke from that of Mary and hers, and who takes pains to appreciate the details by the help of a commentator like Godet, will admit that on the historical and psychological side it is worthy of the occasion.

The question remains, whether it aids us much, or at all, in a metaphysical comprehension of the incarnation. I do not think it does. We do not *understand* any better than before what is meant by the rich One becoming poor, or He who was in the form of God assuming the form of a servant. The supernatural birth only secures the uniqueness of that life which came into the world in Christ, and

[1] *Jésus Christ*, vol. i. p. 424 *n.*

gives His pre-eminence an essential basis, instead of leaving it a merely accidental affair. It does not make it more intelligible, it does not enable us to define the relations between the pre-existent and the historical Christ more closely than John or Paul had done, it does not enable us to state precisely what is meant by ἐκένωσεν ἑαυτόν. This only it compels us to say, that in whatever sense personality is to be ascribed to the Word, that same personality is the centre of the life which began at Bethlehem. The doctrine of the Council of Chalcedon, that Christ's human nature is impersonal, has been vehemently attacked as infringing His humanity. It was certainly not meant in that sense, and many of the assaults proceed upon a misapprehension. It is taken for granted in them that there is some inconsistency between personality in the Logos and personality in a truly human life.[1] But the New Testament doctrine, as far as one can make it out, is all in favour, not of an inconsistency, but of a kinship between the two. All human personality, we are led to think, is rooted in the Logos, and the Logos made flesh could be the personal centre, not of a life alien to men, but of a life truly and purely human. This, no doubt, was the idea of those who framed the creed, and it is truer to the New Testament than a conception of Christ's humanity which makes it impossible to understand how He could be in any unique sense divine. There is no *mere* man in the world, in the sense of a man whose nature is entirely alien to God, out of relation to

[1] See Orr's *Christian View of God and the World*, pp. 282-285.

the Divine; but the completeness with which God is present in Christ depends upon a unique incarnation; and the integrity of Christ's humanity is not affected by this, for the Divine which is incarnate in Him is, at the same time, the principle of all self-consciousness, of all reason and goodness, in all men. In other words, it is a Divine which is at the same time essentially human, or at least essentially akin to man.

This discussion of the apostolic or New Testament doctrine of Christ has, as far as possible, avoided technicalities foreign to the New Testament itself. A statement like that of the Westminster Confession, 'that two whole, perfect, and distinct natures, the Godhead and the Manhood, were inseparably joined together in one person, without conversion, composition, or confusion,' may once have seemed to help intelligence; at the very utmost it can do no more now than guard against error. Orthodox and heterodox alike, theologians have returned to Christ Himself; they have sought to know Him, not by deducing the consequences of an arbitrary definition of God-manhood, but by actually looking at Him and listening to Him. The formula of two natures in one person does not adequately reproduce the impression which He makes. He is all one—that is the very strongest conviction we have: the simplicity, the unity, the consistency of His life, is the final impression it leaves. The divine and the human are not distinct, and the incomprehensible artificialities of the *communicatio idiomatum* cannot avail at once to maintain their distinctness and deny it. All that is divine in Him is human, all that is human is divine. He is not separately, or even distinctly, Son of God and Son of Man; it is the Son of God who is Son of Man; the Son of Man who is Son of God. Great is the mystery of godliness: great, that is, is the open secret of the true religion—*God* was manifested *in the flesh.*

This is the proper place to refer to a subject on which I have not time to dwell at length; the change in the conception of God which followed, as it was necessitated by, the New Testament conception of Christ and His work. The apostles were all Jews,—men, as it has been said, with monotheism as a passion in their blood.[1] They did not cease to be monotheists when they became preachers of Christ, but they instinctively conceived God in a way in which the old revelation had not taught them to conceive Him. The Word which was in the beginning, which was with God, which was God; the pre-existent One, who subsisted in the form of God, and did not think equality with God a thing to be held fast; the Lamb who is so supremely exalted that the heavenly throne is described as the throne of God and of the Lamb; all these conceptions reacted on the idea of God, and gave it a new content. Distinctions were recognised in what had once been the bare simplicity of the divine nature. The distinction of Father and Son was the most obvious, and it was enriched, on the basis of Christ's own teaching, and of the actual experience of the Church, by the further distinction of the Holy Spirit.

[1] Fairbairn's *Christ in Modern Theology*, p. 377.

Not consciously, not reflectively, but instinctively and spontaneously these distinctions find expression in the New Testament. I do not need to point out their recurrence in its pages. The language of St. Paul—the most Jewish of them all—will serve as an illustration. 'There are diversities of gifts, but the same *Spirit*. And there are diversities of ministrations, and the same *Lord*. And there are diversities of workings, but the same *God,* who worketh all things in all.' Or again, 'The grace of *the Lord Jesus Christ,* and the love of *God,* and the communion of *the Holy Ghost,* be with you.' Or once more, 'Through *Him* we both have access by one *Spirit* unto *the Father.*' These are the beginnings of what was elaborated in the course of centuries into the doctrine of the Trinity. That doctrine, it is not superfluous to remark, is nothing if not historical and Christian. It is not a motiveless speculation; it is not the analysis of an arbitrarily chosen idea like knowledge, love, or spirit, as some philosophers and theologians have tried to show; it proceeds from the actual manifestation of God in Christ, and from the actual reception of a divine life through the Holy Spirit. When it departs from this ground it ceases to possess either significance or authority. The great difficulty of comprehending eternal distinctions in the unity of the Godhead has led to many speculative and many popular attempts at restatement of the doctrine of the Trinity; and the fascination which some of these possess for the untaught makes it worth while to remark upon them. A very common type is that which makes Father, Son, and Spirit, three successive, or at least three distinct, manifestations of God, not obviously or essentially related to each other. This is a common device with those who would mediate between Orthodoxy and Unitarianism, but it only needs a glance to show that it is not what is hinted at in the New Testament. There, the Father and the Son can only be known through each other, and the Spirit is that which the Father gives to testify of the Son. The three are one. Though this is as obvious as it is possible for words to make it, it is very frequently missed. Thus a recent English writer, in a work with the somewhat pretentious title, *The Scientific Study of Theology*, interprets the divine Fatherhood as God manifested in nature, the divine Sonship as God manifested in Christ, and the Holy Spirit as God manifested in all the higher aspirations of men. This is simply beside the mark. The divine Fatherhood, or God the Father, is not manifested in nature, but only in Christ: no man knoweth the Father save the Son, and he to whomsoever the Son willeth to reveal Him. It is an illusion, and a departure from Christian ground, to think otherwise. In the same way it is an illusion to speak of God the Father as God in a transcendent sense, apart from all relations or distinctions; God in this sense is not a Christian conception at all, nor a rational conception either, for that matter. To us there is but one God, and He the Father whom we have learned to know through the Son; Fatherhood is His essential, eternal, and only character, and therefore we believe in the eternal sonship, and in the eternal Spirit of the Father and the Son. This faith is not speculative nor fantastic, but it becomes so whenever we separate it from its basis in history and experience, and give deductions of the Trinity, or popular statements of it, which do not rest on and revolve round Jesus Christ and the new Christian life bestowed through His Spirit. Once the doctrine, even in vaguest outline, has been truly grasped, its Christian character becomes apparent; and its real value for the interpretation of nature and of human life is evidenced by the fact that all the higher speculative philosophies develop something as nearly akin to it as they can. Apart from other applications of it, when we see that it is solidly based on the divine sonship of Christ, and remember that this Son of God is Son of Man, we can understand better what is meant by saying that God is eternally love, that Christ is eternally the Son of His love, and that the Son of God's love is the firstborn among many brethren, the Eternal Head of a race of redeemed men.

LECTURE IV

MAN AND SIN

THE Christian religion involves a certain conception
of man—of his nature, his state, and his destiny.
In dealing with these questions we might seem to
be on ground quite different from that which we have
hitherto occupied. Of God we can know nothing
except what He is pleased to reveal; revelation,
therefore, is our source and authority in theology
properly so called. But of ourselves and our condition we may be assumed to have knowledge more
immediately. We do not depend on any revelation
from without. This is in a sense true, but the
limitations of its truth immediately appear when
we consider that our nature and destiny involve
relations to God, and that our state, as far as
theology is called to regard it, is neither more nor
less than our existing relation to Him. Hence the
doctrine of man, as well as the doctrine of God, is
a subject for Biblical treatment, and it is our first
task to apprehend that conception of man which
is assumed throughout Scripture.

On a broad view of this subject there is not
much room for difference of opinion. The inspired
writers, without distinction, regard man as a being

in nature akin to God, capable of fellowship with Him and designed for it, conscious of moral freedom and responsibility, and therefore morally responsible and free. The relation of man to nature is not in the strict sense a religious question, and is never separately discussed in the Scriptures. It is quite consistent with their teaching to recognise fully the palpable truth that man is, on one side, or in one aspect, a piece of nature. His life is rooted in nature; it grows up in the soil of nature; it is incorporated, so to speak, in the general life of the world; no man can disclaim physical antecedents and a physical environment; no man can deny that these are as necessary to him as to the meanest animated creature in nature. All this is quite consistent with Scripture, but it is not much insisted on except for the purpose of rebuking human arrogance. The Bible speaks of man, as a rule, not in his relation to nature, but in his distinction from it. It assumes that the life which is in him, with that reflecting consciousness, that sense of freedom and responsibility, that affinity to and capacity for the divine, is specifically distinct from life in any other form. It assumes that man is not merely *in* nature, but *over* it; that he is, so to speak, not only its crown, but its sovereign. In virtue of that relation to God, that kinship to Him, which is of His very essence, man is destined to have dominion over creation; he is to assert his freedom, and to put all things under his feet.

This conception of man's nature may seem very vague, and very much in want of definitions and distinctions, but I am inclined to think it is sufficient for our purpose. The elaborate treatment of the subject by what is called the science of Biblical psychology has never produced anything truly scientific. To disintegrate human nature into body and soul, as two separate substances, does not help us; body and soul exist only in and for each other; the body is not *a* body, but the body of the soul; the soul is not *a* soul, but the soul of the body; in our consciousness of self the two are one. Just as little are we helped by the tripartite analysis of man's nature into spirit, soul, and body : the popular expression by which St. Paul describes our nature in its whole extent ought never to have been so misapplied. Man is a unity, not a tying together of separate parts or even of separate faculties, and the Bible deals with him as such. On the one hand he is related to nature, grows out of it, strikes his roots into it, is conditioned by it; on the other he is related to God, and in virtue of this relation is lord of nature, regards himself as its chief end, holds himself entitled to use all its resources for his own purposes, and in point of fact finds himself, to an indefinite extent, capable of doing so. This intellectual superiority to nature, in virtue of which man subdues it to himself, is a part of that relation to God which expresses itself otherwise in the consciousness of freedom and responsibility; in other words, the consciousness of being subject, not merely to natural, but to ethical and divine law.

This is one of the points—to which allusion was made in the first lecture—where theology and physical science come into contact. Theology requires that conception of man's nature which

I have just explained ; it does not deny any of the
natural conditions under which that nature comes
to be what it is, but it cannot let go its essential
superiority to nature and its essential relation to
God.   The assaults which some students of science
have made on these last are only what might have
been expected, and though significant are not important.   The chemist and the biologist work with
certain ideas or categories as their implements ; they
are the forms to which they have to reduce all
things in order to their explanation.   But there are
some things which they cannot explain : they cannot explain self-consciousness, nor anything of which
self-consciousness is a presupposition.   They cannot
explain the consciousness of freedom, of sin, of God,
of estrangement, of reconciliation.   But that does
not matter.   It is not their business to explain
them.   If these things could be explained by the
categories of the chemist or the biologist, they
would not be what they are ; they would have been
explained out of existence ; a higher kind of being
would have been reduced to a lower.   It is very
natural for the student of a special science like
biology, which carries us so far into the secrets of
life, to think that what his science cannot explain
cannot really exist ; but it is the very nature of self-
consciousness, and of all that is conditioned by it, to
transcend physical explanation.   The psychologist
and the metaphysician join hands with the theologian
in declining a doctrine of man which makes him
no more than a piece of nature.   A piece of nature
could never form the conception of nature, could
never interpret and use nature, could never conceive

ends, and regard himself as under a moral and not a natural law. If there were nothing but matter, as M. Naville has wittily said, there would be no materialism; if there were nothing in man but what the chemist and the biologist can discover, there would be no chemistry and biology, to say nothing of superior sciences. The fact, for it *is* a fact, that there *is* more than they can discover, leaves the field open to the metaphysician and the theologian.

It is unfortunate, I think, that the questions as to man's nature have been usually discussed in theology in connection with what is called his original state. The question What is man? has been treated as if it were convertible with the question What was Adam? But it is plain that we do not stand in the same relation to these two questions. Man is before us, or rather in us; we have the amplest opportunity for investigating his nature and constitution, and we have the whole range of Scripture to guide and correct our interpretation of these accessible facts. But Adam is not within our reach at all; and it is simply exposing ourselves, without any necessity whatever, to refutation by the progress of physical or archæological science, when we advance statements about the primitive condition of man which have not only a religious, but a physical and historical content. No one who knows what science or history is can imagine that either science or history is to be found in the first three chapters of Genesis; and it will be plain, I think, at a further stage, that to seek for them is quite unnecessary to the Christian position. Man's nature is revealed by what he is, interpreted by the course of God's

dealings with him; it is revealed above all, and
his destiny along with it, in Jesus Christ our Lord;
and it is as gratuitous as it is futile to seek to
discover it in all its integrity in a first man. The
plain truth, and we have no reason to hide it, is
that we do not know the beginnings of man's life,
of his history, of his sin; we do not know them
historically, on historical evidence; and we should
be content to let them remain in the dark till science
throws what light it can upon them. The unity of
the human race—the organic connection of all its
members—the identity in all of that double relation
to nature and to God—the universality of the consciousness which Christians call sin—these are facts,
whatever our ignorance may be of the original state
of man, and of his original righteousness.

Next in importance to the Scripture conception of
man's nature is the Scripture conception of his condition. The two are constantly represented as at
variance with one another: man's nature is contradicted by his state. Man as made in the image of
God is destined for fellowship with God, a fellowship
to be realised in obedience to that higher law to
which he instinctively acknowledges obedience to be
due, and in which Scripture teaches us to recognise
the will of God. The will of God has been revealed
to all men—for the present, it does not matter how;
in conscience, in the ethical framework of the
society into which they are born, in special revelations, in the sending of the Son of God in human
nature; and there is not in human nature one who
has made that will his own. There is not one who
has not felt the pressure of that will and carried

his own will against it by a counter pressure; there is not one who has not sinned against God. I speak of this in the most general terms, because the consciousness of sin is a thing which has to be explained at every moral level. I do not think we should say that sin is to be defined in relation to original righteousness: original righteousness is a perfectly obscure and unknown thing. But neither do I think with Ritschl that sin should only be defined in relation to Jesus Christ and the supreme ethical good which has been revealed in Him, viz., the Kingdom of God. The inference which he draws from this, that all that we call sin, coming short, as it does, of the definitive rejection of Christ and the supreme ethical good, is not sin in a really condemning sense, but merely sin of ignorance, seems to me to contradict the most unquestionable pronouncements of conscience.[1] There are, of course, degrees of sin, and the worst of all, which make restoration impossible, is the deliberate rejection of what Christ has brought us; but the sins which precede and lead up to this are just as real, and as really sinful, as this crowning sin itself. In every case the discord is realised between man's nature and his state; he is destined for fellowship with God by acceptance of His will, and he asserts a contrary will of his own against it, and lives without God, in the world.

Sin always emerges in man's consciousness as an incident. It is *a* sin of which he accuses himself— a disobedience which he can isolate in his life, regarding it as a blot, a stain, an exceptional phenomenon to be dealt with by itself. There is an

[1] See Note A.

element of truth, undoubtedly, in this way of looking at it; it seems to emphasise the voluntariness of
the bad act, and the completeness of the individual's
responsibility for it. It is our own act, and in the
full consciousness of what it is we take it sadly to
ourselves. This is the aspect in which sin was
regarded by Pelagius, and in spite of all that theology
and science have done, it is the aspect in which it is
still regarded by many. But it needs very little
experience or observation to see that there is nothing
in man's life that has this purely incidental character.
Our life is all of a piece, and the most seemingly
isolated actions have both their antecedents and
their consequents. The will is not a mere form of
choice, which remains unaffected by the actual
choices which a man makes; it *is* affected by them;
it gains contents, character, we might almost say
nature, from them. If the atomic theory of sin
were true—that it consisted only in separate actions
—there could be no such thing in man as moral
character, either bad or good; for such character is
produced by the abiding and cumulative effect of
precisely such actions. The will is not a neutral in
the moral conflict, even at the beginning; still less
is it a neutral when we wake up to the fact that it
has a character of its own. It has absorbed a moral
quality from the nature of the individual, and from
his actions; and in the consciousness of this we are
led past the view of sin as an incident to regard it
as a state.

Sin as a state or condition refers, of course, not to
actions, but to persons; it is a conception which bids
us think not of what man has done, but of what he

is. The sinful action is the symptom or the outcome of a sinfulness which already characterises the actor; it proceeds from a corruption or depravity of nature which may be a far more serious thing than any given manifestation of it. It is in this aspect mainly that the New Testament presents sin to our view, and it is in this aspect also that it has given most trouble both to moralists and theologians. The questions to which it gives rise—leaving out of account in the meantime the question of its origin—concern in the first instance its extent, and in the second its consequences.

Its extent is characterised in traditional orthodox theology as 'total depravity,' or 'the corruption of our whole nature'; and probably the strongest expression ever given to this is that of the Westminster Confession (ch. vi. § 4), which declares that by this corruption 'we are utterly indisposed, disabled, and made opposite to all good, and wholly inclined to all evil.' A simple .reader coming across these words would probably feel that there is an element of exaggeration in them, and that though they may seem to be supported by an occasional strong expression in Scripture, they are really not a scientific description of man's actual condition. This has been so strongly felt that most of the churches holding this Confession have modified its declarations on this point. Thus the Free Church of Scotland, in the Declaratory Act of 1892, qualifies its adhesion to the statement of the Confession by saying 'that, in holding and teaching, according to the Confession of Faith, the corruption of man's whole nature as fallen, this church also maintains that there remain tokens of his greatness as created in the image of God; that he possesses a knowledge of God and of duty; that he is responsible for compliance with the moral law and with the gospel; and that, although unable without the aid of the Holy Spirit to return to God, he is yet capable of affections and actions which in themselves are virtuous and praiseworthy.' One does not need to quarrel with any part of this statement in order to maintain the legitimacy of such an expression as 'total depravity.' What it means is not that every individual is as bad as he can be, a statement so transparently absurd that it should hardly have been attributed to any one, but that the depravity which sin has produced in human nature extends to the whole of it. There is no part of man's nature which is unaffected by it. I repeat what I said before, that man's nature is all of a piece, and that what affects it at all affects it altogether. When the conscience is violated by disobedience to the will of God, the moral understanding is darkened, and the will is enfeebled. We are not constructed in water-tight compartments, one of which might be ruined while the others remained intact; what touches us for harm, with a corrupting, depraving touch, at a single point, has effects throughout our nature none the less real that they may be for a time beneath consciousness. This is the doctrine of sin as a state which answers to the experience of religious men. At a primitive stage of advancement, indeed, just as in childhood, men repent of what they have done; but at a more mature stage they repent of what they are. At first they feel that they must make amends; but when they come to know themselves, they feel that they must be born again. 'Oh for a man to arise in me that the man I am may cease to be!'—that is the prayer which answers to a true consciousness of the extent of human depravity; and it is justified by the words of our Lord Himself about the necessity of the new birth.

In a sense, the question as to the consequences of the sinful state is included in the question as to its extent. The one consequence on which the attention of theologians has been concentrated is the consequence to man's will, or to his moral freedom. On this every possible opinion has been expressed. Pelagius, as is well known, denied that sin had any consequence for the will at all; man was as free after he had sinned as before, and could make his next choice as easily and independently as before. The will is simply a form of choice, its liberty a liberty of indifference, and it never gains any moral character or indeed any character at all. At this time of day it is not worth while to refute the atomic theory of morals any more: it makes a moral order in the world impossible, and everybody has the refutation of it in his own heart, if he chooses to consider what he finds there. At the other extreme, it has been held that sin simply annihilated human freedom; and in the desire—a thoroughly legitimate desire—to secure for God the whole glory of man's salvation, man was reduced to a stone or a trunk (Luther), not only incapable of working out salvation for himself, but incapable even of being saved. But there are two interests that Christian theology must keep in view. On the one hand, the effect of sin on human nature, and especially on the human will, must be such that

man *needs* a redeemer; on the other hand, it must only
be such that he remains susceptible of redemption.
There is no harm at all, and no danger, in giving
this last side its due, either in theology or in preaching. God, a witty French moralist has said, does
not need to grudge His enemies even what they call
their virtues; and neither do God's ministers. It is
only when we fully recognise what men have, even
while they disregard the gospel, that we can hope-
fully call their attention to what they have not. It is
only when we recognise what they have done that
we can insist on what they are unable to do. And
the doctrine of spiritual inability, as consequent on
the corruption of man's nature by sin, remains and
will always remain to represent the great truth that
there is *one* thing which man cannot do *alone*. He
cannot bring his state into harmony with his nature.
He cannot fulfil the destiny for which he was
created. He cannot enter into peace with God, as
if his sin and its consequences were nothing; he
cannot annul the past; he cannot overcome it; he
cannot, in spite of it, enjoy the glorious liberty of the
children of God. It is a mistake, in all probability,
in discussing this subject, to enter into metaphysical
considerations at all; the question of man's inability
to any spiritual good accompanying salvation is a
question as to matter of fact, and is to be answered
ultimately by an appeal to experience. When a
man has been discovered, who has been able, *without
Christ*, to reconcile himself to God, and to obtain
dominion over the world and over sin, *then* the
doctrine of inability, or of the bondage due to sin,
may be denied; *then*, but *not till then*. If Christ is

invariably needed to bring sinful men to the Father, and to give them that peace with God in which all spiritual achievements have their root, then man, so far as experience goes, has been completely disabled by sin; and though he may have the right to boast among his equals, in his dealing with God boasting is excluded. He can do nothing in this relation apart from Christ; spiritual inability is the simple description of this invariable and indubitable fact.

But the consideration of sin as an incident, and as a state or condition of individuals, or of human nature in individuals, does not exhaust its significance. Reflection soon shows us that in this respect also no man liveth to himself; that actions and their consequences affect others besides the actors to an indefinite and incalculable extent; that sin is not only personal, but social; not only social, but organic; that character and all that is involved in character are capable of being attributed not only to individuals, but to societies, and eventually to the human race itself; in short, that there are not only isolated sins, and individual sinners, but what has been called a kingdom of sin upon earth.

It is in connection with this conception that the difficulties of the subject come to a height. The relations of the individual to society, even when we conceive him as mature and free, and the spiritual influences to which he is there subjected, simply elude us; they are infinitely beyond our power to trace or estimate. The relations of individual to corporate responsibility in the same way defy elucidation: we have no moral calculus adequate to such complicated problems: we can only believe that God

can do justice where it is out of our power even to
see what is just. The difficulties, however, which
the relations of men in society raise as to the distribution of responsibility are mitigated by the consideration that there *is* a relative independence of
men here, and that the power of example, of law,
and even of custom, is not that of a purely physical
necessity, but is often freely and deliberately admitted to the individual life. It is different when
we come to consider the organic connection of the
generations of men, and those phenomena which are
summed up in the name 'heredity.' Here the
physical world and its laws seem to make a rude
irruption into the spiritual; a physical relation seems
to have moral consequences, and these often of the
most serious kind; we are born with a history in us,
with an accumulation of consequences derived from
the past, to which the future is mortgaged; we are
not allowed to choose our fathers and mothers, and
in comparison with that fundamental choice which is
made *for* us, any other choice we are free to make
for ourselves is not worth speaking of. Considerations of this kind have immensely impressed the
minds of men during the last generation. The
Darwinian theory of the origin of species—probably
the most immediately and widely influential theory
ever introduced to human intelligence—has the law
of heredity, and of accumulation by heredity, as one
of its essential levers; and through it that law has
taken possession of the common mind as it had never
done before. It has concentrated attention, too, on
the law in its purely physical aspects, and has made
men feel more keenly the difficulty of giving it a

moral interpretation consistent with individual freedom. Many of the most popular of modern writers
—novelists and dramatists especially—seem positively crazed by it; one would think that the problems of heredity constituted the sum and substance
of life, and that a man was nothing but a sum of
tendencies transmitted from his ancestors.

There are two preliminary remarks I should make
here before speaking more directly to these difficulties.
(1) The moral problems connected with heredity are
not made a bit easier, or a bit harder, by going further
back, or not so far. It is the bare fact that a physical
connection has, apparently, moral consequences, which
is perplexing; not the scale of the fact or its duration.
Whether we had an ancestor who lived in a state of
original righteousness, a state in which he came
directly from the hand of God, or not, does not
here matter; the conditions under which we are
born into the world are what they are, and labour
under the moral difficulties under which they do
labour, all the same, whether the traditional or the
Darwinian account of man's origin be accepted. (2)
The fact that there is such a thing as heredity does
not destroy the moral consciousness. I revert here
to what I said at the beginning—man is not merely
a piece of nature, but has a superiority over against
nature. He is rooted in it, as the law of his birth
and inheritance shows, but he is also its sovereign.
The facts which are summed up in heredity do not
exhaust his being; they only show what he is *as* a
part of nature, and this character which they bear is
modified when we view him, as his self-consciousness
and consciousness of ethical law compel us to do, as

more than a part of nature. That which would be
merely physical in the lower animals is *not* merely
physical in him; it is not a bare, ultimate, uninter-
preted fact; it presents him with moral problems; it
becomes the means of moral probation, of moral education; in contact with it his freedom asserts itself, or
is defeated; but in either case the moral consciousness
maintains itself, and no man ever with a clear conscience put down his sin to his father's account.

It is important to remember here, that though
the physical conditions of heredity have been more
minutely studied in modern times, the moral perplexities of it were keenly felt long ago, and are
expressly noticed in Scripture. Nor when all has
been said is there any sign that philosophers and
theologians, not to say novelists and poets, have got
beyond the insight of the prophet Ezekiel.[1] When
the Jews in Babylonia commented on their condition
in the cynical sceptical proverb, 'The fathers have
eaten sour grapes, and the children's teeth are set
on edge,' they had the spiritual riddles of heredity
as clearly before their minds as any Darwinian or
Ibsenite of the present day. They put the same
sinister interpretation, also, on the apparent facts, as
many of our pessimistic writers do. Man's antecedents, they said, constitute his fate; the past of
his family and of his race holds him in its relentless
grasp; he has no hope; freedom is an illusion; God
is unjust.

The message of Ezekiel is addressed directly to
this despairing unbelief, and the prevalence of
similar intellectual and moral conditions in our own

[1] Ezekiel xviii.

time renders it specially important and interesting to us. It has two great enunciations. First, 'As I live, saith the Lord God, . . . All souls are mine; as the soul of the father, so also the soul of the son is mine.' In other words, every individual soul alike, the last in the descent as well as any other, has an immediate relation to God. This is what I have said so often already; man is not constituted simply by what he inherits; he is not an incorporated piece of nature merely; he is connected as truly with God as with his natural ancestry, and that connection with God prevents his relation to the past from becoming a mere bondage. Heredity is *not* fate—what we have received from our parents does not weave around us a net of guilt and misery through which we can never break—if it be true that we belong to God as well as to the past. Of course no proof is given of this, just as no proof is given of any prophetic word. But we may confidently say of this, in the word of Jesus, 'Every one that is of the truth heareth this voice.' It is immoral, it is the sign of a cowardly, unbelieving, willingly sceptical spirit, to say the fathers have eaten sour grapes, and the children's teeth are set on edge. It is immoral, because it is a way of evading that direct relation of the soul to God which raises human life to its highest intensity, which makes us feel responsibility in all its strength, and bids us fight the good fight in His name to the last.

The second proposition of Ezekiel is a corollary from this one, and runs: 'The son shall not bear the iniquity of the father: the soul that sinneth, *it* shall die.' Sometimes this verse is quoted as conveying

God's judgment on sin; the soul that sinneth, it
shall *die*; but this is a misapplication. It is rather
a text in which God's righteousness and mercy are
asserted against the sceptical misconstruction of His
dealings by despairing men : The soul that sinneth
—*it* and no other—shall die : the son shall not bear
the iniquity of the father ; heredity shall not amount
to a moral fate. And this reminds us of the truth
that the sins of fathers are only ruinous when sons
make them their own. The inherited bias may be
strong, but it is not everything that is in any man's
nature, and it is only when he ignores or renounces
the relation to God, and freely makes the evil
inheritance his own, that he makes it into a condemnation, and puts it between himself and life.
What we inherit, strictly speaking, may be said to
fix our trial, but not our fate.[1] Every man is to
be put to the proof somehow, and to a certain extent
his natural ancestry determines the mode of it : it
depends on them, so to speak, whether his temp-
tation is to be anger, intemperance, lust, greed,
duplicity, or whatever else. But it does not depend
on them what the issue of this trial is to be. It
depends on the man himself, and above all on his
faith in God. All souls are His; even the soul of
the man who seems most heavily weighted by the
past ; and *He* is able to make him stand. The facts
on which physicists lay such stress are not to be
denied, but they are not to be allowed to claim the
whole field. Side by side with them we must maintain the spiritual facts—that an evil nature only con-

[1] I think this contrast of trial and fate is borrowed from
something in Dr. Dale.

demns us when we make it our own ; and that man is always accessible to God Almighty as well as to the influence of the past. When due weight is given to these considerations, we need not be afraid to contemplate the laws and facts of heredity in all their extent. They give mystery and immensity to the spiritual life of man, and, so far from qualifying his responsibility, they widen its range enormously. They redeem life from that mere individualism which really makes ethics, and even character, inconceivable ; and they remind us that, for good and evil alike, no man liveth to himself and no man dieth to himself. They supply a physical basis for a life which is much more than physical, and they give far more than individual importance to what we might think merely individual acts.

We have now considered sin as an incident emerging at isolated points in consciousness; as a state, or character, of individual men; and as organic, or related to the natural connection of all men with one another as members of the same physical species. But we have considered it only in a general way as a discord or disproportion between man's nature and his state; as a failure to be what God destined him for. We recognise that there is a law or will of God to which our life should conform, and the consciousness of sin is the consciousness that we have set aside that law or will in favour of some end of our own. If this consciousness is analysed, it is always found to include the element which theologians specifically describe as guilt. Sin, that is, is something for which we are answerable to God ; the act passes,

but the responsibility for it remains. Guilt, as a
feeling, always includes fear; an apprehension of
the consequences which sin may bring. Quite apart
from any special conception of consequences this
fear asserts itself; it is a shrinking from the condemnation, the judgment, the punishment, the
wrath of God. This feeling has been very severely
treated by some theologians; it has been censured
as due to an unworthy conception of God and His
attitude and disposition to His sinful children. I
confess myself quite unable to sympathise with this
way of looking at the matter. Sin is a real thing; a
real violation of the will of God, which ought to be
our will, and it brings real responsibility along with it.
I say real responsibility; for it is not an illusion that
we have to answer to God for what we have done.
But it would not be real—it would be a subjective
conception, a pure hallucination—unless God's condemnation were real also. This witness of the
conscience is confirmed by everything we read in
Scripture. A bad conscience is never treated there
as a groundless fear of God; it is a reflection, all too
feeble at the best, of God's awful judgment upon
sin. A great mass of modern theology denies this.
It has a conception of God's love, borrowed I know
not where, in presence of which distinctions of good
and evil seem to vanish, and all experiences dependent on such distinctions to lose their meaning and
reality. When God's righteousness is simply
identified with His grace, when His holiness is
treated as an obscure conception, which cannot be
defined, and seems indeed to be physical rather
than ethical in import; when His wrath is simply

eliminated, or declared to stand in no relation whatever to the work of reconciliation, it is evident that these same characteristics or attributes of God cease to have any relation to sin. *It* cannot be connected with the righteousness, the holiness, or the wrath of God; in other words, it cannot be treated as having reality for God at all. But to make sin unreal is to make redemption unreal also; it is to cast the shadow of illusion over the whole extent of man's relations with God. There is nothing, I believe, which at the present time needs more to be insisted on, in theology and in gospel preaching, than the objectivity and reality of guilt. It is not a subjective illusion, which we should be taught to disregard in view of God's infinite love; it is as real as life or death, a gigantic problem alike for God and man. His condemnation of sin, His wrath repelling sin, resting over sin, are not figments of our ignorance and fear; they are absolutely real things, to which our conscience bears a true though awfully inadequate testimony.[1]

Remembering what has been said already as to the unity of man's being, we should expect to find sin have other than merely spiritual consequences; we should expect it to betray its presence not merely in the consciousness of guilt, and in the corruption of our nature, but on the physical side of our being as well. In other words, we should expect to find a connection between what we are accustomed to call moral and physical evil.

This is a very difficult subject, and as far as Scripture teaching goes we are rather warned not to

[1] See Note B.

make rash judgments than provided with the means
of making true ones.   The difficulty arises in part
from this, that 'physical evil' is an extremely vague
expression, and that what would bear this character to
one person might have quite the opposite character to
another.   A degree of cold which would be fatal
to one might to another be merely exhilarating.
The pressure of danger which paralyses one only
serves to lift the faculties of another to their height.
For those who love God, too, all things work
together for good—tribulation, affliction, distress,
persecution, nakedness, famine, and sword; the
extremest physical evils lose the character of evil
altogether; they become the foil to Christian faithfulness; nay, it is Christian faithfulness which brings
them upon men, and they are a seal set upon it.   But
with those things in our mind we can still say
something on the general question.   *In the first place,*
no man is entitled to judge others.   The calamities
which come upon men may have explanations of
which we are quite ignorant; they may be the
cross due to faithful following of Christ; they may
be the proof to which God is putting them, and in
no sense judgments.   A man is made for far more
than his own private interest, and the physical evils
he has to bear may find their explanation far beyond
himself.   Neither this man, says Jesus, did sin, nor
his parents, that he was born blind; neither guilt of
his own, nor inherited guilt, is the explanation of it.
God had another purpose to serve in sending him
into the world thus, and the final cause of his blind-
ness is to be sought there.   Obviously this consideration takes the right to judge largely out of our hands.

Largely, I say, but not entirely; for if we are to be at home in the moral order of the world it must not be quite opaque, but more or less capable of being construed by us. *In the second place,* while not entitled to judge others, we are often compelled to judge ourselves. Other people do not know why certain things befall us, but *we* may know nevertheless. We do not need to experiment, like the Philistines with the ark, to see whether the Lord has smitten us, or whether it is a chance that has befallen us; there is something within us which points the moral too unambiguously for evasion. I do not speak only of cases in which sins against the body are avenged, in the order of nature, upon the body, but of experiences in which the connection is less apparent. Paul knew why the thorn in the flesh was given him—knew, perhaps, from the service which it rendered him; and many a man is just as certain, though of course he could not communicate his certainty to another, that definite painful experiences in his life have had a definite disciplinary purpose of God in them; in other words, that certain physical evils, to use a not very happy expression, have been put in a divine relation to certain moral evils—perhaps as a punishment, certainly as a corrective and a check upon them. If it is a mistake to be too confident and familiar here, and to speak as if we had found out the Almighty unto perfection, it is at least as bad a mistake to renounce the spiritual interpretation of life altogether, and on the ground that God is present everywhere to refuse to think what He means anywhere.

There is one special question here to which Scripture teaching gives a peculiar importance—the question as to the connection of sin and death.[1] In the Old Testament and in the New alike the connection is maintained : man dies because of sin; or, as St. Paul puts it, the wages of sin is death. It is not necessary to discuss here the precise significance of death either in the book of Genesis or in the Epistle to the Romans; make it mean as much as you please, and at least it always includes what the man on the street means when he says, All men must die. Mortality is a consequence of sin.

But is this true? Is it really because of sin that men die? The consenting voice of science seems to say no: death reigned in the world long before man, and what theologians call sin, appeared. Death is a law of nature; it is an essential lever in the great machine of the world. Every living creature is born with the seeds of decay in it; it is like a clock, wound up to go for a certain number of hours, but liable, of course, to be stopped by a thousand accidents before it has run down of itself. This line of argument, backed up by the actual universality of death, has something imposing about it, and a good many theologians accept it without more ado. Possibly they try to secure the truth of the Scripture idea by making death mean something else than death means in common language : they darken it by shadows of spiritual and eternal separation from God, as distinct from the purely natural experience ordinarily indicated by this

[1] See Orr's *Christian View of God and the World*, pp. 228-233.

name. I do not think these distinctions avail at all to secure the Scripture doctrine, and if it is to be maintained, as I think it ought to be, the line of defence must be drawn further back. The scientific assertion of the natural necessity of death, closely considered, really amounts to a begging of the question. Man, it means, *must* die, must *always* have died, because he is a natural being, subject to the universal natural law of birth and decay; there is nothing but this for him. But the whole ground on which the Bible doctrine is based is that man is *not* simply a natural being, with nothing but the destiny which awaits all nature awaiting him. He is a being invested by his very constitution with a primacy over nature ; he is related to God in a way which makes him specifically distinct from every merely natural being, in a way which those who understand it regard as containing at least the promise and the possibility of immortality. To say that he *must* die, because he is a natural being, ignores all this : it amounts to a proof of man's mortality only in the sense that it is a disproof of his immortality. But this disproof carries us too far : it would not be recognised as valid by most of those who have too hastily accepted the inference which it includes, viz., that death is inevitable for man, simply because of his incorporation in nature. Once we understand what man is, we see that death in him demands an explanation which is not demanded in the case of creatures whose whole life is bounded by nature; and that explanation is supplied by Scripture when it makes death the punishment of sin. Death means, in this case, what we see when we stand beside the dying, or rather what the dying experience as their connection with this present order ceases. It is a mistake to minimise the significance of this by speaking of it as if it were only natural, by speaking, as people sometimes do, even where Christ is concerned, of 'mere physical death.' There is nothing whatever, in human experience, which is merely physical; death is not merely physical; it is human; one, awful, indivisible experience, which cannot be analysed, and which is profaned when it is identified with anything that could befall a lower than human nature. We can be redeemed from the fear and bitterness of it by Jesus Christ; but in itself it has not a natural but a spiritual character: to the consciousness of man, in which it exists in its completeness, it is not the debt of nature, but the wages of sin. What might have been the line in which man's destiny would have been fulfilled had sin not entered into the world, and death by sin, no one can tell; but the fact that man is constituted for immortality, and has the promise of it in his being from the first, forbids us to ascribe to death a natural and inevitable place in his career. It is an intrusion, and it is to be finally abolished.[1]

[1] See Note C.

LECTURE V

THE WORK OF CHRIST IN RELATION TO SIN—THE NEW TESTAMENT DOCTRINE OF ATONEMENT

THE subject of this lecture is the work of Christ in relation to sin. There have been speculations in the Church, from a very early period, which have busied themselves with a wider question. Men have asked whether the Son of God would not have assumed our nature, even had there been no sin; and once they have answered that question in the affirmative, as many have done, they have tried to interpret the work of Christ, as it is historically known to us, as the modification necessitated by sin in an event which would have taken place under any circumstances. The motives of this speculation are plain enough. It seems unlikely that an event so stupendous as the Incarnation should come to pass, as it were, by accident, and not be included in the original design of the world. A kind of unity is secured in the whole work of God—creative and redemptive—if this view is adopted. Creation, as a recent theologian has put it, is built on redemption lines.[1] A perfect revelation of God is

[1] Dr. Orr's *Christian View of God and the World*, pp. 319 ff.

100

secured in humanity, which is as necessary, or at
least as congruous to the divine nature, in a sinless
as in a sinful world. These considerations are not
without plausibility, and will weigh with some
minds. But there are considerations on the other
hand to which we cannot be indifferent. In the
first place, there is the broad fact that Scripture
never gives the faintest hint of any opening for the
mind in this direction. It dwells on the fact that
Christ came into the world to save sinners—that
man's desperate need drew Him from heaven to
earth ; and it never suggests, even in the remotest
way, that He would have come anyhow. If it does
not peremptorily exclude the idea of an Incarnation for other than redemptive purposes, it may be
said to do so tacitly, by always connecting the
Incarnation with the purpose of redemption, and
that from Eternity. Further, the result of such
speculations, or rather their tendency, may be
alleged against them. Without entering into proofs
I can only here express the conviction that they do
tend to obliterate the distinction between nature
and grace, to blur the definite outlines of that work
of Redemption wrought by Christ, which mark it
out as the supreme revelation of God and His love.
Passing from these more general questions, what is
to be specially before us now is Christ's work in
relation to sin.

It has been common here to start with the consideration of the effects of sin in man, and to argue
from the effects of Christ's work upon these to the
nature of that work itself. This is fair enough as
far as it goes ; the only question is, if it goes far

enough. Thus sin, it has been pointed out, pro-
duces in man a sense of distrust in the presence
of God; he has misgivings about God's attitude
towards him; he suspects and dislikes Him.
Christ's work, then, is to overcome this dislike and
suspicion; it is to disabuse the sinner of his false
thoughts about God, and prevail on him to put
them away, and come to the loving God in faith.
The question *how* Christ does this is often vaguely
answered, or not answered at all. Again, sin is
conceived in its effect on man's character. It has
degraded and debased him, so that his nature needs
to be morally renewed; and the work of Christ is
to exercise a regenerating and restoring influence
on this corrupted nature, so that it may answer to
its destiny, and be able to meet God without fear.
If we ask *how* Christ does this, the answers are again
hard to find, or hard to understand. Yet it is this
ulterior question which really goes to the root of the
matter, and it is on it that the whole of Biblical teaching converges. When, however, we follow the lead
of Scripture, we put the question in a different form.

The gospel is the revelation of God's redeeming
love, made in view of a certain situation as existing
between God and man. Now what is the serious
element in that situation, as Scripture unfolds it?
In other words, what is the serious element in sin,
as sin stands before us in Revelation? Is it man's
distrust of God? man's dislike, suspicion, alienation?
Is it the special direction of vice in human nature,
or its debilitating corrupting effects? It is none of
these things, nor is it all of them together. What
makes the situation serious. what necessitates a

gospel, is that the world, in virtue of its sin, lies
under the condemnation of God.   His wrath abides
upon it.   That wrath is revealed from heaven
against all ungodliness and unrighteousness in man ;
and it is in view of this, it is as the exact counterpart
of this, that the righteousness and love of God are
revealed in the Gospel.   This conjunction of ideas
is specially but not specifically Pauline ; if there is
an idea with which every New Testament writer
would have been at home, it is this, that because of
sin the world lies under condemnation, and that
this is the situation with which the gospel deals.   I
am not enough of a lawyer to say whether 'forensic'
is the proper word to describe this idea; I rather
think it is not; but I have no doubt of its truth.
In other words, I have no doubt of the *reality* of
God's condemnation of sin, whether it is to be
called forensic or not.   It is as real as a bad conscience, as real as the difference between right and
wrong, as real as the consciousness of guilt which is
but the echo of it, as real as spiritual impotence and
despair, which are the effects of its paralysing touch.
The thing that has to be dealt with, that has to be
overcome, in the work of reconciliation, is not man's
distrust of God, but God's condemnation of man.

It is this condemnation, then, as a real and
serious thing—it is sin in this especial character of
that which draws down God's condemnation on
man—with which Christ deals.   And He deals with
it in a great and serious way.   He does not treat it
as if it were merely subjective,—an illusion from
which man has to be delivered.   He does not put
it away by disregarding it, and telling us to disregard

it. He puts it away by bearing it. He removes it from us by taking it upon Himself. And He takes it upon Himself, in the sense of the New Testament, by submitting to that death in which God's condemnation of sin is expressed. In the Bible, to bear sin is not an ambiguous expression. It means to underlie its responsibility and to receive its consequences : to say that Christ *bore* our sins is precisely the same thing as to say that He *died* for our sins ; it needs no other interpretation, and admits of no other.

This, as I have said, is most expressly brought out in the epistles of St. Paul; but before commenting on any of the classical passages it is worth while to insist on the fact that the New Testament everywhere, in all its books and all its authors, connects forgiveness with the death of Christ. When St. Paul defends his gospel to the Corinthians (1 Cor. xv. 3 ff.), he reminds them that he delivered to them *imprimis* what he had also received, viz., that *Christ died for our sins* according to the Scriptures ; and after some further particulars sums up thus : Whether therefore it be I or they—*i.e.* whether it be the apostle to the Gentiles or the apostles of the circumcision—this is how we preach, and this is how you believed. In other words, there was no gospel known in the primitive church, or in any part of it, which had not this as its foundation—that God forgives our sins because Christ died for them. We ought to be very sure that we know what this means before we begin to criticise it ; we ought to have that impression of its greatness, of its soul-subduing power, which the apostles had, before we begin to make small remarks about it. We ought to appre-

ciate it in its completeness and integrity before
we submit it to a disparaging analysis. We ought,
I think, to resent, as well as to repel, that paltry
unintelligence which seeks to belittle the solemn
truth that Christ *died* for our sins by speaking
slightingly of what it calls 'mere physical death,'
or ' das abstracte Factum des Sterbens,' or of death
as a mere 'Widerfahrniss,' a thing that simply
happens. The death with which we are concerned
here is never spoken of in the New Testament
except in its completeness, as what it actually was.
It was that experience which the Son of God anticipated in Gethsemane, and underwent on Calvary.
That is what the apostles thought of, that is what
we are to think of, when we say Christ *died* for our
sins. To separate out what we call *the spirit* of His
death, and say that the virtue of it lies in that,
and not in the mere abstract fact of dying, or in
the death as a merely physical occurrence, is to
draw distinctions which the apostles did not draw,
and to miss, in doing so, the very nerve of their
gospel. The answer to the question, 'What did
Christ do for our sins?' can only be given in one
word—He *died* for them ; and neither the evangelist nor the theologian who finds this unimpressive
will prosper in the attempt to unfold its contents.

There are some theologians who, in their consciousness of the great difficulties of the subject,
would like to halt at the bare fact just stated.
They admit that the New Testament everywhere
teaches that the putting away of sin is accomplished
by Christ's death ; but the two things—Christ's
death and forgiveness—stand for them in no dis-

coverable relation to each other. To use the current expression, they profess to believe in the fact of the atonement, but they despair of finding any theory of it. There are even some who glory in this situation; it is not with despair, but with triumph, that they find at the very heart of the gospel a mystery which is simply insoluble, in the very focus of revelation a spot of pure impenetrable black. This is a mental attitude which it is not easy to understand, and which cannot possibly be final. A fact of which there is absolutely no theory is a fact which stands out of relation to everything in the universe, a fact which has no connection with any part of our experience; it is a blank unintelligibility, a rock in the sky, a mere irrelevance in the mind of man. There is no such thing conceivable as a fact of which there is no theory, or even a fact of which *we* have no theory; such a thing could never enter *our* world at all; if there could be such a thing, it would be so far from having the virtue in it to redeem us from sin, that it would have no interest for us and no effect upon us at all. In spite, too, of confident assertions to the contrary, this distinction of fact and theory— this pleading for the fact as opposed to the theory— is very far from finding support in the New Testament. For my own part, I have no doubt the New Testament does contain a theory, or, as I should prefer to say, a doctrine of the atonement. The work of Christ in relation to sin is not a naked fact, an impenetrable unintelligible fact; it is, in the New Testament, a luminous, interpretable, and interpreted fact. The love of Christ, says St. Paul,

constraineth us, because we thus judge; *i.e.* because
we can and do put a certain intellectual construction
upon it. When it is said that the preaching of the fact,
apart from any theory, is blessed to reconcile men
to God, and that therefore theorising about it may
well be dispensed with, I imagine there is imperfect
observation of what takes place. The truth rather
is that the fact, as Scripture presents it, lends itself
so readily to one interpretation, and is indeed in
the New Testament so completely identified with
it, that a soul anxious for forgiveness sees and
assents to that interpretation as if by instinct; no
other lies on the surface of the fact, or meets the
soul's needs, and this one justifies itself by proving
the key to the whole of New Testament teaching. The apostolic doctrine of Christ's work in
relation to sin—if you prefer it, the apostolic theory
of the atonement—is the thing which gives one his
bearings in the Bible. Without it, there is a great
deal that has to be explained away; a great deal
that is disproportioned and awkwardly expressed; a
great deal that is simply baffling; but with it the
whole falls into shape and order. And this is only
what we should expect. The work of Christ in relation to sin is the culminating point in revelation; not
the insoluble problem, but the solution of all problems. It may have depths in it that we cannot
fathom, just as the divine nature itself has; but it
will not be unintelligible any more than God Himself is unintelligible; if God is more fully present in
it than in anything else in the world, it ought to
be of all things the most luminous, and the most
susceptible of rational treatment.

I have indicated, in a summary way, what the New Testament 'theory' of Christ's work is. His death is conceived as putting away sin, because in that death our condemnation came upon Him. That is the apostolic interpretation, the apostolic theory, of the atonement. That is the ultimate fact which gives significance to Christ's death, and makes it a sin-annulling death. It is a death in which the divine condemnation of sin comes upon Christ, and is exhausted there, so that there is thenceforth no more condemnation for those that are in Him. If we cannot say *this* of His death—that in it God's condemnation of sin fell upon Him—then we must either show *other* reasons for saying that His death is the ground of forgiveness, or give up the idea that there is any connection between the two. In other words, if we do not accept the apostolic theory of atonement, we must either provide a more adequate one, or else, as intelligent creatures, renounce what we have distinguished as 'the fact.' An absolutely unintelligible fact, to an intelligent being, is exactly equivalent to zero.

It will be proper, at this stage, to exhibit the New Testament evidence of what I have called the New Testament doctrine. In doing so, I shall begin with passages from St. Paul, because it is in his writings that the doctrine is most explicit; but I hope to show that what is explicit in him is in no way peculiar to him, but can easily be made out in the other New Testament writers. And I think it worth while to call attention to the fact that a theology which treats the passages I am about to adduce as mere excrescences on the gospel, or even

on the Pauline gospel, is utterly at variance with
the New Testament. It is in passages like these
that the Christian consciousness in all ages has
found the very core of the gospel, the inmost heart
of God's redeeming love; they have been the
refuge of despairing sinners from generation to
generation; they are not 'faults,' as a geologist
would say, in the structure of Christian thought;
they are not erratic boulders that have been carried
over somehow from a pre-Christian—*i.e.* a Jewish or
pagan—condition of mind, to a Christian one; they
are themselves the most profoundly, purely, and
completely Christian of all Scripture thoughts.
The idea they contain is not an irrational or immoral something that we must eliminate by one
device or another—by exegetical ingenuity, or
philosophical interdict; it is the diamond pivot on
which the whole system of Christian truth revolves,
and to displace it or tamper with it is to reduce the
New Testament to an intellectual chaos.

I have already quoted the passage in 1 Cor. xv.,
in which St. Paul makes Christ's death for our sins
the foundation of the only gospel known to the
primitive church. The next in order in which he
refers to the subject is in 2 Cor. v. 14. The words
are : 'The love of Christ constrains us, because this
is our interpretation of it : One died for all : so
then all died.' Battles have been fought here over
the preposition 'for,' which is ὑπέρ, on behalf of,
not ἀντί, instead of. This, it has been said, excludes
the idea of substitution. This is a hasty inference.
Paul might very well wish to say that Christ died
on our behalf, without, so far as the preposition

goes, thinking *how* it was that Christ's death was to be an advantage to us. But observe the inference he draws: One died for all; so then *all* died. That is to say, His death was as good as theirs. That is *why* His death is an advantage to them; that is what rationally connects it with their benefit: it is a death which is really theirs; it is *their* death which has been died by *Him*. If any one denies this, it rests with him to explain, in the first place, how Christ's death advantages us at all; and in the second place, how Paul can draw from Christ's death the immediate inference, 'so then all *died*.' We do not need to fight about the prepositions ὑπέρ and ἀντί. Christ's death benefits us, we are all agreed, whatever be the preposition used to express its relation to us, or to our sins, or to our good; but there is no coherence between the apostle's premises and his conclusion, except on the assumption that that death of Christ's was really our death which had come upon Him. It is on this deeper connection that all the advantages to us of that death depend.

This interpretation is confirmed when we turn to the last verse of this chapter, which is virtually the apostle's own comment on verse 14: 'Him that knew no sin God made sin on our behalf, that we might become the righteousness of God in Him.' We sometimes hear the New Testament doctrine of the atonement objected to, on the ground of the contradictions it involves. I do not think the objection is very serious. St. Paul, when he wrote this sentence, had them all in his mind, logical and ethical, in their acutest form. He probably felt, as most people feel when redemption from sin becomes a

practical interest to them, that the point at which
God comes into contact with sin, even as a Redeemer, *must* involve contradictions of every kind :
for it means that God is taking part with us against
Himself.   That in the atoning work a sinless One is
made sin, and sinful ones become the righteousness
of God, is not a *prima facie* objection to the work
in question ; it is the very condition under which
alone the work can be carried through.   Paul con-
denses in this proposition, not only the infinite
difficulties of the question, but its adequate solution ;
it is in these sharp, undisguised contradictions—if
you like to say so, it is in this tragic, appalling event,
the sinless One made sin *by God*—that the condemned soul recognises the very stamp and seal of
a real work of atonement.   That meeting of con-
tradictories, that union of logical and moral opposites,
is here the very guarantee of truth.   But the passage
deserves a closer study.   The idea underlying it is
plainly that of an interchange of states.   Christ is
the Person who knew no sin, *i.e.* to whose conscience and will, though He confronted it all His
life, sin remained an absolutely alien thing.   The
negative μὴ (τὸν μὴ γνόντα ἁμαρτίαν) means that
this is conceived as the judgment of another upon
Christ ; it is conceived as the judgment of God.
He it is to whom Christ is sinless.   As He looks
down from Heaven he sees *Him alone*, among the
children of men, free from evil, and therefore free
from condemnation.   He alone is absolutely good,
the beloved with whom the Father is well pleased.
Yet Him God made sin, that by so doing He might
destroy sin, and have the good news of reconciliation

to proclaim to men. What is it, then, that this 'making sin' covers? What are we to understand by it? It means precisely what is meant in the verse already quoted: that Christ died for us, died that death of ours which is the wages of sin. In His death, all sinless as He was, God's condemnation of our sin came upon Him; a divine sentence was executed upon the sin of the world. It is all-important to observe that it was *God* who made Christ sin; the passage is habitually quoted 'He became sin,' or, indefinitely, 'He was made sin,' in a vague sense unconsciously willing to leave God out; and then the mind goes off at a tangent, and seeks moralising or rationalising senses in which such an expression might be used. But God is the subject of the sentence: it is God who is presented dealing in an awful way with the awful reality of sin, for its removal; and the way in which He removes it is to lay it on His Son. That is done, not in anything else, but in this alone, that Christ, by God's appointment, dies the sinner's death. The doom falls upon Him, and is exhausted there. The sense of the apostle is given adequately in the well-known hymn:

> ' Bearing shame and scoffing rude,
> *In my place condemned he stood ;*
> Sealed my pardon with his blood :
> > > Hallelujah. '

It is *not* given adequately, it is not given approximately, it is not given in any degree whatever, it is not seen even afar off, by the most refined theology which leaves the condemnation out of the cross, and

invents a meaning of its own, for the phrase of its
own invention, that Christ *became* sin for us.

The Epistle to the Galatians was written at no
great interval from the Corinthian epistles, whether
before or after. It also contains one of the great
texts bearing on the subject before us: ch. iii. 13,
' Christ redeemed us from the curse of the law,
having become a curse for us; for it is written,
Cursed is every one that hangeth upon a tree.'
There are two ways in which the essential value of
this passage is missed.[1] The first is to take it as
referring, not only primarily, but exclusively, to the
Jews; and, on the ground that they only were
under the law and its curse, to deny that what
St. Paul says has any bearing on Christ's work in
relation to sin in general. Most people will feel
that this is artificial and evasive. The peculiar
knowledge which the Jews had of God's will
certainly trained conscience, and intensified the
sense of sin among them as it was not intensified
elsewhere, but the will of God is known really, if
not adequately, by all men; and it is not Jews only,
but all men, who know what it is to live with God's
condemnation hanging over them. This it is which
Christ has arrested, and arrested by His death; He
has redeemed us from the curse of the law by
becoming a curse for us. Curse passes away from
us because it falls upon Him: in His death He is
identified with that doom which rests upon the
sinful world. The other way in which the meaning
of the passage is evaded is to point to the interpretation which Paul himself gives of Christ's

[1] See Note A.

becoming a curse : He became a curse for us, it
is said, because, according to Scripture, every one
who is hanged on a tree is cursed.   The curse then
would simply be equivalent to the crucifixion ; it
would be dependent on the particular mode in
which Jesus happened to be put to death ; there
would be no such appalling meaning in it as that
our condemnation came upon Him.   I confess
myself unable to take this seriously ; the virtue of
Christ's death, its redemptive efficacy, could not
depend on the historical accident that He met His
death in this way and no other.   An apostle would
be as incapable of believing this as we are.   The
quotation about the tree is not so much *the expression*
of a thought, as *the symbol* or *index* of one.   The
Scripture that says, Rejoice greatly, O daughter of
Zion ; behold, thy King cometh unto thee, is not
to be defined by the fact that Christ rode into
Jerusalem on an ass's colt.   The Scripture that
says He was numbered with the transgressors has
not its signification exhausted in the fact that Christ
was sent to death along with two robbers.   And no
more is a word so profound, and so entirely in
harmony with the whole construction of apostolic
thought on the atonement as this—Christ redeemed
us from the curse of the law by becoming a curse
for us—to be made insipid and ridiculous by having
the curse reduced to the crucifixion as one mode
of death and not another.   The analogy of other
passages is peremptory.   We lay under the divine
curse, under that divine condemnation of sin which
expresses itself in death ; and with that curse and
condemnation Christ was identified in *His* death.

The *mode* of His death—crucifixion—may have given a hint, through the very senses, to a Jew, of the mystery underlying it; just as the riding into Jerusalem on the ass, a proceeding arranged by Jesus Himself, called attention to His sovereignty; but the ass's colt no more *explains* the Kingdom, than the cross explains the curse. The explanation is to be sought in that circle of ideas with which we are already familiar, and with which Paul's readers in Galatia were no doubt as familiar as we. He became a curse for us, and so redeemed us from curse, is precisely the same as He was made sin for us, that we might become the righteousness of God in Him. The form is varied, but the substance is indistinguishable.

Let us turn now to the last Pauline passage I mean to adduce—the elaborate statement of Rom. iii. 21 ff. There is no mistaking the connection of ideas here. All men have sinned, and fall short of the glory of God : if the Mosaic law has given a more adequate experience of this to the Jew, it is an experience which is perfectly familiar and in-telligible to the Gentile also. One condemnation impends over a sinful race, because one God is the God of all. Hence it is one justification which is proclaimed for all in the gospel, and proclaimed on the same condition of faith. Men are justified freely by God's grace, *i.e.* it is absolutely unmerited on our part; it costs nothing to us. But it does not cost nothing to Him. On the contrary, it costs an infinite price. We are justified for nothing, by God's grace, but through the redemption that is in Christ Jesus, whom God set forth as a propitiatory sacrifice through faith in His blood, with a view to demonstrate His righteousness. Every syllable of this has been contested, and the most various meanings forced into the words, or forced out of them; but I do not think they will really seem ambiguous to any one who has accepted the results of our study of other passages. God's forgiveness, the apostle virtually says, must not obscure but display His righteousness: when justification comes to sinful men, it must not make void, but establish the law. It costs nothing to us, and if we could say also that it cost nothing to God, that would mean that there was no moral order in the world at all, and that God was indifferent to the distinction between right and wrong. The great lesson that the Cross teaches is the very opposite of this. It tells us that justification comes through faith in a propitiatory sacrifice; in other words, that God's mercy to the sinful comes through His judgment upon sin. The pardon which is preached in Jesus Christ has the awful virtue of God's condemnation in it as well as the tenderness of His love to the sinful; it expresses the self-preserving as well as the self-communicating side of the divine nature; it is wrought, as it were, in one piece out of the judgment and the mercy of God; and in this is the secret of its power. I will not go into details of exegesis, but only express the opinion, or rather the conviction, that the same great idea underlies this passage which we have found in all the others, viz., that in Christ's death God's condemnation of sin fell upon Him, that God might be just even while justifying sinners who believe in Jesus.

It is true, indeed, that all this may be described as Paulinism, and on that ground treated with scant consideration. People will point, on the one hand, to what they call independent and divergent views in other New Testament writers; and on the other, to the alleged absence of any views whatever upon this question in the teaching of our Lord; and on the strength of these phenomena, they will feel at liberty to regard this Pauline doctrine as a private theologoumenon of the apostle, a device by which he explained to himself the transition from life under the law to life under grace, a sort of rickety bridge by which he had made the eventful passage from Pharisaism to Christianity, a bridge therefore of no value, and indeed of no meaning, to those who avoid Paul's original mistake of beginning the religious life on Pharisaic principles. This last method of discrediting the Pauline doctrine of the atonement seems to me of a piece with the interpretation of that passage in Galatians which would limit its application to the Jews. It is quite true that Paul was a Jew and a Pharisee; but the question which his gospel solved for him was not, How shall a Jew or a Pharisee, but, How shall a sinful man, be just before God? The presupposition of his doctrine is, not that all men are Pharisees, nor that the constitution under which God deals with men is forensic, nor that the moral order of the world is that of an abstract inexorable legalism; it is simply this, that all men are sinners lying under God's condemnation. No presupposition could be conceived which has less the character of an idiosyncrasy; it is indeed its perfect generality, the perfect simplicity and universality with which it applies to the whole human race, on which the apostle insists. It was this which made him the apostle of the nations; the very thing his gospel is *not* is a private construction, adapted to a singular experience.

I am far, indeed, from saying that this interpretation which I have given of Christ's death from St. Paul is all that the New Testament has to say upon the subject, but I maintain that it is fundamental, that nothing can displace it, and that nothing else can keep its significance without it. As for the alleged independence and diversity of views in the New Testament, it certainly ought to count for something that Paul asserts as strongly as he does his entire agreement with the Jerusalem apostles as to the contents of the gospel. 'Whether it be I or they . . . this is what we preach,—that Christ died for our sins.' It is not conceivable that he should have written thus, if *they* meant by Christ's death for our sins something else than *he* meant, or, as those who distinguish fact from theory would have us believe, nothing definite at all. When we look to the other New Testament books, this impression is confirmed. Peter speaks of Christ's work in relation to sin in precisely the same way as Paul. 'He did no sin, neither was guile found in His mouth . . .' But 'He Himself bore our sins in His body on the tree, that having died to sins we might live unto righteousness: and by His stripes we were healed.' Our death to sin, our emancipation from it, our new life, depend on this, that at the Cross our sins were laid on the sinless One. That

any real meaning can be given to these words
except the meaning already explained I cannot see.
The same remark applies to a later passage, in
which Peter expresses himself, if possible, with
greater emphasis. 'Christ suffered—the true text
is, Christ died—once for all, in relation to sins,
righteous on behalf of unrighteous ones, that He
might bring us to God.' In what way, we ask
again, can the death of the righteous be an advantage to the unrighteous, in virtue of its relation
to their sins, unless the divine condemnation of
those sins, which kept them at a distance from
God, fall on the righteous and be exhausted there,
so that it is no longer a separative and repellent
power for them? There must be *some* rationale of
this effect, some intelligible link between the means
and the end; and this, which is expressed with
entire freedom from ambiguity elsewhere, is instinctively supplied here. A mere exegete is sometimes tempted to read New Testament sentences
as if they had no context but that which stands
before him in black and white; they had from the
very beginning, and have still, another context in
the mind of Christian readers, which it is impossible
to disregard. They are not addressed to minds in
the condition of a *tabula rasa*; if they were, they
could hardly be understood at all; they are addressed
to minds which have been delivered—as Paul says
to the Romans: a church, remember, to which he
was personally a stranger—to a type or mould of
teaching; such minds have in this both a criterion
and a clew to the intention of a Christian writer;
they can take a hint, and read into brief words the

fulness of Christian truth. I have no doubt that it was in this way such expressions were interpreted as we find all through the New Testament: 'Christ was once offered to bear the sins of many;' 'He loosed us from our sins by His blood;' 'Behold the Lamb of God that taketh away the sin of the world;' 'He is the propitiation for our sins.' To say that words like these express a fact but not a theory—a fact as opposed to a theory—is to say that they mean nothing whatever. A member of the Apostolic church would be conscious of their meaning without any conscious effort; what they suggested to him would be precisely that truth which is so distasteful to many of those who plead for the fact as against 'theory,' that in Christ's death our condemnation was endured by Him. This theory *is* the fact; there is nothing else in these various expressions either to accept or to contest.

It is perhaps of more importance to consider the other objection, that in the gospels there is practically nothing of all this. Here there is undoubtedly a concession to be made. It stands to reason that Christ could not say much of the meaning of His death, when He could not get His disciples even to believe that He was going to die. But then, as Dr. Dale has put it, Christ did not come to preach the gospel; He came that there might be a gospel to preach. And surely to the significance of His death, if to anything, we may refer the well-known words of John xvi. 12 f.: 'I have yet many things to say unto you, but ye cannot bear them now. Howbeit when He, the Spirit of truth, is come, He shall guide you into all the truth; for He shall not speak from Himself . . . He shall glorify me: for He shall take of mine and shall declare it unto you.' Assuming that these are the words of Jesus, they anticipate an apostolic teaching going far beyond the express words of the Master Himself. It may be precarious, but I think it is worth noticing that the very word used to describe the Spirit's work— He shall *glorify* me—is the word appropriated in this gospel to describe Christ's death. At all events, glory is connected with Christ's death by John in a way in which it is not by the other evangelists, and it is in what I have called the apostolic interpretation of that death, as the bearing of our sins, that its spiritual glory is completely revealed.

But this is not all that has to be said. When we read the gospels with care, Christ's death is seen, if not to bulk more largely, at least to be more pervasively present, than one would have supposed at a hasty glance. It was much in His own mind before those last days when, as Bengel says, He dwelt in His passion; even before those last months in which He tries to find entrance for it into the minds of His apostles. I see no difficulty in the Baptist's recognition of Him, at the very beginning, as the sin-bearing lamb.[1] It is at a comparatively early date that He Himself speaks of the mournful days when the bridegroom shall be taken away from the children of the bride-chamber, and fasting shall come unbidden. It is with His death in His mind that He cries, I have a baptism to be baptized with, and how am I straitened till it be accomplished! In this lofty poetic word the death of

[1] See Note B.

Jesus is transfigured to His imagination ; it is a kind
of religious consecration as well as a pain. And
still confining ourselves to sayings of Jesus, there
are the two which stand pre-eminent in the gospels
in this connection : The Son of man came not to be
ministered unto, but to minister, and to give His life
a ransom for many : and, This is my blood of the
covenant, shed for many, for the remission of sins.
It is impossible to enter into the conflicts which
have been waged, and are still being waged, over
these great sayings. It is sufficient to remark that
they are at least congruous with the doctrine which
has thus far engaged us. The presupposition of
the first—that Christ gives His life a ransom for
many—is surely this : that the many lives are
forfeit and that His is not; so that the surrender
of His means the liberation of theirs. This is the
precise equivalent—in a figure—of the fact that the
sinless One was made sin in order that the sinful
might become the righteousness of God in Him.
The second, which describes the forgiveness of sins
as the end contemplated in the shedding of Christ's
blood, has been questioned on grounds of higher
criticism, and made insoluble by being made to
depend for its interpretation on an exact appreciation of the Mosaic institute of sacrifice ; but assuming its genuineness, it at least puts the actual
dependence of forgiveness upon Christ's death into
the teaching of Christ Himself. But far above
words for the significance of that death to Christ
Himself is the story of the agony ; far above words
for its significance to the church is the space filled
in all the gospels by the story of the passion.

Christ shrank from His death in deadly fear, for
that, and not vehement prayer, is the meaning of
ἀγωνία ; as it came near, the prospect appalled Him.
It is hard to believe, hard even to impossibility,
that it was simply the anticipation of pain which so
overcame Him.   It was the condemnation in the
Cross which made him cry, O my Father, if it be
possible, let this cup pass from me ; it was the
anticipation of that experience in which, all sinless
as He was, the Father would put into His hand
the cup our sins had mingled.   It was not possible
that this cup should pass.   There was no other way
in which sin could pass from us than by being laid
on Him ; and it was the final proof of His obedience
to the Father, the full measure of His love to us,
when He said to God, Not my will, but thine, be
done : and to the disciples, The cup that my Father
giveth me to drink, shall I not drink it ?   Not to
speak of Christ's opening the minds of His disciples
in the forty days between the resurrection and the
ascension — an interval too lightly disregarded by
many who study the New Testament — there is
surely in these words and experiences of Christ a
sufficient mass of evidence to repel the idea that
the atoning significance of His death is foreign to
the gospels.   His death is the great fact, the great
mystery, the great problem of the gospels ; it
dominates them as truly as it does the epistles ; and
every glimpse we get of its meaning in them is
congruous with what is more fully expounded later.
Under these circumstances, the doctrine of Christ,
or His want of doctrine, cannot be pleaded against
that of the apostles ; if His death has the supreme

importance which even the gospels assign it, it is absurd for us to go back and assume our Christian relation to Him at a time when He has not yet died. You cannot get the Cross nor its meaning out of the New Testament by going behind it: you must stand in front of it to see what the gospel is; and if you do so, with the New Testament in your hand, the meaning will not be obscure.   The Cross is the place at which the sinless One dies the death of the sinful: the place at which God's condemnation is borne by the Innocent, that for those who commit themselves to Him there may be condemnation no more.   I cannot read the New Testament in any other sense.   I cannot see at the very heart of it anything but this—grace establishing the law, not in a 'forensic' sense, but in a spiritual sense; mercy revealed, not over judgment, but through it; justification disclosing not only the goodness but the severity of God; the Cross inscribed, God is love, only because it is inscribed also, The wages of sin is death.

LECTURE VI

THE WORK OF CHRIST IN RELATION TO SIN—INADEQUATE DOCTRINES OF ATONEMENT

THE work of Christ in relation to sin is the great thing in the gospel. It is the centre of interest and devotion, the main object both of attack and defence; for our understanding of the Christian revelation as a whole, everything depends upon the clearness of our vision here. It is tempting, indeed, to think that because of its very greatness we can only have partial and fragmentary views of it, discerning this element and that aspect according as our eyes are opened by grace or by our own extreme need; but the more we reflect upon it, the more we shall be convinced that it is as simple as it is great, and that there is one element in it, one aspect of it, which is omnipresent, constitutive of the thing itself, and not to be denied or overlooked except at the cost of denying the reality of Christ's work altogether. Having explained and justified in the last lecture what I conceive this element to be, I might have passed on; but in view of the immense importance of the subject, and the quantity of theological writing, popular and scientific, in which the problem is inadequately stated and the solution completely missed, I think it better to take a further survey of the whole question.

Theories, or doctrines, of the atonement may be arranged on a kind of scale. At one end would stand what I have expounded as the apostolic doctrine. This doctrine puts the work of Christ in a real relation to man's sin. It treats God's condemnation as a real thing; and it establishes a real and intelligible connection between Christ's death and our forgiveness. It declares that God forgives our sins because Christ died for them; and it maintains unambiguously that in that death of Christ our condemnation came upon Him, that for us there might be no condemnation more. This is the truth which is covered and guarded by the word Substitution. It is, of course, a word to which there are objections, and a word which may be abused. If any one takes it as it is defined in the dictionary, and from that definition draws inferences which he imports into theology, he is likely enough to be guilty of heresies; but it is his own behaviour, and not the word, which is responsible for them. A man who treated the word Person or Trinity in the same way would have the same experience. What the word substitution expresses, in the doctrine of the atonement, is the truth—for it *is* the truth—that man is unconditionally and for ever dependent for his acceptance with God on something which Christ has done *for* him, and which he could never have done, and never needs to do, for himself. Christ died for our sins. *That death* we do not die. Because He bore our sins, we are accepted with God; and we are to

eternity absolutely indebted to Him.   We have no
standing in grace but that which He has won for us :
nothing but the forfeiting of His free life has freed
our forfeited lives.   That is what is meant by
calling Christ our substitute, and to that use of the
word no objection can be taken which does not
strike at the root of New Testament teaching.
There are two practical considerations which are
worth mentioning in support of this view of the
atonement.   The first is, that it can be preached.
You can tell men what it is.   You can appeal to
them with it in God's name.   There are many 'interpretations,' so called, of Christ's work, to which
the fatal objection can be made, that they are
unintelligible.   You could never use them to
evangelise.   They supply no practical or convincing
answer to the question, What must I do to be
saved ?   Now I do not hesitate to say that a
doctrine of atonement which cannot be preached
is not true.   If it cannot be told out, lucidly, un-
reservedly, passionately, tremblingly, by any simple
man, to gentle and simple alike, it is not that word
of the Cross which Paul describes as the power of
God unto salvation to every one who believes.   The
other consideration is this, that the view of the atonement in question binds men for ever to Christ by
making them for ever dependent on Him.   There
is never any standing for them before God but that
which He has bought with His blood.   I have a
friend in Scotland, a convert, I daresay you will be
glad to hear, of Mr. Moody during his first visit
to us in 1874, who has himself been wonderfully
blessed by God as an evangelist and carer for souls.

He is a fishing-tackle maker and an enthusiastic
fisherman, and told me once of losing his bait in a
mysterious way without catching anything. The
explanation was that by some accident or other the
barb had been broken from the hook. It was my
friend himself who made the application of this,
when he said that this was exactly what happened
when people preached the love of God to men, but
left out of their gospel the essential truth that it is
Christ on the Cross, the substitute for sinners, in
whom that love is revealed. In other words, the
condemnation of our sins in Christ upon His Cross
is the barb on the hook. If you leave that out of
your gospel, I do not deny that your bait will be
taken; men are pleased rather than not to think
that God regards them with goodwill; your bait
will be taken, but you will not catch men. You
will not create in sinful human hearts that attitude
to Christ which created the New Testament. You
will not annihilate pride, and make Christ the
Alpha and the Omega in man's redemption.

If this apostolic doctrine of atonement be put at
one end of the scale, at the other will appear
Socinianism, which is virtually the denial of atonement altogether. I do not propose to consider this in
the historical form which is suggested by the name of
Socinus; that form was determined by the exigencies
of controversy, and the actual content of Socinus'
teaching, and especially the spirit of it, are much
more widely diffused. To all intents and purposes
they are found wherever the assertion is made that
God is love, and out of pure goodness, without any
special work at all, forgives the sins of the penitent;

wherever, in other words, love is pleaded against
propitiation. There are various grounds on which
this whole way of looking at forgiveness may be
decidedly rejected. There is first the ground, at
once theological and ethical, that it annihilates the
moral order of the world altogether. God is conceived as an individual who deals with other
individuals, each by himself, in a way of good-
nature and consideration; there is no principle in
the forgiveness which He dispenses; no conception
of a moral organism the constitution of which must
not be arbitrarily dissolved, of a moral system the
integrity of which must be maintained by and
through all God's dealings with men. Then there
is the ground which it is not too much to call
specifically Christian, that the Socinian view is
false, because it deprives Christ of any essential
significance in the work of redemption. God's forgiveness is not identified with Him more than with
anybody else; it is not dependent on Him more
than on any other. He proclaims it, but He does not
procure it; He is not the gospel, but only its supreme
minister. All conceptions of the gospel which, when
reduced to their simplest terms, come out thus, are
to be decidedly rejected. If our religion is to come
from the New Testament, Christ must have a place
in it which no other can share. Not apart from
Him, but *in Him*—the apostles declare with one
voice—*in* Him we have our redemption through
His blood, even the forgiveness of our trespasses.
God's forgiveness does not come to us independent
of Christ, past Him, over His head, so that we can
count Him as one of those who best knew and most

fully proclaimed an unimaginable mercy, which
would have been all that it is even had He never
lived; it comes only in Him, and through His death
for our sins. That this is the distinctively Christian
position is clearly seen by those who have been
brought up in other religions. An interesting illustration of this was given some time ago in India.
A Hindu Society was formed which had for its
object to appropriate all that was good in Christianity without burdening itself with the rest.
Among other things which it appropriated, with
the omission of only two words, was the answer
given in the Westminster Shorter Catechism to the
question, What is repentance unto life? Here is
the answer. 'Repentance unto life is a saving
grace, whereby a sinner, out of a true sense of his
sin, and apprehension of the mercy of God in Christ,
doth with grief and hatred of his sin turn from it
unto God, with full purpose of, and endeavour after,
new obedience.' The words the Hindus left out
were *in Christ*; instead of 'apprehension of the
mercy of God in Christ,' they read simply, 'apprehension of the mercy of God.' But they knew
that this was not compromising. They were acute
enough to see that in the words they left out the
whole *Christianity* of the definition lay; they felt
that here was the barb of the hook, and as they
had no intention of being caught, they broke it off.
I entirely agree with their insight. If the mercy
of God is separable from Christ, independent of
Christ, accessible apart from Christ, as the theory
before us would teach, there is no need and no
possibility of a Christian religion at all. A final

ground for rejecting all Socinian and Socinianising explanations of forgiveness is that, in opposing to each other love and propitiation, they run directly counter to the whole teaching of the New Testament. I say in opposing love and propitiation, for that is what it comes to. God, the argument runs in its simplest form, is love, and therefore does not need to be propitiated. To say that He does need to be propitiated is to make of Him not a Father, but a cruel tyrant. It is a barbarous idea, which is common enough in heathen religions, which may have been natural enough in the early and imperfect stages of revelation, which may even have left its traces, in the New Testament itself, in the minds of men who had only assimilated imperfectly the final revelation made in Christ, but which is radically, essentially, and for ever alien to the true Christian faith—a mere falsehood against which the Christian faith has perpetually to assert the truth, that God is love, and that propitiation is needless. I do not think it is necessary here to do more than confront this doctrine with what I have no hesitation in calling the unanimous and unambiguous testimony of all New Testament writers. God is love, say those of whom we have been speaking, and therefore He dispenses with propitiation ; God is love, say the apostles, for He provides a propitiation. In the New Testament, the propitiation is the contents of love ; it is that in providing which love goes to the utmost length, makes its most stupendous sacrifice, reveals its length and breadth and depth and height. ' Herein is love,' says John, ' not that we loved God, but that He loved us, and sent His Son *as a pro-*

pitiation for our sins.'   'God,' says Paul, 'com-
mendeth His own love toward us '—*i.e.* presents
His love to us as a great and indisputably real
thing—'in that, while we were yet sinners, Christ
died for us.'   These two sentences mean the same
thing; for Christ's death, as we have already seen,
is the propitiation.   They mean that the measure of
God's love is given in this, that He made Christ to
be sin for us with a view to our justification; that
He laid our sins on Him, that they might lie on us
no more.   This combination of ideas gives a real
meaning and content both to love and to propitiation.   We see what the propitiation was; we see
what an immeasurable sacrifice it involves both for
the Father and the Son; and because that sacrifice
was actually made we know that God is love.   That
God is love is in the New Testament a conclusion
from the fact that He has provided in Christ and in
His death a propitiation for sins; but for this, the
apostles would never have known that God is love;
apart from this, they could never have found meaning
for the phrase, God is love.   The whole proof, the
whole meaning, contents, substance, and spirit of
that expression, are contained in propitiation, and in
nothing else.   What, then, are we to say of those
who appeal to love against propitiation, and argue
that because God is love the very thought of propitiation is an insult to him?   We can say this, at
least, that they have fundamentally misunderstood
the New Testament.   We can deny their right to
use apostolic language, like 'God is love,' after carefully emptying it of apostolic meaning.   We can
protest against the use of such language to cover a

meaning which is not at all its New Testament
meaning, just as we could protest against putting
the Queen's head on base metal. No content but
the apostolic content does any manner of justice to
words so great, and when that content is not only
ignored but denied, it is high time to be outspoken.
Under whatever ingenious disguise, to separate love
from propitiation—to evacuate love of that propitiatory import which in the New Testament literally
constitutes it what it is—amounts, in the long-run,
to the subversion of moral distinctions. Propitiation, in the sense of an absolutely serious dealing
with God's condemnation of sin for its removal,
is essential to forgiveness, as long as we regard
God's condemnation of sin as an absolutely real
and serious thing.   Of course *we* cannot provide
the propitiation—that is the assumption on which
the gospel proceeds—but God provides it; and
the fact that He does so, in the sin-bearing death
of the sinless One, is the final demonstration of
His love.   Apart from this, His love is at best
meaningless, and ethically indifferent. The Cross,
with His condemnation in it, reveals at once the
immensity and the sanctity of His love.

The two doctrines I have just described as apostolic and Socinian or Socinianising are the extremes
upon the scale.   The apostolic doctrine is a real
doctrine of propitiation; it represents Christ as
doing a real work in relation to sin, a work which is
essential to forgiveness if forgiveness is not to treat
God's condemnation of sin as unreal; a work also
which we were incapable of doing for ourselves.
The Socinian doctrine, on the other hand, is not a

doctrine of propitiation at all; it refuses to contemplate the necessity of any such work as constitutes in the apostolic doctrine the very soul and substance of what Christ has done for us. It is easy to understand the blank opposition of the two to each other; and in time we come to see that all other doctrines, when thought out to simplicity and clearness, resolve themselves into one or other of these, or are made up inconsistently of elements from both. The number of such doctrines is beyond calculation; the histories of theology are baffled when they attempt to classify them. I do not propose to examine any of them in detail, but to indicate where they all seek their strength, and where, as I think, they all betray their weakness.

They seek their strength in a rigorously historical treatment of the work of Christ, which brings His death into line with His life, and makes it, not a separate or independent thing, but simply the consummation of His life. In other words, they seek their strength in the ethical interpretation of Christ's experience as a whole. His vocation, they say, was all of a piece; He had to live a certain life and do a certain work; and His death, with all its attendant circumstances, was only one of the difficulties which He had to face, one of the sufferings which He had to endure and overcome, rather than fail in His vocation. There are many who even deny that Christ's death has any essential significance in His work at all. Wendt, for instance, argues that He began His public ministry with no anticipation of such a doom, but rather hopeful that Israel might receive Him; and that though His idea of the Kingdom, and of His own work in establishing it, never varied, it was only in the last months of His life that the certainty of His death in conflict with the world began to dawn upon Him, compelling Him to consider in what way even such a destiny could be subsumed under His vocation, and actually further it.[1] Without going as far as this, there are many who insist that Christ did nothing at all for others which He did not also do for Himself—that His whole work was the fulfilment of His vocation, and nothing else—that when He died, it was His own death He endured, a death which presented precisely the same problem to Him which death presents to every man.[2] Now it may freely be granted that in all He did and suffered Christ fulfilled His vocation; even when He died, He became obedient unto death, His death being the climax of His obedience to the Father; but it cannot be granted that His vocation was ethical in a sense which simply identifies it with the vocation of any other man. His vocation was not only ethical, but unique. As a recent English theologian has put it : 'there were certain functions which He performed which cannot be explained out of His character as ideal man.'[3] Supreme among these functions is that of bearing sin. It is this function that constitutes death for Christ a task and a problem which it is not for those who believe in Him. It does not affect the essential character of His death that it actually came to pass in a particular way. He did die a good man in conflict with the

[1] See Note A. [2] See Note B.
[3] T. B. Strong : *Manual of Theology*, p. 291.

evil in the world; He did die a martyr's death; martyrdom, in other words, is included in His vocation; it is included in it, but it does not exhaust it; His vocation was, in a martyr's death, to do what no martyr did or could do—to bear the sin of the world. If death was precisely the same problem for Christ that it is for us, then the New Testament way of speaking about His death is simply incom ehensible. If the first Christians had been of this mind, the phraseology we find in every page of Scripture could never have arisen. But they were not of this mind. They believed that Christ was sinless, and therefore that death, although included in His vocation, had a unique significance, and presented a unique problem to Him. His death is a solitary phenomenon—the one thing of the kind in the universe—a sinless One submitting to the doom of sin. It was *His* death, certainly, for He had *come* to die; but it was *not* His, for He knew no sin; it was *for us*, and *not for Himself*, that He made death His own.

The most important representative of this line of thought in theology is Ritschl. He starts by giving prominence to the conception of Christ as religious subject, *i.e.* as a person who is himself religious, and in whose religious life the destiny of man is ful-filled. Man's vocation, according to Ritschl, is to have dominion over the world; in the possession of a spiritual life he is to be superior to all that is out-ward, temporary, local, painful, or repressive. In other words, he is to exercise sovereignty over the world, and the exercise of that sovereignty is the same thing as the possession of eternal life. Religion is meant to put man in this sovereign position; it is through the power which religion gives that he is able to put all things under his feet, to feel sure that all things work together for his good, to make what are usually called 'evils' minister to his higher life instead of suppressing it, to overcome the consciousness of limitation and restraint which particular evils and even particular situations, not at all evil, necessarily beget, and so to find rest for his soul.   Ritschl conceives Christ from beginning to end as the ideal religious man, whose religion gives Him this practical sovereignty over all things, this perfect peace, freedom, and life. This is what he means by calling Christ a King, and it is under His Kingship that He subsumes His other functions or offices.   Whatever He is, He is royally.   It is absurd, Ritschl thinks, to derive from Christ's exaltation, a state of which we know nothing, our ideas of His Kingship; if the word has any meaning at all, it has to be derived from His earthly life; it is there that we see His sovereignty in exercise, and can discover its contents.   And these contents, as I have said already, are simply Christ's power to lead a perfectly religious life under actual earthly conditions, never allowing these conditions to triumph over Him, but by heroic patience, even when they came in the form of ignominy and death, triumphing over them.   To live this life was His vocation, and He lived it; but He did nothing whatever for us, in doing so, that was not at the same time done for Himself.   Christ living the ideal religious life, which is essentially that of sovereignty, is in it at the same time prophet and priest. He is prophet, inasmuch as in that life He represents God to man. It is throughout a divine revelation, an absolute manifestation of grace and truth. It is not this or that element in it which belongs to the prophetic office, and reveals God; every word, every deed, every suffering endured, everything that can be seen, felt, or inferred, is divinely significant. On the other hand, the royal Christ is priest, inasmuch as in that ideal religious life He represents man to God. Here, again, we are not to pick and choose. It is not this or that in Christ's life which has priestly significance, but everything. We never see Him in any act, in any posture, in any sorrow, in which He is not representing man to God, offering to God in human nature the sacrifice of a will which perfectly consents to and accepts the will of God Himself. We must not divide Christ among His offices, nor even distribute His acts or His sufferings among them. The fundamental category is Kingship; and Christ is King inasmuch as He lives the life of dominion over the world for which man was made, and in fulfilling His own vocation fulfils man's destiny as well. But the Kingship, considered from one point of view, becomes a Kingly prophetship, for the King is representing God to man; and from another a Kingly priesthood, for the King is representing man to God. Everything we know of Christ comes under all these heads, and the ordinary distribution of what He does or suffers under separate heads of Christ as prophet, as priest, and as King, is hopelessly arbitrary and illogical. According to Ritschl, this ideally religious life, in which the man Christ

Jesus fulfils the destiny of the race by His sovereignty over all things, and in which, in the exercise of that sovereignty, He piously accepts death rather than allow sin to enter His soul, commending Himself in so doing to the Father,— this ideally religious life is itself the reconciliation or the atonement.   Christ lives it in His character of Head of the Church; and God reckons to believers for righteousness their fellowship with Christ in the Kingdom He founded.   All Christ's offices, because the aspects of His religious life, are communicable.   He imparts to men the sovereignty which He exercised over all things; it is exercised by those who can say, We know that all things work together for good to them that love God; or, All things are ours, whether Paul or Apollos or Cephas, the world or life or death.   He imparts His prophetic office; it belongs to all who share His spirit, and reveal God to men.   He imparts His priestly office also: it belongs to all who draw near to God in Him.   What is incommunicable is treated as unintelligible, irrelevant, unreal: the ethical interpretation of Christ's vocation—the conception of Christ Himself as religious subject—have their value in this, that they bring the Person and the Work well within our grasp.   The only question that has to be asked is, Whether this interpretation of the work of Christ satisfies the New Testament on the one side, and the human conscience, and the facts of sin and condemnation, on the other.

It may be freely granted, to begin with, that there is an imposing consistency and simplicity in this way of reading the life and death of our

Saviour. It seems to me also abundantly success-
ful in its criticism of the *munus triplex* of traditional
theology. When Christ is spoken of as prophet, as
priest, and as king, it is usually in a way which
divides His life and experiences among these various
functions. Thus Amesius, one of the best orthodox
writers, explains Him as designed to meet the need
of men who labour under three ills : (1) ignorance
of God, which is removed by Christ the prophet ;
(2) estrangement from God, which is removed by
Christ the priest; and (3) incapacity of returning to
God, which is overcome by Christ the King. It is
hardly scientific simply to co-ordinate these three
without explaining their relations to each other;
and there is much to be said for Ritschl's view
which, taking Christ essentially in His character of
founder of the kingdom of God, makes His kingship the supreme category, and co-ordinates the
prophetic and priestly offices under it. There is
much also to be said for the inclusion of the whole
of His life and experiences under each of these
heads, and for the abolition, which this necessitates,
of the distinction between Christ's active and His
passive obedience. Christ's fulfilment of His vocation
was all of a piece ; in all that He did and bore from
beginning to end, He freely accepted His Father's
will and made it His own. Active and passive
obedience interpenetrate in this willing fulfilment
of His vocation, and they neither can be nor should
be separated from each other. By introducing the
conception of vocation, or at least by giving it a
dominant place in the interpretation of Christ's
life, Ritschl has given unity to a department of

theology which had suffered much from excessive analysis; and by viewing everything afresh from the historical and ethical standpoint, he has vivified what had become a rather lifeless subject, at least in books. These services may be, and ought to be, gladly and heartily recognised, even by those who cannot accept his conclusions in all their compass; and in proceeding to make some critical remarks upon his opinion, I do it as one who gladly acknowledges a great debt to the person from whom he dissents.

Three things strike one on a view of the whole position. (1) Underneath it there lies an inadequate conception of Christ's Person. Ritschl often speaks of His Godhead, but he means by this nothing more than that Jesus in His actual situation was as good as God could have been. He refuses to raise any question whatever—historical, physical, or metaphysical—as to the origin of Christ's Person; there He is; He is what He is, and what we see; the secret of His being lies with the Father, and has nothing to do with either religion or theology. These things may be said reverently, or they may be said insolently; but no matter how they are said, what underlies them is the tacit assumption that Jesus is in the world exactly as we are. Now that excludes *a limine* a great deal that we have been accustomed to think essential to the Christian religion, and it is certainly not the view either of the first Christians, or, as we have seen in an earlier lecture, of Christ Himself. (2) But in the second place, this inadequate view of Christ's person necessarily brings with it an inadequate view of

His vocation. He is in the world exactly as we are, and life presents exactly the same problem for Him as it does for us. What He has to do is to be Man, as man's destiny is foreshadowed in the 8th Psalm and in the first chapter of Genesis. He is to fulfil the vocation assigned to Adam—have dominion. He is to reign on earth, asserting and maintaining the sovereignty of the spiritual life over all things—over the body and its infirmities, over the limitations and inevitable constraints of external nature, over the ceaseless pressure of evil, over the last enemy—death. Death, as the debt of nature, is the inevitable issue for Him as for all men; only it is made more terrible, and harder to overcome, by being encountered prematurely in conflict with the evil in the world. Christ maintained His sovereignty even here; He reigned in the very presence of death; He enjoyed, in the very instant of dying, the eternal life, when He said: Father, into thy hands I commend my spirit. I do not think any one who appreciates the New Testament at all will be able to rest satisfied with this. It is an interpretation of Christ's life simply *a parte ante*, not at all *a parte post*. In ignoring the Resurrection, which is Christ's real triumph over death; in ignoring the gift and the teaching of the Holy Spirit, which so interpret the life and death of Christ as to make them the foundation of the Christian religion, it seems to me to abandon the New Testament altogether. Why should we shut our eyes to Easter and Pentecost, for that is what it comes to, in endeavouring to make Christ's life and death intelligible? Why should we insist upon it that life and death were precisely the same problem for Him as for us ?   Certainly the apostles ascribe a meaning and virtue to His death which belong to it alone; and that plainly implies that though death was included in His vocation, and came to Him in a particular way as He fulfilled that vocation, it was nevertheless an essentially different thing in His case from what it is in ours. What Ritschl's theory amounts to is, that Christ redeemed us from death as the debt of nature, by showing us how to trust God's love even in that extremity; what the apostolic doctrine shows is how Christ redeems us from death as the wages of sin by dying *our* death Himself, and bearing our sins for us. (3) And that leads me to the third remark which this theory suggests.   It does not treat sin with the seriousness with which it is treated in the New Testament, and it does not put the work of Christ in any precise relation to sin at all.   Christ is a person in whom man's destiny is fulfilled in a world of sinful men, and of course the sin which is in the world affects Him in innumerable ways, as everything else does; but there is no reason why His vocation should be defined in relation to sin, or why His life or His death should be described by their effect upon sin, more than on anything else.   If the Ritschlian interpretation of the whole phenomenon be correct, why should it ever have occurred to any one to call Christ the Lamb of God, which taketh away the sin of the world? or to say that He bore our sins, or that He died for our sins, or that He loosed us from our sins by His blood, or that God made

Him to be sin for us, or condemned sin in His flesh, or that in Him we have our redemption through His blood, even the forgiveness of our trespasses? The truth is, that all the great passages in which the simple Christian consciousness has instinctively sought and found the very pith and marrow of the gospel present insoluble problems to this school; instead of furnishing criteria and clews they are stumbling-blocks that have to be cautiously evaded or laboriously explained out of existence. There is hardly a word in the New Testament about the death of Christ which would have been written as it stands—there is hardly a word that does not need to be tortured in defiance of exegesis—to fall into any appearance of consistency with the views of this school. And at the bottom of it all lies the refusal to treat God's condemnation of sin as that absolutely real and serious thing which it is declared to be in Scripture. God's righteousness is substantially identified with His grace; it is His steadfast faithful purpose freely to impart His own character to men. God's holiness is an obscure attribute, half physical, half ethical, of which no exact account can be given, and of which no account need be taken in explaining the work of reconciliation. 'Wrath,' 'curse,' and 'penalty' are ideas or things which do not from the divine point of view (*sub specie æternitatis*) come between God's love and the persons who are or are to be reconciled and saved. It is extremely important, Ritschl says, to maintain the distinction between our individual religious reflection on the one hand, and the form of theological knowledge

sub specie æternitatis on the other.[1] But to maintain this distinction by saying that wrath, curse,
penalty, etc., are ideas or things which from
the divine point of view (*sub specie æternitatis*)
do not come between God's love and sinful men,
seems to me precisely equivalent to saying that
the *real experiences* through which men are prepared to welcome redemption are after all *not
real*, but merely illusions. Christ redeems us simply
by undeceiving us. He persuades us that we
have been frightened for nothing. This is not a
gospel that a man whose conscience is stricken
will take seriously; nor is it a gospel that one who
knows the need of the conscience will seriously
preach. Our sin, our evil conscience, our sense of
condemnation, are absolutely real things; and in
the New Testament work of redemption they are
treated *as* real, and not as illusions. Christ bears
our sins; *that* is the very soul of His vocation; He
bears them in His body on the tree; and there is
therefore now no condemnation to them that are in
Him. He does not disillusionise us; He ransoms
us with His blood. Unto Him be glory for ever.

The school of Ritschl is at this time dominant
in Germany; indeed, he is the only theologian
since Schleiermacher who can be said to have
founded a school at all. It is exciting the liveliest
interest, and has provoked some lively discussions,
in the Protestant churches of France and Switzer-
land. Partly in direct, much more in indirect
ways, it has very great influence both in England
and Scotland. That is by no means to be re-

---

[1] See Note C.

gretted, for however inadequate it may be to the
fulness of New Testament teaching, its thinking
is at all events live thinking, and its representative
men are animated by a real enthusiasm for the
man Christ Jesus, and a real desire to get as close
as possible to the life which He lived and the
death which He died.   Their devotion to the
ethico-historical line of interpretation has brought
undoubted gains with it : it has restored to the
consciousness of many Christian people a great deal
that the traditional orthodoxy was at least in danger
of losing.   But it is possible for us to appropriate
all that it has won without letting go our hold
of those still deeper and greater things which it
either ignores or denies.   The conception of Christ's
vocation, on which the whole scheme depends, can
be enlarged so as to include a death which is not
what ours is, but what ours could not be—a real propitiation for the sin of the world, regarded as itself
real.   Christ's death need not cease to be ethical,
because it is not the same as ours ; it is the cup which
the Father has given Him to drink, and therefore
the drinking of it can be ethically interpreted,
though not His sins, but ours, explain its bitterness.   It is a mistake, of course, to make a doctrine
of atonement which serves no purpose but to be a
touchstone of orthodoxy ; but it is a mistake, too,
and surely as bad a mistake, for men who have to
go out into a sinful world with a gospel for sinners,
to elaborate interpretations of the life and death of
Christ, which show how rich in significance that
life and death are, but which contain no doctrine
of atonement at all.   The traditionally orthodox

and the Ritschlian may have much to learn from each other; but the New Testament is always able to teach us all.

When we fix the death of Christ in this significance which belongs to it alone, we see that it necessarily puts a limit to the communicableness of Christ's experience, and to the possible interpretations of such language as that we are identified with Christ in His sacrifice for sin, that we are crucified with Him, that we are in Him in His death, that *we* die that death as well as He. Expressions of this sort have something in them which is hardly amenable to logic, and the rigorous treatment of them by the understanding is very likely to mislead. But we cannot allow ourselves to forget that the very apostle who used 'in Christ' almost as his sign-manual is he who teaches with the utmost plainness the doctrine that makes Christ's death a solitary phenomenon in the universe; and that though he calls himself 'a man in Christ,' he exclaims with bewilderment and indignation, Was Paul crucified for you? The spirit in which Christ lived and died ought certainly to be our spirit; we are to be identified with Him in His utter renunciation of evil, and in His complete devotion to God; but no similiar renunciation, no similar devotion on our part, even though they ended in literal crucifixion, could make our death identical in nature with that of the sinless One, who, in dying, bore our sins. It is in this that the atonement lies. Christ finished it. He finished it alone. No one can do it after Him. No one needs to do it. The utmost conceivable closeness of union and communion with the Redeemer never brings us to anything like an identity of experience with Him here. We are not saved because of anything we do, or bear, or feel, in fellowship with Christ; but because, when we were yet without strength, in due time Christ came and bore in our stead the burden which would have crushed us to perdition. The New Testament, I believe, carefully guards this distinction, even while it insists on the union of the Christian with Christ through faith.

This suggests the last remark which I would make on the subject. Reflection on the atonement, a recent theologian has observed, has in our time proceeded mainly under two impulses: (1) the desire to find spiritual laws which will make the atonement itself intelligible; (2) the desire to find spiritual laws which connect the atonement with the new life springing from it.[1] The legitimacy of these desires no one will contest. There is certainly work for theologians to do under both of them. It has always been too easy, referring to this last point first, to treat the atonement as one thing, and the new life as another, without establishing any connection whatever between them. It has always been too easy, in teaching that Christ bore our sins and died our death, to give conscience an opiate, instead of quickening it into newness of life. It is a task for those who hold such a doctrine of Christ's work in relation to sin, as I have just been asserting, to show that there is a natural, intelligible inspiration to a new life in the acceptance of it, and that it cannot be lodged in the

[1] See Note D.

heart, in all its integrity, and leave the life, as it
was before, under the dominion of sin. Even in
New Testament times the gospel which Paul
preached was accused of antinomianism; and so
will every gospel be accused which makes pardon
a reality. But in the death of Christ, and in faith
laying hold of that death, we have the security
against such abuses of the grace of God. To
accept the forgiveness so won is to accept forgiveness which has in it God's judgment upon sin, as
well as His mercy to the sinful; it is to have the
conscience awed, subdued, made tender and sensitive to the holy will of God, and the heart bowed
in infinite gratitude to His love. It is not the law
which can secure its own fulfilment; it is not by
gazing on the tables of stone that we are made
good men. It is by standing at Mount Calvary, and
taking into our hearts in faith that love which for
us men and for our salvation bore our sins upon
the tree. It would be a miserable theology that
by any defect in this direction gave room to think
of Christ as the minister of sin. But what are we
to say of the other desire which animates reflection
on the atonement—the desire to find spiritual laws
which make the atonement itself intelligible? Put
into different words, this means the desire to find
human analogies for the work of Christ in relation
to sin; things which people can do for one another
like that which He did for the world. This line of
thought does not seem to me very likely to lead to
theological progress. The New Testament is not
afraid to bring Christians into the fellowship of
Christ. ' Bear ye one another's burdens, and so fulfil

the law of Christ,' says St. Paul. 'I fill up that which
is behind of the sufferings of Christ in my flesh, for
His body's sake, the Church.' 'Who is weak, and I
am not weak? Who is made to stumble, and I am
not on fire with pain?' But that does not disturb in
the least the simple perception of all the New
Testament writers that Christ is our Saviour just
because He does for us a work that we could *not* do
for ourselves, and cannot do for each other. 'None
can by any means redeem his brother, nor give to
God a ransom for him; for the redemption of their
soul is costly, and must be let alone for ever.' In
the sinless bearing of sin—the one thing that
needed to be done for man's redemption—Christ
has a solitary greatness. We understand the motive
of it, as we understand the motive of the incarnation; it was because He loved us that He took our
doom upon Himself. Every action, then, and every
suffering, which pure love prompts, is in the line of
Christ's work; but that work, though its motive is
thus brought within our reach, is not assimilated to
anything we can do for each other. The scale of
it is different—love made a sacrifice there to which
earth has no parallel; and the inmost nature of it
is different—there only God made to be sin for the
world Him who knew no sin. The love of a father
for his erring son, the love of a patriot for his
country, the love of a martyr for his faith, and all
the sufferings and sacrifices these various kinds of
love make, are included in the love of Christ; they
are included in it, but it transcends them all.
Herein is love—not that we loved God, not that the
world has had the passion of parents, of patriots, of

martyrs, but that God loved us, and sent His Son
as a propitiation for our sins. The other loves do
not explain this; it is here and here only—in the
Cross, where the sinless Son of God died for the
sins of men—that we see what love itself is, and
find a scale for the measurement of all these lesser
loves. This solitariness of Christ, this uniqueness
of His work, is to be maintained over all analogies;
and modes of speaking which outrage it, such as
that Christians should themselves be Christs, minia-
ture Christs, little Christs, are to be decidedly rejected.   It is little to say they are in bad taste;
they are as false as they are offensive, for salvation is of the Lord.

CHRIST IN HIS EXALTATION

WITH the death of Christ upon the Cross, His work in relation to sin may be said to have come to a close. He Himself cried, It is finished, before He bowed His head and gave up the ghost. He had finished transgression and made an end of sin. But the statement needs to be qualified. Christ did not cease to be when He died and was buried. He rose again from the dead on the third day ; He ascended into heaven; He sits at the right hand of God the Father all sovereign. In this exalted heavenly life He continues, in a real sense, the work in which He was engaged on earth. Here He obtained eternal redemption for men, and now He applies that redemption. He actually makes us partakers of the salvation which He wrought out for us in our nature, especially in the garden and on the Cross. The Christian religion, as the New Testament exhibits it, is the religion of men who believe that Christ lives and reigns in grace, and that they themselves are in living fellowship with a living Lord, who does all things perfectly in them and for them.

On this extremely obvious truth I wish to insist for a moment ; for there are tendencies at work in the world, and even in the Church, which go to

obscure it.   The artificiality of some traditional
conceptions of Christ's person has driven men back
upon the gospels for a more living contact with
Jesus Himself.   Back to Christ is as favourite a cry
in theology as Back to Kant in philosophy, and the
reason is the same.   People had lost themselves in
a maze of words and ideas which they had no means
of testing or verifying, and found it necessary to
start again *ab initio*.   But, in theology, what is the
result of this?   There are many cases, I believe, in
which it is unmixedly good; Christ becomes a real
person, and the Christian religion regains the
ethical content it had lost.   But there are many,
also, in which it is anything but good.   There are
men who go back to what Christ was in His life on
earth simply because they have no belief any more
in His existence, or in His sovereignty in heaven.
They go back to gaze upon the great Teacher of
Nazareth, as they call Him, not in the spirit of
religious faith, but simply in that of æsthetic
appreciation.   They introduce into the gospels the
realism of the modern novelist, and try to reproduce
Christ as He lived, moved, taught, and suffered
nineteen hundred years ago; they dwell tenderly—
not to say sentimentally—on the figure they evoke;
and there is a kind of emotion accompanying this
contemplation, which is supposed to be religious, and
to have some kind of healing or saving efficacy in
the soul.   I do not refer to this to deride it—far
from it; but surely it is obvious that the historical
imagination, carried even to its highest power, and
suffused with the tenderest feeling, is not the same
as religious faith, and cannot do its work.   The

Christian religion depends not on what Christ was, merely, but on what He is; not simply on what He did, but on what He does. It might sound, perhaps, too paradoxical to say that no apostle, no New Testament writer, ever *remembered* Christ; yet it would be true in the sense that they never thought of Him as belonging to the past. The exalted Lord was lifted above the conditions of time and space; when they thought of Him, memory was transmuted into faith; in all the virtue of the life they had known on earth He was Almighty, ever present, the Living King of Grace. On this conception the very being of the Christian religion depends; but for it, that religion could never have been born, and without it, it could not survive for a generation. When we preach from the gospels, and see what Jesus was, and said, and did, and suffered, let us remember to make the application in the present tense. Never preach about the historical Christ; preach about the living, sovereign Christ—nay, rather preach *Him*, present in the grace of His earthly life and death, and in the omnipotence of His power to save; it is not because He lived, but because He lives, that we have life also; it is not because the historical imagination is highly developed, so that we can make the evangelists' pages vivid, and be affected as by a fine scene in a drama —not for this reason, but because we confess with our mouth and believe in our heart that God raised Him from the dead, that we are saved. Faith always has its object here and now, and without faith there is no religion.

In a complete course of lectures on theology, this,

I suppose, would have been the place at which to speak of the subjective side of the work of redemption; of the appropriation by men of Christ's work in relation to sin; of our reconciliation to God, our justification, our new life in Christ, and all kindred topics. But as it is impossible to include everything in a brief course, I am obliged to dismiss this side in a passing notice. When Christ is preached, clothed in His gospel—Christ the sinbearer, omnipotent to save—He draws men to Himself, and men cast themselves on Him. Faith is not the acceptance of a legal arrangement; it is the abandonment of the soul, which has no hope but in the Saviour, to the Saviour who has taken its responsibilities on Himself, and is able to bear it through. It includes the absolute renunciation of everything else, to lay hold on Christ. It is in idea and in principle the death of the old life in order to a new life in Him; and Christ enables the believer to realise this idea, and to carry out this principle, by imparting His own victorious life to him. He who can endure to cast himself on Christ, and, not for anything he has done himself, nor for anything he means to do, hopes to do, is able to do, or even is destined to do, but simply for that awful death in which Christ bore his sins, to look for God's mercy, he is accepted in the Beloved. He takes into his soul, in that very act, God's judgment upon sin, and God's grace to the sinful. In daily renunciation of evil he dies with Christ; in daily victorious assertion of the new life he lives and reigns with Him. On the one side, these topics belong as much to Christian ethics as to theology; and in the limited time at my disposal, I have thought it better to devote this lecture to Christ's Exaltation and the continuance of His work in that state. There are three subjects included under this head: (1) the giving of the Holy Ghost; (2) the intercession of Christ, or His heavenly priest-hood; and (3) the Sovereignty or Glory of Christ. The last, indeed, as the more general, and as lending its majesty to the other two, might stand first; but there are reasons also for the order I have chosen.

1. The Holy Spirit occupies a place in the New Testament strikingly out of proportion to that which is assigned to Him in most books of theology. Especially in the theological schools of our own day, there seems to be an incapacity, or an un-willingness, to do justice to the Biblical data. Writers of the school of Ritschl, with their insistence on the historical Christ, and their disregard of the Exalted Lord, naturally evade or explain away New Testament teaching: the Holy Spirit is no more than the common spirit of the Christian community; a special gift of the Lord of Glory has no meaning for them.[1] As if to counterbalance this neglect, a special emphasis is laid on the Spirit and on the work of the Spirit, by many of what may be called without offence the pietistic types of Christianity. Most of those who make the attainment of New Testament holiness a deliberate and conscious ideal, and many of those who are engaged in evangelistic work, preoccupy themselves with the doctrine of the Spirit. Let us look at New Testament teaching in its great outlines.

To begin with, the Spirit is the gift of the exalted

[1] See Note A.

Christ. He has Himself received it from the
Father, and He bestows it upon men. 'Spirit was
not yet,' as John says, 'because Jesus was not yet
glorified.' This puts the giving of the Spirit in
direct relation to Christ's work; He was anointed
with the Holy Spirit Himself, but He did not
possess it in such wise as to be able to bestow it on
men till His work on earth was done and His glory
entered. It was the promise of the Father—part
of Christ's reward for His obedience unto death,
even the death of the Cross. The giving of the
Spirit was thus the conclusive sign of God's acceptance of Christ's work, and we should not lose this
signification of it. Pentecost was won for us at
Calvary; it needed the atonement to make regeneration possible. Christ's death was paid as a
price for the new life, and when the new life came,
it demonstrated the value of that death. The
forgiveness of sins was preached in *His* name, who
sent the Spirit. Pentecost is a historical proof—a
proof in the domain of fact and experience—that
sin has been overcome by Christ's death, and that a
divine life is again within the reach of men. It is a
seal of the great reconciliation; in the possession of
the Holy Spirit men are actually united to God in
Christ. For the Spirit is, so to speak, Christ's *alter
ego*; it is He who is with us in the Spirit; it is God
who through the Spirit makes our hearts a habitation
for Himself. I do not know whether the New
Testament ever speaks of believing in the Holy
Ghost as the Creed does, and as we all do of
believing in the Father and the Son; but it is more
significant still that it constantly speaks of *receiving*

Him.   The very word Spirit seems to us a hard
one to deal with; there is something evasive and
subtle in it; its range of meanings is almost incredible, and we hesitate to define it; but plainly,
in the apostolic age, it had a thoroughly *real*
meaning.   Christian experience was a thing so
unique, so entirely apart, so creative, that it could
not be overlooked nor confounded with anything
else.   There had been no time for conciliations, for
approximations, for compromises; that which was
Christian possessed all its originality and distinctiveness; and it was conceived as the gift and work
of the Spirit.   If we are ever to find the language of
the New Testament natural, it must be by a return
to that originality and distinctiveness of the Christian
life which created the New Testament speech.

There are three ways in which, chiefly, the Spirit
is characterised, and to glance at these will at least
suggest lines of study.   (*a*) It is in the first place
the Spirit of truth.   This conception is emphasised
and defined in the last discourse of our Lord Himself
to His disciples.   Only the spirit of man which is
in him knows the things of man, and the same holds
true of the things of God.   To initiate us into
divine truth—into truth as it is in Jesus, who says
'I am the truth'—is the work of the Spirit.   In the
case of the first disciples it was the reception of the
Spirit which turned memory into faith, which made
the past present, which set in the light of God, so
that they could be understood and appreciated, the
whole life and death of Jesus.   The Lord had much
to say to the disciples which in His lifetime they
could not bear, but they were not for that reason to

remain permanently in darkness; when the Spirit of truth came, He would glorify Jesus by taking the things that were His, and reading their meaning to the disciples.   The New Testament is itself the proof that this promise was fulfilled; the New Testament, and the new spiritual life to which it bears witness.   It is the standard interpretation of the life and death of Jesus, the testimony of men specially enlightened by the Spirit to comprehend in their solitary greatness and importance the Person and the Work of the Lord.   In a later lecture I shall have occasion to speak of this more fully; meanwhile, it is sufficient to remark that spiritual things can only be spiritually discerned, and that unless we are enlightened, taught, and guided by the Holy Spirit, it is vain for us to seek an understanding of Him who is true.   No one can understand what Christ is, or what He has done, unless he is led into all the truth by the Spirit, who is the only revealer and interpreter of it.   (b) The Spirit is further, and habitually, designated as *holy*. We might almost say that this is equivalent to divine, for in truth only God is holy, and the Holy One is an exhaustive description of God.   It is through the Holy Spirit that the divine life, or as we read in one passage, even the divine nature, is communicated to men.   The Spirit of God in the Old Testament means God at work, God engaged in exerting His power; and all through the New Testament the Holy Spirit is specifically God at work in the heart of man for the creation and maintenance of a holy life.   There is no experience possible to us as Christians which is not an experience in the Spirit. It is the Spirit which convinces us of sin, it is the Spirit by which we are led as sons of God, it is the Spirit which is our law, it is the Spirit which helps our infirmities, which makes intercession for us and in us with groanings that cannot be uttered ; love, joy, peace, long-suffering, gentleness, goodness, faith, meekness, temperance, all are fruits of the Spirit. The Christian life and character, in their beginning, middle, and end, are the Spirit's work. This truth has a practical importance that is apt to be overlooked. We are all naturally lovers of independence, and slow to learn that it is not the fundamental law of our nature. But just as no one can be good without God, nor a Christian without Christ, so, quite definitely, no one can be holy in the New Testament sense without the Holy Spirit. We ought to acknowledge that practically in our prayers and our thanksgivings. It is the experimental proof of the personality and divinity of the Spirit. It is on the ground of this absolute dependence of the divine life in our souls upon Him, that we say the Spirit is to be worshipped and glorified with the Father and the Son. (c) Thirdly, the Spirit is in the New Testament peculiarly connected with the idea of *power*. 'Ye shall receive power,' Jesus said to the disciples, 'when the Holy Spirit is come upon you.' 'I preached,' says Paul, 'in power and in the Holy Ghost and in much assurance ;' and again, 'in demonstration of the Spirit and of power ;' and again, 'in the power of the Spirit of God.' There is, indeed, a more special application of this to the gift of working miracles of healing, and perhaps of rendering other services in the early church ; but what is in view at present is not this. It is that peculiar reinforcement of the gospel preacher which gives effect to his message. Christ told the disciples plainly that they could not bear witness to Him without it; tarry at Jerusalem, He said, until ye be endued with power from on high. That anointing which makes a man a telling witness to Christ is very likely incapable of being defined. No material guarantee of it can either be given or taken. No human ordination can confer it; no place in a historical succession, however august or venerable, has anything whatever to do with it. We notice its absence, as Vinet has said, more readily than its presence. Nevertheless, it is a real thing; it is the *sine qua non* of effective witness-bearing to Jesus Christ. Self-emptying is an essential condition of it; no man can bear witness to Christ and to himself at the same time. *Esprit* is fatal to unction; no man can give at once the impression that he himself is clever and that Christ is mighty to save. The last impression excludes everything else; the power of the Holy Spirit is only felt when the witness is unconscious of self, and when others remain unconscious of him. No man is being blessed by the Holy Ghost when his hearers say, 'What an able sermon that was to-day!' But when we are content to be weak, then we are strong. The power of Christ rests upon us through the Spirit; and our simplest words that have the truth in them—what at another time would strike men as the merest moral commonplace—will sound in their souls like that searching scripture : The Holy Ghost saith, To-day, if ye shall hear His voice, harden not your heart.

(2) It is by the gift of the Holy Spirit that the exalted Lord carries on His work on earth ; He is with us through the Spirit, and in the work of the Spirit the ends are being secured for which Jesus lived and died. But the New Testament exhibits the Lord Himself as engaged in carrying on His own work above. That work culminates in what is specifically described as His Intercession. The apostles mention this sacred function with a kind of adoring awe which is quite peculiar even in the New Testament. It seems to have impressed them as one of the unimaginable wonders of redemption —something which in love went far beyond all that we could ask or think. When inspired thought touches it, it rests on it as on an unsurpassable height. Remember how it appears in St. Paul. His mind has swept in one comprehensive glance the whole process of redemption from foreordination to glory, and with that great consummation in view he exclaims : What then shall we say to these things ? If God is for us, who is against us ? Then he goes on to describe how completely God is for us. ' He that spared not His own Son, but delivered Him up for us all, how shall He not also with Him freely give us all things ? Who shall lay any thing to the charge of God's elect ? It is God that justifieth ; who is he that shall condemn ? It is Christ Jesus that died, yea rather, that was raised from the dead, who is at the right hand of God, *who also maketh intercession for us.*' Remember how, in the Epistle to the Hebrews, the same idea is in the same way the climax of the writer's thoughts : ' Wherefore He

[1] Romans viii. 29 ff.

is able to save to the uttermost them that draw
near unto God through Him, seeing *He ever liveth to
make intercession for them.'* [1]   Remember, finally, in
St. John, how this is the last line of defence in the
Christian life, the final resource in peril : 'These
things write I unto you, that ye sin not; and if any
man sin, *we have an advocate with the Father,* Jesus
Christ the righteous.' [2]

Christ's intercession is part of His priestly functions,
that part of them in which they culminate and are,
so to speak, perpetuated.   The priesthood itself is
very difficult to define, and has divided theologians
in the most bewildering fashion.   In the Reformation
Theologians it is specially connected with Christ's
death ; the fundamental thing in it is that Christ
offers Himself a sacrifice to satisfy divine justice,
and to reconcile us to God.   In the school of
Ritschl it covers everything which Christ does as
representing man before God ; it is His whole life
and experience in one particular aspect ; Christ is
priest, simply as the ideal religious subject.   In the
New Testament the name and idea are used to
interpret the work of Christ only in the Epistle to
the Hebrews, and there it is not easy to say anything
which could not be contested.   But thus much
seems plain.   The great high priestly act of Christ
is His entrance into the holiest of all, and His
appearing in the presence of God for us.   This
corresponds to the entrance of the high priest of
Israel, once a year, on the day of atonement, into
the holy of holies, the dwelling-place of God.   This
entrance, in which, of course, the high priest

---

[1] Heb. vii. 25.   [2] I John ii. I.

represented the people, embodied as it were the fellowship actually existing, on the basis of the covenant, between the people and God. The people, in the person of the priest, were admitted to the presence of their God. Similarly Christ's entrance into the sanctuary above embodies the new fellowship which, on the basis of the new covenant, exists between God and those who are represented by Christ. But if this entering into God's presence as our representative, this appearing before Him on our behalf, is the characteristically priestly act, according to New Testament teaching, are we entitled to say that Christ is a priest apart from this? Are we entitled, in particular, to say that He was a priest in His death? that His death was sacrificial, and that it was necessary to put away sin as an objective hindrance to fellowship between God and man?

The Socinians, as is well known, answered these questions in the negative. Christ, they said, is only called a priest in the Epistle to the Hebrews, and there His priesthood is only heavenly. It is not exercised on earth at all, and therefore it is not exercised in His death. Hence His death is not sacrificial, and has not the expiatory power which orthodoxy attributes to it. There is a great deal of hastiness and of misapprehension here. Quite apart from any question as to priesthood, scientific exegesis has got beyond the Socinian doubts about the interpretation of Christ's death. Whether its teaching be accepted or rejected, it is universally admitted, by all who are competent to judge, that the New Testament does teach that Christ's death

has an expiatory virtue, and that it does put away
sin as a real obstacle to fellowship between God and
man. This being the fact, it does not much matter,
for practical purposes, whether His death be brought
under the head of His priestly work or not. But if
the question is raised at all, it should be rightly
answered, and the Socinian answer does not do
justice to the facts. The author of the Epistle to
the Hebrews writes with his mind full of the Old
Testament ritual. He does not, with the day of
atonement in his mind, distinguish between the
slaying of the goat and the entrance of the priest,
bearing its blood, into the holy of holies, as two
independent or separable acts ; the whole transaction
was one ; it was only consummated when the blood
was carried into God's presence, and the priest stood
there embodying the fellowship between God and
Israel. So in the New Testament. When he
figures Christ appearing in the presence of God on
our behalf, he figures Him, of course as a priest,
but it is not in separation from what has before
taken place on earth. Christ appears in God's
presence with the virtue of His death in Him ;
He appears there offering to God, as our representative, a life which has passed through that
tremendous experience, in order to put away sin.
If Christ is a priest in one part of these transactions,
He is a priest in them all ; for they are all one,
and derive their meaning and efficacy from each
other.

But to return to the intercession, as the sublime
act in which His priesthood finds full expression.
Christ stands in God's presence representing us ;

exhibiting, as it were, in His own person, what He guarantees *we* shall be; bespeaking for us, as His brethren, the mercy and the fellowship of God. He intercedes for us, as our surety; He is the warrant to God that, all unworthy as we are, we may become worthy of union and communion with Him, if only we draw near through such a mediator. Christ prays for us. The same objections have been raised to this as to every part of the Christian doctrine of redemption. What is there, it is said, in God to be overcome, that any intercession should be needed? Is not God the author of salvation? Is it not His work from beginning to end? Is He not already waiting to be gracious? Such objections, we ought to feel, carry us too far. They are arguments against *all* intercession and indeed against all prayer; and if we see nothing unnatural in the fact that Christ prayed for Peter on earth, we need not make any difficulty about His praying for us in heaven. The relation is the same; the only difference is that Christ is now exalted, and prays, not with strong crying and tears, but in the sovereignty and prevailing power of one who has achieved eternal redemption for His people.

The Epistle to the Hebrews bids us think of Christ's qualifications for priesthood, and therefore for intercession, as resting mainly on His sympathy and on His sacrifice. It is the great lesson-book on Christ's humanity, on the community of nature, of experience, and of interests, between Him and us. His power to sympathise, and to be merciful and faithful as a high priest, was bought with a great price. He became one with us in nature; He

partook of our flesh and blood, and was compassed
like us with infirmity ; He was not ashamed to call
us brothers. He shared not only our nature, but
our experience. He passed through all the stages
of man's life as we do. He was tempted in all
points, like as we are, yet without sin ; He can have
compassion, therefore, on the ignorant and the
erring. Though He was God's Son, He learned
obedience by the things which He suffered ; in the
hour of deadly peril He prayed to God with strong
crying and tears, and was heard because of His godly
fear. It became God, for whom are all things, and
through whom are all things, in bringing many sons
unto glory, to make the author of their salvation
perfect through suffering. This training or discipline
of Christ qualifies Him to intercede for us. He
knows what human life is by actual experience of
it ; He has the capacity for sympathy and appreciation
which nothing but experience gives. The curricu-
lum of suffering educated Him in sympathy, and
it is because He identifies Himself with us to the
uttermost, and makes common cause with us in all
our interests, that He is a true representative of man
with God. But especially ought we to consider
that His intercession rests upon His sacrificial death.
As the high priest entered into the ancient sanctuary
with the blood in his hand, and could not enter at
all without it, so Christ enters for us into the very
presence of God in virtue of the death which He
died upon the Cross. Apart from that, man has no
standing-ground in God's sight ; Christ has no
standing-ground as the representative of man. It
is in this sense that Christ's intercession is said to

be the continuation of His atonement, the pleading of the merits of His blood. The only Intercessor who can plead our cause effectively is the One who has died for us, and by His death put away our sins. He does not intercede apart from that; He is clothed in His crimson robe when He makes Himself our advocate with the Father. These two things, then, ought to go together—His sympathy and His sacrifice—as the basis of His intercession. He is for ever human, and the virtue of His death for ever remains in His humanity; that is how He ever liveth to make intercession for us. The priests of the order of Aaron were a succession, and each, as he died, transmitted the splendid official robes to his son; but the robe in which Christ intercedes—the vesture of humanity, made perfect by sufferings, dipped in blood—is never laid aside; He is a priest for ever. We may sometimes find it difficult to interpret the work of intercession in theological formulæ; but surely every man can feel the graciousness of it. Who, if he had the choice to make, would choose to go into God's presence, unguided, on his own responsibility, rather than with his hand in the hand of One who knew his heart, and was qualified by nature, by experience, and by His sacrificial death, to represent his interest with God? Christ's intercession means practically that one who knows our case, who has access to God, and who is willing and worthy to be our surety, gives us His hand to lead us into the Father's presence. When we present our prayers in His name, He presents them again in our name. He *appears* for us before God, compassionate, sin-

destroying, prevailing.[1]   Christ the Intercessor is
Christ the Redeemer actually carrying out in glory
that work of love of which we have seen the
foundations laid on earth.   It is this figure of
Christ in which, more than in any other, He seems
to have thrilled and subdued the souls of the early
Christians, and bound them irrevocably to Himself.

(3) There is a sense in which the gift of the
Holy Ghost, especially as the Spirit of truth, and as
the Spirit of power, may be said to be the exercise
of Christ's prophetic function in His state of exaltation.   Similarly His intercession is the continuance
in glory of His work as a priest.   But quite apart
from this or that work in which He is engaged, the
New Testament fixes our attention on the mode of
His existence as itself determining the character and
quality of the Christian life.   I alluded to this at
the opening of this lecture, and recur to it at the
close.   The Christ in whom the apostles believed,
the Christ who created Christianity and sustained
it, the Christ who was the object of that faith which
makes the New Testament to this day the most
living book in the world, was the Risen Christ, the
Lord of Glory.   It was not Jesus the carpenter of
Nazareth, it was not even Jesus the prophet of
Galilee ; nay, it was not even Christ crucified, as a
person belonging to history and to the past ; it was
the crucified Christ *in the heavenly places*, the
Lamb as it had been slain *standing in the midst of
the throne*, the Universal Redeemer as *Universal
Lord*.   It was One whose parting word to His own

[1] Hebrews ix. 24.

was, All power is given unto me in heaven and on earth . . . Lo! I am with you alway, even to the end of the world.

A true conception of the Christian life depends very much on the appreciation of this truth. It has been largely lost, *e.g.*, in the Romish Church, with its excessive employment of the crucifix. The Cross is the sign of Christian devotion, the inspiration of Christian service; but the crucifix is no adequate symbol of Christian faith. Christ was crucified through weakness; but He lives by the power of God, and we must not forget His life. Sometimes people do. They look at Christ on the Cross as if that exhausted the truth about Him, or even the truth about His relation to sin. They forget that He is not on the Cross, but on the throne; that He has ascended far above all heavens, separate from sinners, inaccessible to sin. They forget that the keynote of the Christian life as it is related to the Ascended Christ is one of victory and triumph.

There is an *imitatio Christi* which loses sight of this, and offers to the world, under the name of Christianity, a life which has not the remotest resemblance, especially in temperament, to that of the New Testament. The highest note it strikes is that of resignation; it could never have invented, and never dare appropriate, such an outburst as that of St. Paul: 'in all these things we are more than conquerors.'[1] The beauty of Christ's earthly life it is not for us to praise; we worship as we look upon it; we try with all humility to take His yoke upon

[1] Romans viii. 37.

us, and learn of Him. The passion of His death constrains us; it takes hold of our hearts, and puts a pressure on us under which self-will dies, and we are crucified with Christ to the world and the flesh, and conformed unto His death. But neither His death nor His life exhaust the knowledge of Christ which we possess, nor the likeness to which we are to be assimilated. It is of the exalted Saviour that the apostle says, 'We all, beholding as in a mirror the glory of the Lord, are changed into the same image from glory to glory, even as by the Lord the Spirit.'[1] It may seem at first sight meaningless to say that Christ in His exaltation is to be included in the *imitatio Christi*; but is it so absurd when we think of it? The exalted Christ is through His Spirit the author and giver of our life as Christians, and the life which He communicates is His own. It is essentially a victorious, triumphant, joyous life. It is such as we see it in the apostolic writings, and as such we ought to see it everywhere. Christianity has been named, sometimes patronisingly, sometimes sentimentally, sometimes honestly enough, the Religion of Sorrow; but there never was a more complete misnomer. It is not the religion of sorrow, but the religion which, because it is inspired by One who lives and *was* dead, gives the victory over every sorrow, even the crowning sorrows of death and sin. There is not in the New Testament from beginning to end, in the record of the original and genuine Christian life, a single word of despondency or gloom. It is the most buoyant, exhilarating, and joyful book in the world. The men who write it

[1] 2 Cor. iii. 18.

have indeed all that is hard and painful in the world to encounter; but they are of good courage, because Christ has overcome the world, and when the hour of conflict comes, they descend crowned into the arena. All this is due to their faith in Christ's exaltation, and in His constant presence with them in the omnipotence of His grace. Their world had prospects and horizons which the world of many so-called Christians wants, and no one could do a better service to the Church than to work for their recovery by working for faith in the reign of Christ in grace.

LECTURE VIII

THE CHURCH AND THE KINGDOM OF GOD

In the previous lectures of this course I have been dealing with what are in the strictest sense theological subjects. God, Christ, the Holy Spirit, the nature of sin, and the nature of Christ's work as related to it; these are all felt to be properly theological topics. But many, I have no doubt, are less interested when we come to the Church. Many will ask whether the Church is a necessary conception in the Christian view of the world at all, and whether there is, or ought to be, or even can be, anything entitled to the name of a theological doctrine of the Church. I can understand that feeling, and sympathise with it to a certain extent; but there are obvious considerations which put a limit to the indulgence of it. For one thing, the Church undoubtedly occupies a large place in the apostolic writings. To the original and inspired teachers of Christianity it was a grand and inspiring conception; its origin, its functions, its nature, its destiny, commanded both their imagination and their hearts. Further, Christianity has always assumed social forms; it has taken shape in the world at the bidding of the spirit within it, or under

173

the constraint of external forces; and these forms demand to be understood by the theologian. And finally, the Church has a place in all the creeds in which the self-consciousness of the Christian community has found expression. Not only in the distinctively Romish and Protestant confessions— which are elaborate in definition, because the conception of the Church was one of the chief points on which Papal and Reformation Christianity diverged—but in the symbols of early Christianity, the Apostolic and Nicene creeds, the Church finds a place. Christians professed to believe that there is a holy Catholic Church, or, in fuller form, one, holy, catholic, apostolic Church. We do not indeed believe *in* it, as we believe in God or in Christ; we do not commit ourselves to it for salvation as we do to the Redeemer Himself; but from the very beginning Christian men acknowledged their belief in the existence of a society called by this name, and more or less fully described by the attributes just quoted. Even at the Reformation, the representative men on the Protestant side were very jealous of their own legitimacy. They laid great emphasis on the idea of the Church, and on what they called the catholicity of their position; in other words, on the lawfulness of their own place in the historical Christian succession, and on their right to serve themselves heirs to all the inheritance of the saints. Now individualism and sectarianism destroy the historical sense, and perhaps we who have been born and bred in freedom and self-reliance, even in the Christian life, have more need than others to appreciate the idea of the Church.

Nay, even the actual Church, with all its faults, may be entitled to more credit and consideration than it receives at our hands. This is how so free a spirit as John Calvin spoke of it: 'Let us learn by the mere name of mother how profitable, indeed how necessary, is the knowledge of her; since there is no other entrance into life unless she herself conceive us in her womb, unless she bear us, unless she foster us at her breast, unless she guard us under her care and government, until we put off this mortal flesh, and become like the angels.' Here is one who represents the very Protestantism of the Protestant religion speaking with almost papal fervour: it recalls the famous saying of Cyprian, He who has not the Church as his mother has not God as his Father. A conception that impressed so strongly men otherwise so remote from each other must deserve our earnest study.

Our Lord, we know, spoke little of the Church, but habitually of the Kingdom of God. The Kingdom is indeed so central and so comprehensive in His teaching that it is difficult to speak of it without introducing the whole contents of the gospel. Jesus spoke of it as present, and also as future; as in process of development, and as yet to be revealed in power; as among men, and yet as transcendent. The question that is principally before us in our present situation is whether Jesus conceived the Kingdom of God as a separate society in the world. I think there is no difficulty in answering that He did. He called men who were living in the world, in all the various lines of life, into the Kingdom. He associated them with Himself and with one another in the consciousness of being the citizens and subjects of the Kingdom. Faith in the fatherly love of God, binding them to love one another, and to live in humility, patience, and prayer, was what united them among themselves. There is in the Kingdom a real union of persons who are conscious that they have what binds them to each other, and separates them from the world; but there is nothing formal or institutional about it. The Kingdom of God is not a kingdom of this world; it is not a society which is in any sense the rival or the competitor of any other social organisation which Providence has evolved in the history of man; it does not supplant the family, the nation, the state, the federation of states, the economic or industrial organisation; it recognises the divine right which all these social forms possess, though it need not regard any of them as perfect; but it is too great—too profound in its principle—to come into collision with them on their own ground. It can render to Cæsar the things that are Cæsar's, without being hindered, for that, from rendering to God the things that are God's. It is not destined, as a visible society, to absorb every other, or to assert its superiority over, and its right to interfere in, every other; but it is destined, by the free action of its members, to give a new character to all. It is destined to carry into all that law of love which Christ has revealed, and, as it does so, to transform, or rather to transfigure them. The Kingdom of God becomes a conquering and transfiguring power —the leaven exerts its virtue, the salt its savour— in proportion as the citizens of the Kingdom are intensely conscious of their new relation to God, and of the new obligations it imposes. Of course the Christian community will have a mind of its own about what these obligations are in any particular case. The Christian community will foster in its members the sense of obligation to God and to the brethren. The common conscience and enlightenment will invigorate and enlighten the conscience of the individual. But it is not by corporate, legislative, compulsory action of the Christian community; it is by free, spontaneous, spiritual action of Christian individuals, each in his own sphere, each in the calling in which his life is to be given to God, that God's Kingdom comes.

The generality of these propositions will be illustrated before I close, but here I wish to call attention to the fact that Jesus does, in the gospels, speak twice, by name, about the Church. Both the passages, as you are aware, are in Matthew, and both have been questioned on critical grounds, that are not very easily appreciated. For my own part, I see no difficulty in treating both as genuine. The first is that in which the ministry of Jesus is at the turning-point, and He sets His face like a flint towards the Cross. The Jewish nation as a whole has rejected Him; the historical people of God are not to be His people; it is evident that He must form a society of His own, a New Testament Church. It is at this point in His fortunes that He first uses the word—On this rock, the believing Peter, will I build my Church.[1] The occasion suggested the idea quite distinctly, and

[1] Matt. xvi. 18 ff.

as Beyschlag has acutely remarked, the magnificent
idealism with which the Church is here spoken of,
the poetic figures, the high attributes and functions
assigned to the representative of her faith, authen-
ticate the word as genuinely Christ's.[1] Who but
Christ was capable of saying, Thou art Peter, and
on this rock will I build my Church, and the gates
of Hell shall not prevail against it? Who but
Christ was capable of saying, I will give unto thee
the keys of the kingdom of heaven, and whatsoever thou shalt bind on earth shall be bound in
heaven, and whatsoever thou shalt loose on earth
shall be loosed in heaven? That is obviously,
almost palpably, Christ's anticipation, Christ's
ideal of the Church; it is the grand style of the
Master; no ordinary man who saw the form in
which the Church actually became historical, could
have spoken of it in this lofty strain. The paltry
Papal interpretation, in which the whole soul
and originality of the words are lost, is beneath
contempt. It is worth remarking that in this
passage the Church and the kingdom of heaven
are apparently alternative expressions for the same
thing. 'On this rock will I build my Church. . . .
I will give unto thee the keys of the kingdom:' it
is impossible to ignore the connection. The other
passage in which Jesus speaks of the Church is in
the 18th chapter of Matthew, and refers to the
Christian treatment of the erring. When a brother
has sinned, He says—and a brother means one
who, like you, is a child of God, and a citizen of
the Kingdom—no pains are to be spared for his

[1] See Note A.

restoration.   You are first to go and tell him his
fault in private; if he disregards that, you are to
take one or two witnesses; if he makes light of
them, you are to tell the whole Church; if he disregards the Church, he is to be treated as a heathen
man and a publican, *i.e.* as a rank outsider, whose
privileges as a citizen of the Kingdom are not to
be recognised.   In this passage there is, no doubt,
a descent from the idealism of the one in the 16th
chapter, to something like the formality of legislation; but how worthy, on the other hand, is the
spirit which breathes through it all; how like
Christ it is, how Godlike, to say that the initiative in
the work of reconciliation is to be taken by him
who has been wronged; that a bridge is to be built
for the return of the offender; that no pains are to
be spared for his restoration; and that not till the
whole community has brought the pressure of its
moral judgment to bear on him in vain, is he to be
treated as one without.   All this, it seems to me,
is evidence for the genuineness of the words.   And
the closeness of the connection between Church and
Kingdom, in this passage as in the other, is shown
by the fact that, when Peter asks Jesus a question,
arising out of this discourse, about the limits of forgiveness, he is answered by a parable concerning
the kingdom of heaven.   The Kingdom as organised
and as acting collectively for the moral discipline
of its members seems to be called the Church.

But this marks the transition to a larger question.
When we pass out of the gospels into the later
books of the New Testament, we pass also into a
new custom of speech, if not of thought, as to the

Christian community. The Kingdom of God does not, indeed, disappear, but it is no longer so obtrusive. It has still the same two sides that it has in the gospels; it is with us, and it is to come; it is spiritual, and it is transcendent. It may be regarded from either point of view—the Kingdom of God is righteousness, and peace, and joy in the Holy Ghost; or, flesh and blood cannot inherit the Kingdom of God.[1] But it is perhaps doing no injustice to the apostolic writers to say that the Kingdom tends to be identified more and more with the future and the transcendent; while side by side with it the conception of the Church grows continually in meaning and importance.

This phenomenon has given rise to an immense quantity of discussion, instructive enough at times, but not very satisfying, as to the relation of Church and Kingdom. Those theologians who have made much of the return to Christ, and are disposed to magnify the idea of the Kingdom as the compendium of all He taught, have sometimes done less than justice to the idea of the Church. Those, on the other hand, who have tried fairly to construe the two ideas as the New Testament exhibits them, but have felt bound, after doing so, to define them as in some organic relation to each other, have, I am disposed to think, been misled by this assumed necessity. That something, at all events, is wrong, in the various attempts to explain Church and Kingdom in relation to each other, is proved by the fact that the explanations diverge in the most extraordinary way, and that none of them can stand the

[1] Romans xiv. 17; 1 Cor. xv. 50.

test of comparison with New Testament teaching. Take, for instance, the most famous of all—that which is given by the theologian who claims to have restored the Kingdom to its proper place in the scheme of Christian thought—I mean Ritschl. He recognises that the persons composing the Church and the Kingdom are the same; but on the background of this sameness He defines the difference. 'The community of believers, as subject of the worship of God and of the juristic institutions and organs which minister to that worship, is Church: as subject of the reciprocal action of its members, springing from the motive of love, it is Kingdom of God.'[1] This must be an attractive distinction, for it has attracted many persons. It is just, I think, to the Kingdom; the Kingdom is not unfairly described as the community of those whose mutual action is ruled by the law of love. But is it fair to the Church? It may be fair enough to the church of which Ritschl was a member, it may be fair enough to any given society, or to the sum of existing Christian societies, to call them the Church, in the sense that they are subject of the worship of God, and of the juristic institutions and organs which minister to that worship; but is it fair to the idea of the Church, as that idea is outlined, say in the Epistles to the Colossians and Ephesians? I am sure it is not. We find nothing there of juristic institutions and organs, and we find precisely what Ritschl excludes from the Church, and assigns to the Kingdom, viz., the conception of the community of believers as subject of the

[1] See Note B.

reciprocal action of its members, springing from the motive of love. It is the Church which is Christ's body. It is the members of the Church who, living truly in love, grow up in all things into Him who is the head; and from Him the whole body—*i.e.* the Church—fitly framed and knit together through that which every joint supplieth, according to the working in due measure of each several part, maketh the increase of the body unto the building up of itself in love. Here, I say, the whole description exactly suits what Ritschl calls kingdom, and does not suit at all what he calls church; yet it is church, and not kingdom, that the apostle is describing. Ritschl's distinction has often been seized and used by men who had an interest in maintaining that the Kingdom of God was a greater thing than any of the institutions recognisable on earth as churches; but those who so use it overlook the fact that the Church of God, as the New Testament describes it, is also a greater thing than any of our existent churches. Hence it is not on this basis that Church and Kingdom can be distinguished; and when they are, the distinction does not belong to Christian, or at least to New Testament, theology, but only to the prepossessions of the person who makes it.

I imagine it is a distinction essentially similar which would characterise the Church as religious, the Kingdom as ethical; and which, on the ground of this, would subordinate the Church to the Kingdom as means to end. This is done by a theologian of your own, the late Professor Stearns, who mentions the Church and the Family side by side as 'teleo-

logical organs' of the Kingdom.[1] But this distinction cannot, any more in this than in the other
form, stand comparison with the New Testament
use of the words. It is at bottom quite arbitrary;
even if it has conveniences in view of a given
situation as presently existing, it is sure, sooner or
later, to mislead. The Church is *not*, in the New
Testament, a religious community which has to be
supplemented by the idea of the Kingdom as an
ethical community. In degenerate times the
Church may lose the true consciousness of itself
which the New Testament exhibits; it may lay
stress on dogma, or on ritual, or on organisation,
as its basis; it may make common worship, and the
juristic institutions and organs which minister to it,
its be-all and end-all; it may be invaded by a
spurious individualism, or corrupted by the decay
of moral interest; any or all of these things may
happen. But when they do, we are not to seek
the remedy by acknowledging that the idea of the
Church is inadequate to the moral demand, and
must be supplemented by that of the Kingdom; it
will be quite sufficient to revert to the New Testament idea of the Church itself. It is ethical through
and through. The acceptance of the love of God
in Christ, the offering of soul and body a living
sacrifice to God, are free ethical actions. The very
first time an apostle mentions the Church, he calls
it 'the Church . . . in God the Father and in the
Lord Jesus Christ.'[2] A church in God the Father
and in the Lord Jesus Christ is a community not
only organised for worship, but inspired by re-

[1] See Note C.   [2] I Thessalonians i. I.

ciprocal action springing from the law of love. It is not only religious, but ethical; though, since Jesus lived, that distinction has lost its validity. If the Church has ceased to be ethical, if love is not an inspiration in it, if it is not full of moral idealism and originality, it is not that the conception of the Kingdom has been overlooked; the conception of the Church itself, as apostles saw it, has been lost.

What, then, you may ask, *is* the distinction between the two? I am not confident that in principle there is any. The explanation of their use in the New Testament is to be sought, I imagine, rather in historical than in dogmatic considerations. When Jesus appeared among the Jews, preaching the glad tidings of the Kingdom, He proclaimed the grace of God the Father in a form which made it accessible to Jewish minds. They had already the idea that God was their King, and that they themselves were, or were to be, citizens in the divine kingdom. True, this idea was very far from corresponding to the idea which Christ brought; it was narrow, carnal, confused; the child of bigotry and pride as much as of divine inspiration; and a great part of our Lord's teaching consisted in purifying it from base elements and raising it to the height of the truth. Nevertheless, the idea was there; it was a beginning of interest on which He could count; a point of attachment in their minds to which He could fasten what He wished to say. But when the gospel passed out of the Jewish circle altogether, what was the value of this form for the expression of it? In all probability it was very slight. In the synagogues it would still

be possible to speak of the Kingdom of God, and
hope to be understood; but to the mass of Gentile
people in Asia, in Macedonia, in Greece, in Italy,
it would convey nothing at all. Hence the apostles
practically dropped it, and represented the social
side of Christianity in the *ecclesia* or church. This
name is not to be defined *a priori*. It is not to be
explained by the use of ἐκκλησία in the LXX. to
render the Hebrew קָהָל, nor by the use of the same
word to describe the citizens of a Greek city assembled for the transaction of public business; it
means whatever the apostles use it to mean, and it
will be very hard, if justice is done to their use of
it, to put it in any subordinate place. In particular,
nothing could be more false than to say, as is sometimes said, that the introduction of this word marks
the failure of the apostles to apprehend the height
and range of Christ's ideas. They did not lapse
from His idea of the Kingdom, and discard it for
an inferior one, because they could not carry all its
contents; they practically exchanged it for another
idea, when they found that through another the
grace of God could find easier access into the minds
of men. The displacement of Kingdom by Church
as we pass from the gospels to the epistles, does
not signify that the apostles had failed to understand Christ; it signifies that in the freedom of the
spirit, and in the consciousness of having *the mind*
of Christ, words, even Christ's words, were of no
consequence to them, and were used or disused as
occasion served. The apostles do not *quote* Christ;
they live in Him, and reproduce His mind in living
ways. A man may define Church and Kingdom in

their relations to each other in a way that pleases himself, because it is his own work; but such definitions never please others, and I believe the reason is to be found in what I have just said. They are arbitrary answers to an unreal question.

In a full study of the Church, as a topic in theology, the New Testament is of course our guide. Principal Fairbairn, in his well-known work—*Christ in Modern Theology*—has given an analysis of apostolic doctrine on this subject, which seems to me almost the best thing in his book. He shows the idea of the Church in all its aspects, and while persisting, with his irrepressible philosophical determination, in defining the mutual relations of Kingdom and Church, does ample justice to the grandeur of the church idea in St. Paul. 'The Kingdom,' he says, ' is the immanent Church; the Church is the explicated Kingdom, and nothing alien to either can be in the other. The Kingdom is the Church expressed in the terms and mind and person of its founder; the Church is the Kingdom done into living souls and the society they constitute.' For reasons already stated, I think these decisions are superfluous, and not free from an element that may mislead; but they show that the writer has appreciated New Testament teaching on the Church, and that is the main thing.[1]

The Church, then, is at first a local community. It is the totality of those who have accepted the salvation which is in Christ, and who are living in mutual love as children of God. It is filled with the Holy Spirit, which is the Spirit of Jesus; and

[1] See Note D.

it is this which is the bond of union among its members. In every community there must be some kind of organisation, but certainly in the original Christian community none seems to have been prescribed. The twelve men who had been with Jesus had a natural and proper ascendency in it; but when necessity arose to organise the work of charity, the whole community chose persons who were set apart to this task. At a later stage apostles and apostolic men—Paul, Barnabas, Peter, and James —state cases, and plead causes, before the assembled community, which is nothing if not autonomous. When the gospel spreads into foreign countries, we see the same kind of phenomenon repeated. There are other local churches which have to organise themselves for Christian worship *and for Christian life.* Their internal independence is plain from every page of the epistles : even Paul cannot lord it over their faith—*i.e.* cannot impose his authority on them as Christian men, as a master imposes his will on his slaves. He must convince, persuade, prevail, by spiritual means, even when he is in the right; he was the great teacher of liberty, and could not defy the principles he had himself inculcated. But these local churches, reciprocally independent as they were, were nevertheless one ; they were *a* church ; they were *the* church of the living God. The bond that united them to each other as churches was the same as the bond which united the members in any one of them among themselves ; it was their common reception of the love of God in Christ Jesus ; their common accept-ance of the obligations which receiving that love imposed. They freely recognised each other's Christianity — each other's membership in the Church—in various effective ways. They sent commissioners, duly elected, to each other; they gave letters of commendation to their own members, which found welcome for them in Christian societies elsewhere; they had a lively interest in each other, and in times of distress contributed liberally for the relief of those most hardly pressed. They formed a living and sympathetic unity, a new humanity within the bosom of the old; but 'the new humanity,' as Dr. Fairbairn happily puts it, 'created and penetrated by Christ, was as little dependent for its being as the old humanity on specifiç forms of polity.' It was one body, only because there was one spirit in it.

This is the actual Catholic Church as the New Testament exhibits it to us—the totality of those who in every place call upon the name of Jesus Christ our Lord, both their Lord and ours. I do not think the New Testament contemplates the existence of unattached Christians—persons who have accepted the Christian salvation, and embraced the Christian ideal and vocation—but who are not members of a church. The Christian end can never be attained, either for ourselves or for others, except by the mutual action and reaction, the reciprocal giving and receiving, of all who are in fellowship with Christ. What the brethren have is indispensable to us; what we have is indispensable to them. In this sense the dogma is true—*extra ecclesiam, nulla salus*. It is the recognition of this truth on which the vital unity of the Church depends. The Church is united, it is *one* Church, because it is the body of Christ, and because every member is necessary to all the rest. It is united, because to *every* member grace has been given according to the measure of the gift of Christ; because to *every* one the manifestation of the Spirit is given, not for his private satisfaction, but to profit withal; in other words, for the furtherance of the common good. It is not united by offices, nor even by officials; it is not united by a documentary constitution or creed; it is not united by a uniform and all-embracing government—not one of these things is mentioned by the apostles. Christ's gifts to it for the maintenance and furtherance of its unity are not offices nor officials, but spiritually endowed men; it is not in the fellowship of a priestly or episcopal order— much less in the fellowship of a Pope—that it is one; it is one in the fellowship of the Holy Ghost.

Men are gradually coming to see, what your branch of the Church saw earlier than most, that 'particular churches, with their specific polities, do not break the unity of the Catholic Church visible, while their faith and love constitute the unity of the invisible.'[1] The Church is truly one, though its organisation is diverse. A world-wide sympathy, in virtue of a common life, is great and inspiring; it tends to enlargement of mind and heart; it tends to generate the most various and independent types of goodness. A world-wide uniformity of ecclesiastical organisation, on the other hand, may be great and inspiring to some; to multitudes, and especially to free men, bred in democracies, it is oppressive as a

[1] *Christ in Modern Theology*, p. 547.

nightmare ; it suffocates all originality and enterprise in the Christian life.   It materialises the very conceptions that should make materialism impossible, and puts fetters on the soul in what ought to be the citadel of freedom.   A Congregationalist or a Presbyterian believes as devoutly as an Episcopalian or even a Romanist in the unity of the visible Catholic Church ; but he knows better than to seek the signs of it in any external badge, in any formal order of priesthood or of ritual.   He knows that it is unity of life, not of organisation or of forms ; he knows that the life which manifests itself everywhere under the inspiration of Christ is too rich and potent to be limited to any particular order, to the exclusion of all others ; he knows that the more energetic it is, the more will the unity exhibit itself in diverse forms, which do not dissolve it, but only declare its power.

But the conception of local churches, and of a universal church, one in its acceptance of the Christian salvation and in its devotion to the Christian ideal, does not exhaust New Testament teaching.   Over this universal church hangs the figure of the ideal church, 'the symbol,' as Dr. Fairbairn has admirably put it, 'of the completed work of Christ.'[1]   *This* church is not yet, but it is the church which is to be ; it is the bride of Christ, which He loved, and for which He gave Himself up, that He might sanctify it, having cleansed it with the washing of water by the word, that He might present the church to Himself a glorious church, not having spot or wrinkle or any such thing ; but

[1] *Christ in Modern Theology*, p. 526.

that it should be holy and without blemish. In the poetic imagination of the apostle this church is almost personal in its unity. Its members come all together to a full-grown man, to the measure of the stature of the fulness of Christ. It is Christ's body, the fulness of Him that filleth all in all. It is the contents of the divine decree of redemption ; it is in it, that not only to sinful men, but to the principalities and powers in the heavenly places, as age succeeds age, there is revealed the manifold wisdom of God. It is the end of all God's works ; creation and redemption together are consummated in it ; when it is presented to Christ, as the bridegroom to the bride, the goal of history has been reached ; the apostle sees no more, but ascribes glory to God, in the Church, in Christ Jesus, through all ages, world without end.

When we have grasped these New Testament ideas of the local church, the universal church, and the ideal church, and when we have seen in what their unity consists, we are in a position to criticise with some confidence the actual phenomena of church history, the definitions of dogmatic theologians, and even the demands which are being made on the Church in our own time. The first two of these things, the phenomena of church history, and the dogmatic definitions, are more or less dependent on each other ; and I wish to say a few words about them to begin with.

As we have already seen, the primitive church was a community, the bond of union in which was spiritual. It was the *coetus fidelium*, the assembly of the saints ; it had the consciousness of possessing

salvation in Jesus Christ; its various parts were
held together by the *conscientia religionis*, the *unitas
disciplinae*, the *foedus spei*. It would of course be a
mistake to say that the congregations which composed it, or even the universal church itself as a
whole, was without beliefs or without organisation;
but it was no legally formulated belief, it was no
divinely prescribed organisation, which legitimated
the congregations, or guaranteed the Christianity of
the Church.   One of the most interesting and
difficult problems for the church historian is to
trace the influences under which, and the process
by which, the primitive conception was displaced,
and legal conceptions put in its place.   There is
no doubt that the question of creed became important at an earlier date than that of constitution.
The Church had to naturalise itself in the world,
and there was danger of its being swamped in the
process.   As soon as it became a phenomenon,
visible to all, people were attracted into it from
every variety of motive.   They did not leave their
minds behind them when they entered, and in the
attempts which they inevitably made to work up
into one connected whole their pre-Christian and
their new ideas, they were sometimes in danger of
doing less than justice to the latter.   Many of what
are known as the gnostic systems are no less than
deliberate attempts on the part of pagan philosophies,
usually with a moral as well as a speculative interest,
to capture the Christian Church for their own ends,
and turn it into a school.   In self-defence, as it were,
the Church was compelled to become somewhat of a
school on its own account.   It had to assert its facts;

it had to define its ideas; it had to interpret in its own way—in a way which satisfied the Christian consciousness, aware of its connection with Christ—those facts which men were misinterpreting. It had not only to do this, but it had to secure authority for it when it was done, and the process by which all this was accomplished is the process in which the primitive was transformed, it is impossible to say transfigured, into the historical Catholic Church.

The earliest creed, if one may call it so, was involved in the baptismal formula: the name of the Father, the Son, and the Holy Spirit, comprehends all that is distinctive in Christianity. But in a philosophising environment, where persons and facts became ideas, and ideas abstractions, this was not enough; and the baptismal confession was expanded into a rule of faith, for which apostolic authority was claimed. The so-called apostles' creed is an example of what is meant by this rule of faith. It was the basis of the teaching given to catechumens, and, apart from the acceptance of it, no true Christianity was possible, and no membership in the true Church, for either individuals or communities. It is significant that the Church at Rome is the one in which the earliest traces are found of a definite rule of faith to which apostolic authority was assigned. It may have been the practical governmental instinct of the leaders in that Church—though the body of its members was Greek; or it may have been that the need of resisting philosophies which would evaporate the Christian facts, or fanaticisms which would supersede them, was more urgent there than elsewhere; but certain it is that the first embodi-

ment of a rule of faith which can be traced is of
Roman origin. And it is equally significant that in
Rome we find the first approach to a definite conception of a New Testament canon—that is, a
collection of Christian writings on the same level of
authority with the Old Testament. The formation
of the New Testament canon is indeed obscure and
perplexed in the extreme; but thus much seems
certain — that it was formed under the same
influences which led to defining the rule of faith,
and that it was meant in the main to serve the
same purposes. Many things and persons were
claiming to be Christian, or were claiming Christianity for their own, with which the collective
consciousness of the historical Christian community
could hold no terms, and some test of legitimacy
was needed. It was found at first in this intellectual
way. Certain definite statements emerged, which,
as constituting the rule of faith, were regarded as of
apostolic authority; certain books were set apart, out
of a number more or less indefinite, though within
narrow limits, of those that were read in the churches,
and these were regarded as of the same authority;
nothing was Christian, nothing belonged to the
Church, that was inconsistent with either; but everything belonged to the Church which accepted both.

This may seem on the whole an inevitable, and a
quite legitimate process, yet it undeniably affects
the character of the Church. It is no longer the
fellowship of the saints, the community of those
who possess salvation in Jesus Christ; it is the community which confesses certain historical facts, and
recognises certain interpretations of them, and a

certain collection of writings, not perfectly definite
indeed, as religiously authoritative. The spiritual
character of the Church has retired, and it has
assumed an intellectual aspect. I do not mean that
the Christianity of it has been lost; nay, it was an
active effort of the Christianity within the Church
which set up the rule of faith and the canon of the
New Testament in self-defence. It was well meant,
and it was well done, but it shifted the emphasis in
the conception of the Church, and we have had to
pay for that ever since. It became possible then to
look for the marks of the Church, not in the actual
Christianity existing in it, not in the new life which
its members owed to Christ and lived to Him, but
in the correctness of their opinions. The basis was
laid for the dogmatic, as opposed to the spiritual
conception of the Church : the idea of orthodoxy,
which has no doubt a place of its own, got the
opportunity of creeping into a place which does not
belong to it ; and men were inevitably tempted, in
laying emphasis on the need of the time, to overlook the eternal need—that the new life which
came in Jesus Christ should reign in all who called
themselves His. It is always dangerous when we
call in the law, no matter in what shape, to defend
the gospel.

But the process did not stop here—I mean the
process of transforming the conception of the Church.
It was easy to say that the rule of faith, and the
canon of the New Testament, were of apostolic
authority ; but if this were questioned, how could it
be proved ? Critical investigations were out of the
question. The processes they involved were too

complicated, and the results were sometimes inconveniently uncertain; if the rule of faith and the New Testament canon were to serve the purpose for which they had been defined, there must be some short and easy method of demonstrating that they possessed the apostolic character which was claimed for them.   This short and easy method was found when the episcopal constitution which had grown up in almost all the churches was declared to be itself apostolic, and the bishops regarded as successors of the apostles.   The separate churches, or the Church as a whole, were not fitted to give the guarantee required; and hence writers like Irenaeus and Tertullian tell us that the possession of the apostolic inheritance, unimpaired, is guaranteed by the churches only because in them there is found *ordo episcoporum per successionem ab initio decurrens*— a line of bishops following one after another from the beginning.   This answered, no doubt, in a rough way, to the truth: the Church had a continuous history and a continuous consciousness; and it was natural to seek the organs of these in her ministers.   But this general view did not meet the necessities of the case; no merely historical view could do so.   It is impossible to find a material guarantee like this for the possession of Christian truth, to say nothing of Christian life. The pressure of the situation drove those who felt it to supplement the historical by a dogmatic conception : the bishops not only were a line of men going back each after each to the apostolic age, and to the apostles themselves; they received *cum episcopatus successione certum veritatis charisma* (along with their place in the

episcopal succession a sure charism—spiritual gift—
of truth); they were in virtue of their ordination
the depositaries and guardians of the apostolic
inheritance, the custodians of the truth, and, through
the sacraments, of the grace of the gospel.   It is
impossible to trace out these conceptions in detail;
but we can easily see how the original conception of
the Church was lost in them.   At first men said, No
Church without the Spirit, without the salvation, the
life, the holiness of Christ; then they said, No Church
without the rule of faith and the apostolic writings;
then, again, it came to be, No rule of faith, and no
apostolic writings, except under the guarantee of
the episcopal succession.   The Church was originally the community of the saints, of those who knew
themselves saved in Jesus Christ; at the next stage
it became, in self-defence, something of a school; at
the third, it was completely metamorphosed, and
instead of the community of the saved became an
institution in which the means of salvation were to
be found, because there was to be found there a
line of officials intrusted with them.   If we want
catchwords, we can say it was first spiritual, then
intellectual, and finally hierarchical; first a holy
society, then a society of true doctrine, and finally a
clerical polity.   No bishop, no Church; because no
bishop, no apostolic tradition; and no apostolic
tradition, no Christian life.

By the middle of the third century the Church
had got worlds away from the ideals of the New
Testament, and once embarked on the wrong course
it had to pursue it to the end.   The organised
hierarchy, with its apostolic and sacerdotal powers,

its sacraments in which the simplicity of the New Testament had been corrupted not only by the traditions of the Old but by the influence of pagan mysteries, its sacrifices, its legal discipline, and its superstition, grew in process of time into the Romish Church, with the sovereign priest at its head. This historical succession, we may thankfully acknowledge, did not extinguish the spiritual succession of Christian souls and of Christian life from generation to generation, though it often did its best to that end ; and as long as we can serve ourselves heirs to the saints of Jesus Christ, we do not need to mourn that we have broken with an external legal succession. It is a dead weight which some churches carry, and which, though sometimes imposing to the imagination, is never in the truest Christian sense inspiring.

I may assume that in a Protestant seminary such conceptions are refuted even as they are stated : the questions that trouble us are not so much the relation of the Church, as the New Testament conceives it, to the various forms in which Christianity has historically organised itself, as the functions of the Church, such as we know it, in view of the present social situation. Assuming that we have a consciousness of ourselves as Christian men and Christian communities answering to that which is represented in the New Testament, what are we to say to the various demands which the world makes upon us ? I do not know how it may be here, but I know that in Britain the churches are plentifully instructed in their duties by those who are without, and their interposition demanded on all sorts of occasions. Just as men sometimes tried to capture them in early days for a philosophical propaganda, so they would now for a social propaganda; they want the Church, very often, as an ally to fight their own battles. It is in the name of the Kingdom of God that these claims are made. This large conception, it is said, has been lost in the little one of the Church, and the Church needs to be waked up to the true scale of her duties. I have already criticised the relation of the two names, and do not need to say more here than that all that is binding on citizens of the Kingdom is binding on members of the Church. They are to carry the new life into every department of human activity, and by so doing to Christianise all. In the calling in which Christian men are called they are to abide *with God*. Whatever line of business a Christian man works in, he must work in it as a Christian. If he is an artist, he must be a Christian artist; he must recognise a responsibility to Christ and to the brotherhood in all the use he makes of pen or pencil. If he is a capitalist, he must be a Christian in the use of his money, and of the power it gives him, remembering what Christ says about the dangers of wealth, and that the soul of the poorest workman he employs is worth more to God than all the money in the world. If he is a politician—and in a free country every man ought to be one—he will carry Christian conviction, Christian cleanness of hand and of purpose, into his politics, and remember that Christ's will is supreme over nations as over individual men. All this, you will say, is commonplace, and so it is; but it is commonplace the disregard of which has brought upon the Church many of her perplexities and dangers. Take, for instance, those economical questions that arise in disputes between capital and labour. People cry out fiercely that the Church ought to mediate, that the Church ought to be on the side of the poor and oppressed, and so on. The Church ought certainly to be on the side of justice and of mercy; but it needs more than sympathy with justice and mercy to decide on the merits of a given dispute; it needs an accurate knowledge of the whole circumstances of the case, and that, it is impossible and unnecessary for the Church to have. It is no part of my business as a Christian man, or even as a Christian minister, and therefore it is no part of the business of the Church, which is the assembly of Christian men, to understand mining, docks, engineering, railways, or any industry, so as to be able to give sentence in cases of dispute. To do that is the work of Christian men who in God's providence are called to live the Christian life under the conditions in question; and it should be left for them to do. When representative Christian ministers—like Cardinal Manning, or the Bishop of Durham—interpose in economic disputes, in their character as ministers, it tends to put the Church in a false position, and though the present distress may excuse it, it is on larger grounds to be regretted. All life has to be Christianised; but the process is to be accomplished, not by dragging everything under the scrutiny and sentence of the Church as it exists among us, but by sending out into all the departments of life men to live and work there in the Spirit of Christ. The Church is the home of the

Spirit, the nurse and the educator of the Christian life; but her power to leaven society, and to be the salt of the earth, will not be increased if she makes it her policy, in the name of practical preaching, to lay down the law about all the details of existence. Christian ethics is not casuistry, still less is it the doing of other people's duties for them. There were things Christ refused to do; there are things that the Church, and the ministers of the Church, should refuse in His name. We will speak often of money, if we speak as He spoke; but we will not divide the inheritance. We will not assume that because we are Christians we are experts in economy or in legislation, or in any branch of politics, any more than in science or in art. We will believe that the Church which cultivates in all its members the spirit of humanity, the spirit of liberty, justice, generosity, and mercy, will do more for the coming of God's kingdom than if it plunged into the thick of every conflict, or offered its mediation in every dispute. The Church does nothing unless it does the deepest things; it does nothing unless it prevails on sinful men to have peace with God through our Lord Jesus Christ, and to walk in love even as He loved us. Let us fix our minds on this as the first and supreme interest, and everything else will come out in its proper place.

LECTURE IX

HOLY SCRIPTURE

Through these lectures there has been constant
reference made to Scripture, and indeed a constant
appeal to its authority. There are some, I presume,
to whom this will seem quite natural and appropriate; others, no doubt, to whom it will appear like
building in the air, or building at best on a foundation the security of which remains to be tested. This
individual difference of opinion answers roughly to
a confessional distinction to which reference was
made in the first lecture. There are some confessions—*e.g.* the old Scottish one, and the new
English Presbyterian one—which state Christian
doctrine in some such order as I have followed here,
and introduce what they have to say of Scripture
under the rubric of means of grace, and in subordination to the doctrine of the Church; while
others, like the Westminster Confession, make
Holy Scripture the subject of their first chapter,
and treat it as fundamental to everything else.
The arguments seem to me all in favour of the
former course. The Bible is, in the first instance,
a means of grace; it is *the* means through which
God communicates with man, making him know
what is in His heart towards him. It must be

known and experienced in this character before we can form a doctrine concerning it. We cannot *first* define its qualities, and *then* use it accordingly; we cannot start with its inspiration, and then discover its use for faith or practice. It is through an experience of its power that words like inspiration come to have any meaning, and when we define them apart from such experience we are only playing with empty sounds. This is implied in that treatment of Scripture, just alluded to, under the heading of means of grace; and it is expressly admitted by such sturdy upholders of the inspiration, and the consequent infallibility and inerrancy of Scripture, as Professor Warfield and the late Professor Hodge. 'Very many religious and historical truths,' they write,[1] 'must be established before we come to the question of inspiration, as, for instance, the being and moral government of God, the fallen condition of man, the fact of a redemptive scheme, the general historical truth of the Scriptures, and the validity and authority of the revelation of God's will, which they contain—*i.e. the general truth of Christianity and its doctrines.* Hence it follows that, while the inspiration of the Scriptures is true, and, being true, is a principle fundamental to the adequate interpretation of Scripture, it nevertheless is not in the first instance a principle fundamental to the truth of the Christian religion.' I agree with this as far as it goes, but I should go further. 'The general truth of Christianity and its doctrines,'—to quote the words I have underlined—must indeed be established

[1] *Inspiration*, p. 8. Presbyterian Board of Publication, Philadelphia.

'before we come to the question of inspiration;' but it cannot possibly be established without the use of Scripture. On the contrary, it is as we use Scripture, without any presuppositions whatever, that we find it has power to lodge in our minds 'Christianity and its doctrines' as being not only generally but divinely true; and its power to do this is precisely what we mean by its inspiration. We do not use the Bible, as it has been used in the foregoing lectures, because of an antecedent conviction that it is inspired; we are convinced it is inspired because it so asserts its authority over us, as we read, that we cannot but use it in that way. This, I am confident, is the only rational and experimental way of reaching and stating the truth.

But it is when we leave generalities behind, and come to detailed questions of fact, such as are raised by almost all historical criticism, either of the Old Testament or of the New, that difficulties emerge, and men's minds are perplexed. No Christian questions such a proposition as this, that God actually speaks to man through the Scriptures, and that man hears the voice and knows it to be God's. No Christian questions that through the Scripture the believing soul has fellowship with God its Father and Redeemer in Christ Jesus. These are things of experience which need no guarantee beyond themselves. 'If,' said Professor Robertson Smith, 'I am asked why I receive Scripture as the word of God, and as the only perfect rule of faith and life, I answer with all the fathers of the Protestant Church, *Because the Bible is the only record of the redeeming love of God, because in the Bible alone I find God drawing near to man in Christ Jesus, and declaring to us in Him His will for our salvation. And this record I know to be true by the witness of His Spirit in my heart, whereby I am assured that none other than God Himself is able to speak such words to my soul.'* [1] This, it seems to me, is not only true, but self-evident and unassailable; the only trouble is that it is so easily misapplied. It is really a doctrine of the word of God, or of the divine message to man; but it is too apt to be construed as if it were a doctrine of the text of Scripture. It has been used to cover not only certain assumed qualities of Scripture as we have it, but certain alleged qualities of an 'original autograph' of Scripture which no one knows anything about. It will facilitate understanding, if, with such a conception of Scripture as the medium through which God speaks to the believer, we survey the Bible in its distinctive parts, and look at the relation which this conception bears, in each case, to the problems and results of criticism. It is here that the whole difficulty lies; but I believe the result will be not to invalidate, but to vindicate, that use of Scripture which has been made in the foregoing lectures.

Our starting-point in such an investigation as this must be that part of Scripture in which we come most immediately into contact with Christ, viz., the gospels. It is in Christ supremely—there are those who would say in Christ exclusively, which is right in a sense, though misleading here— that God draws near to us, and declares to us His

[1] See Note A.

will for our salvation. No one who admits that God speaks to the soul through the Scriptures will question that the voice of God is peculiarly audible, intelligible, and compelling in Christ. When *He* speaks to us, God speaks to us; when we are brought into *His* presence, and apprehend His mercy and His judgment, we are brought into God's presence, and are judged and redeemed by Him. But, some one will say, the gospels purport to be historical, and all that claims to be historical must be subject to historical criticism. We must be able to show that the life of Jesus actually happened as it is reported by the evangelists—we must have a scientific guarantee of the accuracy of the narrative —before we allow it to have any impression on our minds or hearts at all. What if the gospel narrative should prove, on examination, to be untrue?

This looks a serious, but is in reality a trifling, question. It is by no means necessary that we should know everything that is in the gospels to be true, or that we should be bound to the accuracy of every detail before they begin to do for us what God designs them to do. To any sincere person who raised this difficulty I should say, Read these books with your eye on Christ, and it will be as certain to you as anything is certain to the mind, heart, and conscience of man, that the character of Christ there exhibited is a real character. It is not a fancy character; it is not a work of imagination; the evangelists did not make it out of their own heads. Leaving details on one side, and confining ourselves exclusively to Jesus as a person of such and such a character, a person in whom such and

such a relation is realised to God on the one hand
and to man on the other, a person who, in His moral
temper and in all His words and deeds, exhibits
Himself as the Son of God, the brother, friend, and
Saviour of men; leaving, I say, details on one side,
and confining ourselves exclusively to this, it is
certain, with a certainty no doubt can touch, that
such a one actually lived. We do not need to
become historical critics before we can believe in
Christ and be saved by Him. The Holy Spirit,
bearing witness by and with the word of the evangelists in our hearts, gives us, independent of any
criticism, a full persuasion and assurance of the
infallible truth and divine authority of the revelation
of God made in Him. And if any one still maintains that this does forestall criticism, I should say
that the very meaning of the Incarnation, the truth
on which all Christianity depends, is precisely this,
that there *is* a point, viz., the life of the Son of
God in our nature, at which the spiritual and the
historical coincide, and at which, therefore, as the
very purpose of revelation requires, there can be a
spiritual guarantee for historical truth. The witness
of the Spirit to the believer enables him, not only
de facto but *de jure*, to take the life of Christ recorded in the gospels as a real historical life. If it
were not so, the life of Christ would be absolutely
without religious significance. God could make no
use of it; for if it could not be used till historical
criticism had finished its work upon it, obviously
it could never be used at all.

But on this general basis, criticism is free to do
its appropriate work. A criticism, indeed, which

on principle denies the supernatural, and regards it as one of its most obvious tasks to explain away this element in the story, need not discompose one who has the spiritual certainty referred to, that all through the history, and not merely when what we call miracles are being wrought, he is in contact with a supernatural Person. Christ and His works are all of a piece, and he who has apprehended Christ, or rather been apprehended by Him, will not seek to reduce the self-manifestation of the Saviour to the measure of common humanity. To prove the miracles one by one is as impossible as to disprove them in the same way, but they unite with the Person and the words of Jesus into one divine whole through which God reveals His very heart to man. The gospels have every quality which they need, to put us in contact with the gospel; they do put us in contact with it, and the Spirit makes it sure to our faith; why should we ask for more from them? If they truly represent Christ to us, so that we gain the faith in Him which their authors had, is not that all we can desire? The evangelists may make mistakes in dates, in the order of events, in reporting the occasion of a word of Jesus, possibly in the application of a parable; we may discern here and there, as in Luke, the incipient formalism of the second generation; we may distinguish, as a recent analysis of the gospels has done, between a first, a second, and a third cycle of oral gospel, which preceded our written gospels; we may feel more certain, on bare historical grounds, of details contained in the Apostolic Source as Weiss has extracted it from Matthew and Luke,

than of details the historical authority for which
we cannot define ; we may differ—Christian men do
differ—about numberless questions of this kind ;
but we ought to be able to say boldly that though
all these be left out of view, nay, even though in
any number of cases of this kind the *gospels* should
be proved in error, the *gospel* is untouched ; the
word of God, the revelation of God to the soul in
Christ, attested by the Spirit, lives and abides.
Revelation is ultimately personal, as personal as
faith.   It is to Christ we give our trust, and as long
as the gospels make us sure of what He is, they
serve God's purpose and our need.

It is from the vantage ground of this certainty,
furnished by faith in Christ, that we can most
effectively survey what remains of the field.   Whatever men may say of the authority of Scripture, no
one who agrees with what has been said thus far
will dispute the authority of Christ.   At all events,
I do not speak here to those who would.   And
what every one must feel who has said in the Spirit
of God, ' Jesus is Lord,' is that in a very real sense
His authority may be invoked to cover that of
Scripture.   He was born and brought up in the
Jewish Church, to which had been committed the
oracles of God.   He used the Scriptures of the Old
Testament—the same to all intents and purposes as
we ourselves have—and He used them, if we may
say so, as men legitimately use them still, as a
means of fellowship with His Father in heaven.   He
used them in the crises of His life, in the wilderness
and on the Cross, to fight Satan and death.   If
they served Him thus, it would surely be an extra-

ordinary rashness and presumption to assert that
there is no similar service they can render to us.
But we can go further than this, and point to
express words of Jesus in which the authority of
the Old Testament is recognised, and even used in
argument with the Jews. 'They have Moses and
the prophets, let them hear them.' 'The Scripture
cannot be broken.' 'One jot or one tittle shall in
no wise pass from the law till all be fulfilled.' 'Ye
do err, not knowing the Scriptures.' 'Have ye
never read?' Sayings like these assure us that
Jesus, at all events, found in the Scriptures of the
Old Testament a true revelation of God; as He
read, the Father spoke to Him, and He Himself
had fellowship with Him. More important still is
that testimony to the ancient Scriptures which is
borne by the fact that Jesus saw in them, as has
been remarked in an earlier lecture, foreshadowings
of Himself. If it is too much to say that His coming
and His work are clearly predicted in them, it is not
too much to say that they are clearly prefigured.
The reality is more important than the words
(though articulate predictive words are not wanting),
and the reality, to His own mind, bore directly upon
Him. In other words, the Old Testament is vitally,
and not only casually and chronologically, connected
with the New. Christ was born in that particular
historical connection, and, we may say it reverently,
could not have been born in any other. He came
to fulfil the law and the prophets, and though the
fulfilment exhibited in His Person and Work un-
imaginably transcends all we could have anticipated,
and makes the mechanical correspondences that

have been sought out between the Old Testament and the New as worthless as they are often absurd, it shows indubitably that the Old Testament and the New are included in one purpose of God, and gives to the record of the earlier revelation the same sanction possessed by the later.

From the very beginning, as we are all aware, the Old Testament was in some sort a problem to the Church. The early Christians used it without embarrassment as a Christian book. When they quote from it they always quote in a Christian sense. Their very use of its words makes them, and is intended to make them, New Testament words, and what has just been said is to a certain extent their justification. It is possible to err in detail, if we read the Old Testament in this way ; it may even be possible to err in every detail, and yet not to err on the whole. For it is the same Word of God which became Incarnate in Jesus that speaks to the heart in the ancient Scriptures. On the other hand, men have been as strongly impressed from the beginning with the idea that the Old Testament was *not* a Christian book. This was the view, among others, of Marcion, who, *ipso Paulo paulinior*, simply rejected it. He could only define the relation of it to Christ and the gospel negatively—by contrast, not by connection, or even by comparison. The theology of Ritschl and his adherents, in spite of protests to the contrary, is in this respect passably Marcionitic. 'We cannot,' says Herrmann,[1] one of its representative men, 'we cannot transplant ourselves into the religious life of a pious Israelite so as

[1] *Der Verkehr des Christen mit Gott*, p. 49.

to understand it completely. For the facts, which wrought upon him as revelations of God, have no longer this power for us. . . . Since we cannot be conscious of ourselves as Jews, neither can the revelation which Israel enjoyed any longer satisfy us.' 'Satisfy us,' is perhaps true; but what the argument requires is, 'have significance for us,' and this, in point of fact, is not true. For Christians, the authority of Christ Himself, the use He made of the Old Testament in His teaching, the use He made of it in His personal life, the relation in which He set Himself to it as the Fulfiller of Law and Promise, all these combined secure the Old Testament as a whole in a position from which it cannot be dislodged, and in which no other book can compete with it. It is a part of the divine revelation consummated in Christ, and what has already been said about the gospels has an application here also. The witness of the Spirit, by and with the word in the soul, does not guarantee the historicity of miraculous details, but it does guarantee the presence of a supernatural element in the history recorded. It bars out a criticism which denies the supernatural on principle, and refuses to recognise a unique work of God as in process along this line.

But when this is recognised, we ought to recognise, on the other hand, that within these limits criticism has its own work to do. The Old Testament is not only a book, but a collection of books. It has a unity as the record of revelation, and as a medium through which God still speaks to men and enters into fellowship with them. It is one, because it is the product of one work of God proceeding con-

tinuously through the ages and completing itself in
Christ; and it is one also because all its writers
write out of their faith in the one living and true
God who is the author of this work, and write to
communicate their faith to others.   And indeed
it is nothing else than faith, apprehending the
revelation, which makes this unity apparent.   But
the one revelation came 'by divers portions and in
divers manners,' and in this diversity the literary
and historical critic finds his work prepared.   Who
wrote the books, the time at which they were
written, the historical conditions out of which they
spring, and to which they are addressed, the circumstances of their preservation, collection, transmission,
and so forth; all these are his task.   And a Christian
who knows that God does speak to the soul through
the Scriptures ought not to speak of criticism as
an alien or hostile power, with which he may be
compelled, against his will, to go so far, but which
he must ever regard with suspicion.   There have no
doubt been irresponsible critics, and even profane
and wanton critics—for the way in which men handle
revelation judges them when they do not think of
it; but true criticism is a science, and will go its
own length, and we will all go along with it.   Even
to speak of 'moderate' and 'extreme' opinions in
criticism is out of place.   The answers to the critic's
questions are not moderate or extreme, but true or
false; and of all men a Christian ought to be willing
to go any length with truth.   But let us reflect, for
a moment, on what the general effect of criticism
has been, so far as the Old Testament is concerned.

It has certainly brought into a new prominence

the work, and the works, of the prophets. It has, indeed, altered greatly the use that is commonly made of them. It is no longer an apologetic, but a directly spiritual function, that the prophetic Scriptures fulfil. They are not a waste area in the Bible, with one or two luminous points in it, where coincidences can be detected or imagined between the Old Testament and the New. They have been put, by the labours of criticism, into their original setting; they have been read as the voice of God addressed to discoverable historical situations, and the voice of God has become audible in them again as it had not been audible for long. It is no exaggeration to say that the prophetic Scriptures are at this moment inspiring more men, speaking to more men for God, giving more men larger and fresher conceptions of things divine and human, than at any previous age in the history of the Church. This is only another way of saying that as a result of criticism the inspiration of the prophetic books has had freer play, and is working more powerfully and fruitfully than it has ever done before. If there has been loss, the gain has far outweighed the loss; but it is by no means plain that the supposition should be granted. The old way of vindicating prophecy by pointing to the ruins, or want of ruins, at Babylon, and to the fishermen's nets at Tyre, had something painfully unproductive about it. It might be unobjectionable, but it never took one further forward. The New Testament idea that all prophecy is fulfilled in Christ—and therefore that in Christ only are fulfil-ments of prophecy to be sought—is true, wholesome, and inspiring. How far the revelation fully made in Christ had been brought within the horizon of the ancient men of God,—how far, through the enlightenment of the divine Spirit and sympathy with the divine purpose, they were permitted to anticipate what God was doing for His people,— these are not questions to which there is any mechanical answer. The vital connection between the work of the prophets and the work of Jesus is guaranteed by Jesus Himself; and we have only to be thankful that criticism has enabled us to hear more plainly than before the voice of God speaking to His people in the promises, threatenings, and spiritual teachings of the prophetic Scriptures. We do not need to believe that the prophets could write history beforehand. The revelation they have to make to us is not the revelation of this or that incident in the fortunes of men or nations ; it is the revelation of God. Their writings stand in the Scriptures because they do reveal God ; because they are a mighty and effective means of putting us in communication with Him who spoke to the prophets, and generating in our souls that faith in Him which they possessed. That is what they really have to impart to us,—faith in God the Holy One, the alone living and true, ever present in the life of men and nations, to judge and to save. I repeat that we owe criticism a debt for liberating, as it were, this spirit of prophecy, and giving it free course in the Church.

With the historical books many will feel the case is different. The critical investigation of these has led to results which it is apparently impossible to combine with old ideas of the authority of Scripture.

But let us compose our minds by recalling the point
from which we started. The primary certainty which
ought to be unceasingly present to our minds is that
God speaks to us through Jesus Christ, and that
this final revelation consummated a preparatory
revelation made to Israel in the course of its
history, and very largely by means of its history.
I have said already that this guarantees the presence
of a supernatural element in the history, which
cannot be defined *a priori*, but it does not seem to
me to guarantee any more.   It warrants us to
anticipate, what we find in experience is the fact,
that God speaks to the heart and conscience of men
through the Biblical record ; it does not guarantee
that in this record we shall find nothing but what
is historical in the modern and scientific sense of
history.   In the Hebrew Bible, the writers of what
we call the historical books—Joshua, Judges, Samuel,
and Kings—are called 'the former prophets,' and
this is the right aspect in which to regard them.
They are not annalists merely, or secular historians
tracing out the secondary causes by which the
historical process has advanced, but men of God
reading and interpreting the story of God's dealings
with their race.   That this story is peculiarly
significant, and that there was a peculiar presence
of God in it, is proved by its peculiar and vital
relation to Christ; but the historical writers need
not have been, and evidently in point of fact were
not, miraculously provided with information which
other historians would have required to search out
for themselves.   Regarded simply as historians, their
opportunities naturally varied, and with them the

strictly historical importance of their work. Sometimes one might have lived through all that he
describes. Thus Jeremiah tells with the authority
of an eye-witness, as well as the insight of a prophet,
the story of the last days of Jerusalem. Sometimes,
again, one might have good contemporary evidence
to go upon, such as we often find referred to in the
Books of Kings. For more remote and unsettled
periods, as that described in the Book of Judges,
it may be extremely difficult to appreciate the
evidence historically. Yet God spoke to His
people through all these different kinds of history,
and they heard His voice. All of them are written
by men firmly convinced—and truly convinced—
that God had ever been present in the history of
Israel, and desirous to impart that conviction of
theirs to others. They may have been mistaken
about one detail or another in the story they tell.
They may have had poor facilities for obtaining
information, but their testimony to God is a testimony to which God Himself bears witness, by and
with their word, in our hearts; and in treating the
Bible as the record of revelation it is this alone
with which we are concerned. Perhaps what has
troubled most people in this connection is the
verdict of criticism on the opening chapters of the
Bible. These are in form historical, but they
manifestly treat of prehistoric times. The very
moment we think of it, it is obvious that the story
of the first man cannot be history, as the story of the
siege and conquest of Jerusalem by the Chaldeans
is history. The beginnings of man's life on earth
lie far behind all records, and all traditions too.

Yet here, in the beginning of Genesis, we have what purport to be accounts of these inaccessible things. What are we to call them? Some would say, 'Supernaturally communicated history.' But this would be a thing not only without analogy in the rest of Scripture, but utterly incapable of proof. It is indeed a meaningless, because a self-contradictory, description. The truth is that these stories illustrate, in the race to which God chose to reveal Himself, a stage through which the human mind passes in all races, and indeed in all individuals. Long before man is capable of science or history, he asks himself questions to which only science or history can give the answer, and not only asks, but answers them too. Now what is the technical name for these prescientific answers to scientific questions? for these prehistorical answers to historical questions? The name which is technically given to them is myths. Among people who do not know anything of mythology, myth is usually a term of contempt. But here it is a term of science. There is a stage at which, in this sense, the whole contents of the mind, as yet incapable of science or of history, may be called mythological. And what criticism shows us, in its treatment of the early chapters of Genesis, is that God does not disdain to speak to the mind, nor through it, even when it is at this lowly stage. Even the myth, in which the beginnings of human life, lying beyond human research, are represented to itself by the child-mind of the race, may be made the medium of revelation. God has actually taken these weak things of the world and things that are despised, and has drawn near to us, and spoken to

our hearts, through them. I should not hesitate to
say that the man who cannot hear God speak to
him in the story of creation and the fall will never
hear God's voice anywhere. But that does not
make the first chapter of Genesis science, nor the
third chapter history. And what is of authority in
these chapters is not the quasi-scientific or quasi-
historical form, but the message, which through
them comes to the heart, of God's creative wisdom
and power, of man's native kinship to God, of his
calling to rule over nature, of his sin, of God's
judgment and mercy. It is the contents of this
message also which we use, without misgiving, in
constructing our theology, for these contents are
authenticated by the witness of the Spirit. To
quote the Westminster Confession, ' The Supreme
Judge, by which all controversies of religion are to
be determined, and all decrees of councils, opinions
of ancient writers, doctrines of men, and private
spirits, are to be examined, and in whose sentence
we are to rest, can be no other but the Holy Spirit
speaking in the Scripture '—not the mere letter of
Scripture itself.

The point, however, at which the authority of
Scripture is most discussed theologically is that at
which the authority of the apostles comes into view.
Revelation is summed up in Christ—this is conceded
on all hands. But the question at once arises, What
is meant by Christ? Is it Christ as He lived and
moved among men? Christ as He can be interpreted out of His own express teaching? Christ as
He can be preached on the basis, say, of the second
gospel alone, or on a narrower basis even than that?

There is a large school of theologians who incline to say so more or less dogmatically. For them, our knowledge of Christ ends at the Cross. His resurrection is part of the apostles' faith, but incapable of proof as a historical fact. Words ascribed to Him after the Resurrection may be reminiscences of words He had actually spoken before, only adapted to a new situation; or they may be the product of the loving imagination and reflection of disciples, put without misgiving into the Lord's mouth. This is the attitude on the whole of the Ritschlian school.[1] They ignore Christ's exaltation as something belonging rather to the realm of pious imagination than serious fact. They ignore the giving of the Holy Spirit as a Spirit of truth to enable the apostles to interpret the revelation contained in the life, death, and exaltation of Jesus. They ignore, as I had occasion to point out in an earlier lecture, the many things which Jesus could not say to His disciples while He was with them, because they could not bear them, but which the Spirit was to show them when He was gone. And on the strength of general principles like these, while they accept the apostolic testimony to what Christ said and did, they do not feel bound by the apostolic interpretations of His life and death. Christ they admit to be the perfect revelation, but it does not follow that the apostolic is the final theology. Hence the apostolic theology has no binding authority for us, or for the Church at large.

In another way, also, the authority of the New Testament as a theological standard has been called

[1] See Note B.

in question. The New Testament itself, it is asserted, does not present us with a single type of theology. The Biblical Theology of the New Testament even takes it as its special task to present the conceptions of the various writers in their characteristic distinctness from each other. Thus we have a Pauline, a Johannine, a Synoptic theology; a theology of the Epistle to the Hebrews, and even of Peter. But all that needs to be insisted on is that underneath these there is a Christian theology, a unity to which the Spirit of God bears witness, by and with the apostolic word, in the heart; and a unity, too, in which all the personal distinctions disappear. It is quite misleading to say that because the New Testament writers apprehended Christian truth each with his own mind and in his own way, therefore there is no coherent Christian truth to apprehend, or no authority in the original apprehension of it.

But leaving this point, let us return to the position just defined, that of those who accept the apostolic testimony, but feel no obligation to accept the apostolic theology, and declare expressly beforehand, and on principle, that it has no authority for them. I do not think it is worth while to discuss beforehand, in this abstract way, what authority the apostolic theology *can* have, or *ought* to have. We wish our doctrine of God to rest upon the authority of God; and the Holy Spirit does not bear witness *before* the word, but *by* and *with* the word, in our hearts. Where the human mind is concerned, it is idle to speak of an authority which can simply be imposed. There neither is nor can be any such thing. The real question is whether there is an authority which can impose itself, which can freely win the recognition and surrender of the mind and heart of man. Applied to the matter. in hand, the real question is whether the characteristic teachings of the apostles, which constituted at once their theology and their gospel, are guaranteed by the witness of the Spirit. For 'the authority of the holy Scripture, for which it ought to be believed and obeyed, dependeth not upon the testimony of any man or church, but wholly upon God.'— (Westminster Confession, ch. i. § 4.). Take, for instance, the great doctrine of apostolic theology, which, as I have tried to show (in Lecture v.), is found in substance, and without ambiguity, in all the New Testament 'types of teaching'—the expiatory significance of the death of Christ. A man may say if he pleases that he is not bound to accept this merely because it is taught by Peter and Paul and John; his intelligence is in no predestined relation of bondage to theirs. This is exactly what the confession says: 'the authority of the holy Scripture, for which it ought to be believed and obeyed, dependeth not upon the testimony of any man'—not even of an apostle. But this is an abstract assertion, with no particular application. The doctrine of an atonement for sins, made in Christ's death, has never been accepted in the Church simply as the speculation of three accidentally privileged men—Peter, Paul, and John. The authority it enjoys and has enjoyed from the beginning is due to this, that the Holy Spirit has borne witness by and with that doctrine in men's hearts, making them sure that in accepting Christ's death thus interpreted, they were accepting the very soul of God's redeeming love. If there is one truth in the whole Bible which is covered by the *testimonium internum Spiritus sancti*, and by the consenting witness of Christians in all ages, it is this. It has an authority in it or along with it by which it vindicates itself to faith as divinely and infallibly true; it asserts itself irresistibly, and beyond a doubt, as the supreme revelation of God's judgment and mercy to penitent souls. There can be no authority higher than that. Neither, so far as I can see, can there be any real authority prior to that.

But surely we are bound to consider how the apostles themselves understood the situation. They were conscious that their gospel, with this as its central doctrine, had the authority I have described, and they preached it in this consciousness. It had a divine guarantee in their own souls. It was not taught them by man; they received it by revelation. It was preached with the Holy Ghost sent down from heaven. It was meant to evoke, and did evoke, in the souls of those who heard it, a faith standing not in the wisdom of man but in the power of God. If now we weigh this consciousness of the apostles themselves—and it surely has significance, just as the self-consciousness of the prophet had in the earlier dispensation—and if we take it in its New Testament connection with the exaltation of Jesus and the gift of the Spirit, it becomes necessary, I think, even *a priori*, to concede a far higher importance to the apostolic theology

than is done by writers of the school to which I
have referred. If the revelation made in Jesus had
either to be apprehended in its essence immediately,
or lost—and there is hardly room to doubt that
these were the alternatives; if the apostles themselves claim to have received special spiritual power
to interpret and to teach it; if the claims they make
are attested by the witness of the Spirit finding
entrance for their message into the souls of men; if
they are all at one, as St. Paul asserts they are, and
as the examination of the texts in the fifth lecture
showed, on what they regard as the very heart of
the revelation made in Christ, ought we not to feel
that there is something unreal, and out of proportion
to reality, in the claim to reject the central doctrine
of the apostolic gospel, and the keystone of apostolic
theology, on the abstract general ground that one
man's thought can have no binding authority for
another? That a man should see nothing in the
doctrine is conceivable, but another matter; the
apostles themselves encountered those in whose
case it was veiled. There is something flippant in
a remark like Herrmann's, that what is important is
not that we should have the thoughts of the apostles
about Christ, but that we should have thoughts of
our own. What is important is that our thoughts
should truly interpret the divine revelation; and if
they do this, they are not ours nor theirs but God's.
The very grace of the apostolic Scriptures is, that
God by means of them interprets to us His love in
Christ, and enables us to grasp it with heart and
mind.

It is, I think, along the line followed in this

lecture that the conception of the divine authority of Scripture can be best presented to those whose minds are perplexed about it. A sure starting-point must be acquired, and working out from it the area of certitude may be gradually enlarged. That starting-point for any one at the present day will almost inevitably be the words, or rather the character and Person, of Jesus. It is under His inspiration, under His guardianship, that the Old Testament maintains itself as the medium of a true revelation of God to man; and it is His Spirit which in the apostles justifies itself as the original and final interpreter of His work. But this individual procedure *presupposes* the Bible; the canon of Holy Scripture is there, to begin with; a collection of sacred books to which nothing can be added, revelation being completely recorded in them. What authority, it may be asked, has the collection itself?

This is a question of quite a different kind from that which has engaged our attention hitherto. The process by which the various writings composing the Old Testament and the New were brought into their present relations is one which the historian finds full of difficulty; it raises innumerable questions to which there is at present no answer. It is obviously impossible to pursue it here, but perhaps it may serve some purpose to say that the canon has the authority of the Church, while the divine message which it brings to us has the authority of God. Yet that antithesis is not absolute. The Church is Christ's creation, and did not proceed at random in constituting its Bible; however in details the judgment of the Christian community may have wavered—and we know that there were fluctuations not quite unimportant—the result proves that it was divinely guided on the whole. There is nothing in the canon unworthy of a medium of revelation, and it is certainly a most impressive fact that the experience of nineteen centuries has produced nothing worthy to be added to it. There has been no interpretation of the revelation made in Jesus which has done more than try to grasp the breadth and depth of apostolic teaching; and the perennial impulse which Scripture and Scripture alone communicates to spiritual life and spiritual thought is always sealing its pre-eminence anew. This is especially true in all that the New Testament tells us of the life beyond death. The world in which the Risen Lord reigns is a real world to all New Testament writers, and they never speak of it unworthily, or in language that makes it incredible. Their uniqueness, in this respect, is indisputable and significant; it is another indication that a real divine guidance superintended all their work, and kept it true to God and worthy of Him. The precise limits of the canon are, of course, no matter of faith. Some confessions define them, but none of the great creeds. But it is not too much to say that they are entitled to profound deference, and that though one may, as Luther did, employ the authority of the Word of God, attested by the Spirit, to criticise the limits of the canon, as merely part of a human tradition, it is at least as likely that the individual should be insensible to the divine message in a book, as that the Church should have

judged it to contain such a message if it did not
do so.

One cannot help feeling, at the close of such a
discussion as this, that the Scripture may sometimes
be prejudiced by our best-intentioned attempts to
serve it. It has a greatness and power of its own
which are most free to work when we approach it
without any presuppositions whatever. The less
we ask beforehand from those whom we wish to
read it the better. Words which provoke antipathy
and disputation, like authority, infallibility, inerrancy, and so forth, had better be let alone by
the preacher. The theologian will know how to
distinguish between the letter of the record and
God revealing Himself through it; and he will find
no insuperable difficulty in building his theology,
as on the surest of all foundations on this revelation of God.

LECTURE X

ESCHATOLOGY

ESCHATOLOGY, or the doctrine of the last things, is that one of the topics of theology on which it may well seem most perilous to speak. In the primitive church it probably filled a larger space in the common Christian mind than any other; it was *the* doctrine of the new faith. Up to a comparatively recent period it was a topic on which dogmatism was emphatic and confident; men treated it abstractly, and spoke as boldly as if they had been initiated into all the secrets of God. But a great change has taken place, especially during the last generation. All men are willing to confess ignorance. Ritschl, to whose conceptions reference has been made all through these lectures, has no eschatology at all. He is a theological positivist, who simply abjures the transcendent. The Kingdom of God is among us; it is righteousness, peace, and joy in the Holy Ghost, and that is all we need to know. The theologian is not called on to anticipate its future or its consummation, nor to say anything about the scenic representation of these to be found in the New Testament, or in the pious imaginations of Christian people. Heaven and hell are beyond his beat. This conception is not, indeed, shared by all Ritschl's disciples. Kaftan, *e.g.*, one of the most distinguished, holds that ' the certainty of an eternal life in a Kingdom of God which is above the world, which lies to us as yet in the beyond, is the very nerve of our Christian piety.' But it is widely diffused even where Ritschl is unknown, and there is a certain amount of sympathy with it in those who are puzzled by the apparent teaching of Scripture, repelled by the statements of the creeds, or vexed by obstinate questionings in their own hearts. Particular parts of the large problem of eschatology—such as the destiny of the unbelieving, of the heathen, of those who die in infancy ; or the nature and moral possibilities of the intermediate state—have been earnestly discussed among all Christians, and have excited deep and passionate interest. It is not very hard to give an exegetical statement on the whole subject; neither is it very hard to explain what the teaching of the Church has been; what *is* hard, though perhaps it should not be, is to say precisely what is of faith in the matter, what is made sure to the heart by the witness of the Spirit, what is the religious conviction in the strength of which we face the unknown future. I believe I shall best say what I have to say by making the Bible itself the starting-point : the history of ideas is often the only key to the appreciation of them.

In all the prophets of the Old Testament there is what may be legitimately called an eschatological element. They all deal with the Kingdom of God—they all deal also with the consummation of that Kingdom. They look on to a future in which it will be established without a rival on the earth. There are, of course, varieties in the form of their predictions, but when we look closely into them there is great unity of substance. The subject is always the Kingdom or the people of God—the cause of God on earth, and not the destiny of individuals. The consummation comes on what is called the day of the Lord. The associations of this name may be with battle ('as in the day of Midian'), or with judgment; but the character of it is always the same. It is a day in which God interposes decisively to plead His own cause; all the enemies of His Kingdom, within and without, are destroyed; and after that destruction the Kingdom is established in peace and perpetuity. The day of the Lord usually seems close at hand to the prophets, but not invariably; but whether it be nearer or more remote, it has the character of finality. The enemies of the Kingdom are destroyed for ever; the Kingdom itself is set up in a light that no darkness will ever cloud. As a rule, the Messianic king figures as its head; sometimes as an individual, sometimes, apparently, as head of an endless succession of princes; and under His victorious rule Israel holds dominion over the nations, and extends to all the world the knowledge of the true God. This is the general conception of the last things which we find in the prophets.

But there is one striking exception, which must be mentioned, because it is the explanation of the one striking exception which also exists to the New Testament type of doctrine: I refer to the prophecy about Gog and Magog in Ezekiel. The 37th chapter of Ezekiel, which describes the re-animation of Israel, and their re-settlement in their own land, is in a line with Old Testament prophecy in general. It tells how God will make an everlasting covenant with His people, and set His sanctuary in the midst of them for evermore; and it ends by declaring that the heathen shall know that all this is His work. Usually in prophecy this would be the final stage; it would be *eschatology*; there would be nothing more to wait for. But Ezekiel, perhaps from his enlarged experience in exile, has the idea of nations lying on the outskirts of the earth, distant nations that have not been in contact with Israel, and 'have not heard Jehovah's name, nor seen His glory'; and even after the consummation has come, long after, these remote peoples, with names unknown to history, come up from the farthest corners of the world, to assail the people of God. Only after *their* destruction are the finality of God's Kingdom and the unassailable bliss of His people secured. This conception has no analogue in the Old Testament, but it is precisely reproduced in the New, in the book of Revelation. There also we have a kind of preliminary consummation—a millennial reign of Christ with His martyrs and confessors— which is not the very end. The very end does not come till the innumerable multitudes from the four corners of the earth—the remote outlying peoples that have not known the name of *our* Lord, nor seen His glory—make one more determined attempt to storm the camp of the saints and the beloved city. The attempt ends, as in Ezekiel, with their complete destruction, and with the final manifestation, in glory, of the city of God. Now Ezekiel's prophecy never received a literal fulfilment; no one, I imagine, looks for a literal fulfilment of it, and I cannot see why any one should look for a literal fulfilment of John's. The nature and value of such anticipations are misconstrued when we ask whether Christ's coming is pre-millennial or post-millennial, or who they are who reign with Christ in the millennium, or any of the innumerable questions that have been asked in regard to this subject. To ask such questions is to assume that Ezekiel and John could write history before it happened, which is not the case. Christ certainly comes, according to the picture in Revelation, before the millennium ; but the question of importance is whether the conception of the millennium itself, related as it is to Ezekiel, is essential to faith. I cannot think it is. The religious content of the passages—what they offer to faith to grasp—what the Holy Scripture bears witness to in our hearts—is, I should say, simply this : that *until* the end the conflict between the Kingdom of God and the kingdoms of the world must go on ; that as the end approaches it becomes ever more intense, progress in humanity not being a progress in goodness only, or in badness only, but in the antagonism between the two ; and that the necessity for conflict is sure to emerge even after the Kingdom of God has won its greatest triumphs. I frankly confess that to seek more than this in such Scriptural indications seems to me trifling. We can see why a New Testament prophet should follow in the track of an Old Testament prophet, and we can conjecture why the Old Testament prophet's anticipations took the precise shape which they did ; but the mere form of them does not possess binding authority for us. I say *does* not, for the simple fact is that such conceptions are not able to win for themselves the unhesitating assent of the mind.

But to return to the main line. The subject of eschatological prophecy is the Kingdom of God as a whole—the people of Israel as God's people. It is *its* future which is in view. When it seems as though the nation must perish, and have no future at all, a prophet like Ezekiel is bold enough to predict its resurrection. But it is still the *nation's* resurrection that he predicts, not that of individuals. The resurrection of individuals, I believe, first entered into the scenery of eschatology when religious persecution produced martyrs for the Kingdom of God. It was a thought intolerable to those who believed in the glorious future that the very persons who sacrificed themselves to make it sure should be deprived of their inheritance in it. Rather than those who had laid down their lives in fidelity to God should forfeit their hope of the future, God Himself would restore them to life, and give them their part in His Kingdom. This thought—one which faith in God and in His righteousness had created— took firm possession of the Jewish mind, inspiring and controlling much of its reflection about the last things. It bears, of course, only on the righteous, only on the people of God ; it is only with them that faith has anything to do. We see the influence of it, even when it has been complicated with other ideas, in such expressions as 'the resurrection of the just,' 'the first resurrection,' 'attaining to the resurrection,' 'worthy of the resurrection,' 'a better resurrection'; we see it also in the doctrine of conditional immortality.[1] As far as individuals are concerned, the first resurrection, the resurrection of the just, was, to begin with, the only resurrection; the belief in it was produced by faith in God, and its sole object was to safeguard the interest of the righteous in His Kingdom. Those who had died fighting God's battle must not be robbed, when it came, of the joy of victory. When the idea of a resurrection of all men came in, bad as well as good, it was not from the fidelity of God to His people, but from the necessity of impartial retribution, that it was derived. All were raised, that all might be judged. This idea was not defined in relation to the other, nor was the general resurrection defined in relation to the resurrection of the just. We first find it expressly mentioned in the latest book of the Old Testament— the prophecy of Daniel: 'Many of them that sleep in the dust of the earth shall awake; some to everlasting life, and some to shame and everlasting contempt.' The two sides of the resurrection appear here as co-ordinate, at least they are stated simply side by side. But that does not imply that they are to faith of equal interest. It is an exegetical result that some arise to shame and ever-

[1] Luke xiv. 14; Rev. xx. 6; Phil. iii. 11; Luke xx. 35; Heb. xi. 35.

lasting contempt; but we have not a positive
religious motive for affirming it, as we have for
affirming that God will be for ever faithful to those
who are His, and that not even death will cheat
them of their inheritance in Him. This, at all
events, is true, that it was the interest of the
righteous which produced faith in the resurrection
at first, and that the main import of that faith
always remains there. It is connected not so much
with the necessity that the judgment which has
not been executed in this world should be executed
in another, as with the necessity that nothing, not
even death, should separate from each other the
God who has pledged His love to men, and the
men who have proved their love and faithfulness
to God.

When we put the doctrine of the resurrection in
this light, it falls into line with that dawning hope
of immortality which can be discerned in the Old
Testament even where the resurrection is not
spoken of. Stated, as it sometimes is, in a bare,
authoritative way, the resurrection loses spiritual
meaning and evidence; it strikes one as scenic or
spectacular rather than spiritual. But side by side
with the *resurrection-faith* of which I have been
speaking, there is a belief in immortality to be
found in the Old Testament which is in substance
the same, though it has not taken the resurrection
form. The typical expression of it is to be found
in Ps. lxxiii. 23 f.: 'Nevertheless I am continually
with Thee: Thou hast holden my right hand.
Thou shalt guide me with thy counsel, and afterward receive me to glory.' A person who is con-

stantly in God's presence, who is conscious that God has held his hand all his life, and sure that He will guide him to the end, cannot believe that death is the end. 'Afterward, thou wilt receive me to glory.' Faith in immortality is here an immediate inference from faith in God, and from the assurance of His gracious guidance all through life. And it is well worth remarking that this is the argument which Jesus uses to the Sadducees.[1] God, He says, said at the bush, I am the God of Abraham, of Isaac, and of Jacob, and *therefore* they live. The argument does not depend for its force on the present tense of the verb (I *am* the God); it depends on the fact that the speaker was to the patriarchs all that is indicated by the name *God*. God pledged His love to these men, led them and fed them all their life long, redeemed them from evil, ministered His grace to them, expended the resources of His providence to discipline them, and make them spiritual men: what for? Was it to see the spirits He had so blessed and fashioned expire in a few years, and never miss them? Was it to be bereaved of the children He had taught by all the experience of life to love and trust Him? Surely not. No one, Jesus argues, who knows what God is, and what God is to men, could draw that conclusion. God called Abraham His friend. Was it possible that God could leave His friend in the dust? Enoch walked with God: and what came after that?[2] God *took* him—the same word as in the 73rd Psalm (receive). *God* took him—not nature, nor disease,

[1] Mark xii. 18-27. [2] Gen. v. 24.

nor death, but He with whom he had walked. This is the real spiritual source and support of the faith in immortality, and the resurrection faith among Old Testament believers was only one form which it assumed. Under the New Testament, faith in the resurrection is not the naïve, not to say crude thing which it was in the popular religion of the Jews; but, refined and transfigured as it is, it is essentially related to this profound trust in the faithfulness of God. When the apostles gave their testimony to the resurrection of Jesus, they not only told that they had seen, heard, and eaten with the Risen One; they said also that God had loosed the bands of death because it was not possible that He should be holden by them. It would have been a denial of God's own nature had one like His Son been permanently overcome by death. Thus faith even in the historical resurrection of Jesus is engrafted into and supported by the older faith in the sure mercy of God to His own, and we have the less cause to overlook this, seeing that there are many minds to which resurrection, apart from it, can hardly become a conviction of faith at all.

But this brings us out of the Old Testament into the New, and it is anticipating the natural order to begin with the Resurrection there. Our Lord, like the prophets, spoke much of the future of God's Kingdom. We find, much more distinctly in His teaching than in theirs, the idea of a course the Kingdom has to run, of a development it has to undergo, before the end comes. Jesus presents this coming history of the Kingdom in different aspects in His parables. Sometimes the prospect

is optimistic, as in the parable of the mustard-seed
and the leaven; the Kingdom is a living germ
which expands into a great tree; it is a potent
force which imparts its own qualities to the whole
mass with which it is in contact. At other times,
again, the outlook is depressing, as in the parable
of the sower, or of the tares and the wheat; the
good seed is in great part thrown away, or its roots
are entangled with those of the devil's plants, and
it has to fight for its life with them to the very end.
But whatever the course of the history may be,
Jesus always contemplates a consummation of it.
There *is* an end. There *is* a final separation.
There *is* an expulsion from the Kingdom of all
scandals and of all that do iniquity, and a glorious
perfecting of the righteous. And all this takes
place at the end of the world—the consummation
of the age—when Christ comes again. To use 'the
Old Testament expression which has been carried
on into the New, it all takes place at the day of
the Lord.

These conceptions of the coming again of Jesus,
and of the day of the Lord, have been the subject
of much discussion. It may be frankly admitted
that the return of Christ to His disciples is capable
of different interpretations. He came again, though
it were but intermittently, when He appeared to
them after His resurrection. He came again, to
abide with them permanently, when His Spirit was
given to the Church at Pentecost. He came, they
would all feel who lived to see it, signally in the
destruction of Jerusalem, when God executed judgment historically on the race which had rejected

Him, and when the Christian church was finally
and decisively liberated from the very possibility of
dependence on the Jewish. He comes still, as His
own words to the high priest suggest—From this
time on ye shall see the Son of Man coming—
in the great crises of history, when the old
order changes, yielding place to new; when God
brings a whole age, as it were, into judgment,
and gives the world a fresh start. But all these
admissions, giving them the widest possible application, do not enable us to call in question what
stands so plainly in the pages of the New Testament,
—what filled so exclusively the minds of the first
Christians—the idea of a Personal Return of Christ
at the end of the world. We need lay no stress on
the scenery of New Testament prophecy, any more
than on the similar element of Old Testament
prophecy; the voice of the archangel and the
trump of God are like the turning of the sun into
darkness and the moon into blood; but if we are
to retain any relation to the New Testament at all,
we must assert the personal return of Christ as
Judge of all.

The reasonableness of this, especially as connected
with the judgment, will be seen if we look at the
alternatives. Those who take a materialistic or
naturalistic view of the world do not need to raise
any questions about its end; it is an essentially
meaningless affair for them, and it does not matter
whether or how it ends. But if we take an ethical
view of the world and of history, we must have an
eschatology: we must have the moral order exhibited, vindicated, brought out in perfect clearness

as what it is. It is because the Bible is so intensely ethical in spirit that it is so rich in eschatological elements—in visions of the final and universal triumph of God, of the final and universal defeat of evil. It is not ethical to suppose that the moral condition of the world is that of an endless suspense, in which the good and the evil permanently balance each other, and contest with each other the right to inherit the earth. Such a dualistic conception is virtually atheistic, and the whole Bible could be read as a protest against it. Neither is it ethical to suppose that the moral history of the world consists of cycles in which the good and the evil are alternately victorious. There are, indeed, times when that is the impression which history makes upon us, but these are times when the senses are too strong for the spirit; and as the moral consciousness recovers its vigour, we see how inconsistent such a view is with its postulate, that the good alone has the right to reign. The Christian doctrine of a final judgment is not the putting of an arbitrary term to the course of history; it is a doctrine without which history ceases to be capable of moral construction. Neither does it signify that there is no judgment here and now, or that we have to wait till the end before we can declare the moral significance, the moral worth or worthlessness, of characters or actions; on the contrary, in the light of that great coming event the moral significance of things stands out even now, and when it does come, it is not to determine, but only to declare, what they are. It would be impossible, I think, to over-estimate the power of this final judgment, as a motive, in the primitive church. On almost every page of St. Paul, for instance, we see that he lives in the presence of it; he lets the awe of it descend upon his heart to keep his conscience quick; he carries on all his work in the light of it; 'before our Lord Jesus, at His coming'—that is the judgment by which he is to be judged, that is the searching light in which his life is to be reviewed. And it needs no lesser faith than this to keep character and conduct at that height of purity and faithfulness which we see in him.

Great part of the modern interest in eschatology begins at this point. The fact of a universal judgment by Christ being admitted, questions are raised as to the principle of the judgment, the issues of it, and perhaps one may say the pre-conditions of it. These are not systematically treated in the New Testament, and hence the variety of opinions regarding them. Perhaps there is greatest agreement in regard to *the principle* of the judgment. That is so far determined by the fact that Christ is the judge: it implies that men will be judged by His standard. But it is here that a certain ambiguity comes in. Christ's standard is no doubt Christ Himself—the man Christ Jesus as He lived on earth; the gospel of John expressly says that all judgment has been committed unto Him, because He is the Son of Man.[1] Can men, therefore, be judged by this standard, unless they know it? Can men be condemned because their lives bear no relation to it, if it has never been presented to them? If the grace and truth that were manifested in Him—if the

[1] John v. 27.

eternal life which in Him was put within man's reach—if these have never been offered to some men, can they be condemned because they do not possess them? In other words, can those who have never heard of the historical Christ, or who, though they have heard His name, have never had the opportunity of knowing what He really is, be judged by Christ and by the standard of the gospel in Him?

At first sight we are tempted to answer No: if these people are to be judged at all, it must be by *a different* standard. Or if they are to be judged by *the Christian* standard, then Christ, who is that standard, must be definitely presented to them; they must have the opportunity of accepting or rejecting the righteousness of God in Him. Many theologians, as you are aware, adopt this last alternative. They teach a doctrine of future probation for the heathen, or perhaps for all who in this life have remained in ignorance of Christ and the gospel. In the intermediate state, they are convinced, between death and the consummation of the age, such persons are prepared for judgment by being brought face to face with Christ, and making the great decision. This theory is protected by great and pious names in, I suppose, all the churches of Christendom, except the Romish, and it may perhaps be entitled to assert itself as a pious opinion. I do not think it is entitled, on Scripture ground, to do so much. It is supported not by express Scripture statements—if we except an isolated passage in 1 Peter, the key to which seems to have been lost—but by inferences from

a Christian principle which strike one as logical
rather than real.[1] When we do look into Scripture,
and especially into our Lord's teaching, our
thoughts are taken on to another line. In the 25th
chapter of Matthew our Lord expressly gives, in
pictorial form, a representation of the judgment
of the heathen. All nations—all the Gentiles—are
gathered before the King; and their destiny is
determined, not by their conscious acceptance or
rejection of the historical Saviour, but by their unconscious acceptance or rejection of Him in the
persons of those who needed services of love.
Those who acknowledge the claim of a brother's
need prove themselves the kindred of Christ and
are admitted to the Kingdom; those who refuse to
acknowledge it prove themselves children of another
family and are shut out. This is unquestionably
Christ's account of the judgment of the heathen,
and it does not square with the idea of a future
probation. It rather tells us plainly that men may
do things of final and decisive import in this life,
even though Christ is unknown to them. I frankly
confess that this is the only view of the matter
which seems to me to keep the ethical value of our
present life at its true height. The idea of a
future probation is not to be rejected, indeed, on
prudential grounds, because, forsooth, in the hope
of another chance men would gamble away the
present one; the hypothesis in question is that
only those have a future probation who have *no*
chance here; the real argument against it is that it
depreciates the present life, and denies the infinite

[1] 1 Peter iii. 18; iv. 6.

significance that under *all* conditions, essentially and inevitably. belongs to the actions of a self-conscious moral being. A type of will, as a recent writer on this subject has put it,[1] may be in process of formation, even in a heathen man, on which eternal issues depend ; and 'Scripture invariably represents the judgment as proceeding on the data of this life, and concentrates every ray of appeal into the present.' Any doctrine, of course, may be abused, and I should never make the abuse of a doctrine of future probation an argument against it, any more than the abuse of the doctrine of pardon an argument against the free grace of God ; but we ought to take care that this conception of a suspense of judgment—of a relative unimportance of the present life under given circumstances—does not lower the moral tone of the spirit unconsciously. I dare not say to myself that if I forfeit the opportunity this life offers I will ever have another ; and therefore I dare not say so to another man. And it is going beyond the truth altogether—it is denying the inalienable greatness and significance of human life—to say that there are men who have no conception of a will of God, no idea of a good by which to regulate their conduct. Christ tells us there is a principle on which even the heathen can be judged *by Him,* judged according to the deeds done in the body : and we cannot afford to have life, even at its lowest, robbed of the awfulness, the grandeur, the absolute moral worth which it thus obtains. The life of humanity is really of a piece, from the lowest level to the highest, and it

[1] See Note A.

is only in some such way as this that its unity can be maintained. We feel indeed the limits of our knowledge at every turn, but while cherishing the largest faith in the goodness and mercy of God, what we need to have developed in us is an intense feeling that if God is anywhere, He is here; if He is near to the soul at any time, it is now; if a decision of eternal consequence can be taken under any circumstances, it can be taken in this world. And we ought to be immensely careful that nothing we say should blunt the acuteness of that feeling, in white men or black, in any country, under any civilisation, at any moral level, with any, greater or less, acquaintance with historical Christianity, *or with none.* What came into the world in Jesus Christ was the true light which lighteneth every man, and no man is quite without it. What that light wins from the heathen may not be what it wins from the disciplined Christian, but it may be enough to prove him Christ's kinsman, and secure his entrance into the Kingdom.

The discussion of future probation has been complicated unnecessarily by introducing reference to its bearings, or supposed bearings, on missions to the heathen. The motive of missions to the heathen is not to be found in the belief that all the heathen who die without having heard the name of Christ are lost for ever. It is to be found in obedience to Christ's command, in devotion to His honour in the world, and in that love, learned of Him, which, looking not on its own things but on the things of others also, longs to impart to those who are yet in darkness the blessings of that light in which itself rejoices. It is the love of Christ which constrains the true evangelist, and not the apprehension of an awful future.

Having considered so far the principle and the pre-conditions of the judgment, let us look now to its issues. In the largest sense, it is the decisive step through which the Kingdom of God attains its consummation and the people of God are perfected. This positive way of looking at it, in which the interest of the Kingdom is the main interest, is the one which predominates in Scripture. When the early Christian hope of the speedy consummation had died out, or nearly so, interest began to be transferred from the fortunes of the Kingdom to the destiny of individuals. It began to busy itself especially with the destiny of those who died apparently outside the Kingdom. I believe it is necessary, if we are to reflect in our minds the true proportion and balance of Scriptural teaching, to escape from this pre-occupation with individuals and exceptions, and to get into the centre and fore-ground of our thoughts God's purpose to perfect His Kingdom and glorify His people. That is the main thing, and an interest in that is accessible to all. The inheritance that is incorruptible, un-defiled, and imperishable, is an inheritance to which we are all called; it is a complete misconception of God's purpose, a complete waste of mental and spiritual energy, to dwell upon the condition of those who do not share it. Why should not all share it? I do not wonder, Ruskin says, at what men suffer; I often wonder at what they lose. God has set before us a great future, a great hope, in

His perfected Kingdom; as far as it has positive
contents, Christian eschatology deals with that, and
with that alone.   Those who do not share it lose it,
and when the time comes the exclusion will be
found awful enough.   The last judgment is the
decisive event through which the Kingdom of God
is consummated, and the state of eternal perfection
begins.

But here a number of questions rise upon us.
The judgment is associated in Scripture with the
resurrection.   Those who are to live for ever with
Christ in glory receive then the spiritual body,
glorious, powerful, incorruptible.   Such, at least,
is the ordinary interpretation of Scripture.   There
are indeed interpreters who read a well-known
passage (2 Cor. v. 1) in a different sense: 'We
know that if our earthly house of this tabernacle be
dissolved, we have a building of God, a house not
made with hands, eternal, in the heavens.'   They
argue from this and the following verses that Paul
shrank in horror from the vague conception of a
disembodied existence, and that in the desire to
escape from it his faith produced the idea of a new
body to be assumed, not at the day of judgment,
but in the very instant of death.   I believe this is a
misinterpretation, and that St. Paul held from first
to last the same faith, that the new body was a
resurrection body, and was not put on till the
judgment-day.   Had he then, it may be asked, or
has the New Testament, any definite conceptions
of the intermediate state, of the interval between
death and judgment?   Had he any conception, or
has the New Testament any, of the condition of the

departed, of their consciousness or unconsciousness, of the possibility or impossibility of mutual intercourse or mutual influence between them and us, of their work, their sufferings, or their joys? Here is a wide open field, in which sentimentalism and presumption have roamed at large. It is significant that on the whole subject the New Testament expresses itself with the utmost reserve. It makes plain that for the Christian death is no longer the king of terrors; it has lost its sting. Paul desires to depart and to be with Christ, which is far better. Christ Himself promises the penitent robber that that very day he shall be with Him in paradise. Whatever that means, it means a condition of conscious blessedness, the essential element in which is furnished by the nearness and the friendship of Christ. This is all matter for faith to grasp, but it yields nothing to imagination. We cannot picture it; the moment we try to do so we defeat our intention, and instead of reinforcing dissipate the impression of reality. It is the truth grasped by the soul which is essential here—that neither death nor life, nor angels nor principalities nor powers, nor things present nor things to come, nor height nor depth, nor any other creature, shall separate us from the love of God in Christ Jesus our Lord—it is this which is essential, and not any imaginative representation of it which we can figure to ourselves. How significant is that word of the dying Saviour—Father, into Thy hands I commend my spirit. That is the last solemn act of faith. It is an act of faith which we must all perform for ourselves if we would die Christians. It is an act

of faith which we must all perform for our nearest
and dearest when they are taken from us. It is a
final resignation of all to God, implying an absolute
confidence in Him, and precluding curiosity or more
special prayers.

I choose to dwell on this last point, because it
has recently attracted attention in Britain, and owing
to the interest in the intermediate state is certain to
do so among you also, if it has not done so already.
The practice of prayer for the dead is widely pre-
valent in the Church of England, though it can
hardly be said to be sanctioned at all by its formu-
laries ; and in a qualified sort of way it has been
defended in a sermon—on The Blessed Dead and
their Commemoration in Prayer by the Church on
Earth—preached to the Scottish Church Society by
a minister of the Established Church of Scotland.
Now in the Church of Rome prayer for the dead is
very intelligible, for it is part of a system ; and it
is represented both in the practice of Romanists
and in their teaching on the scale which one would
expect, if the legitimacy of the practice were conceded. The Romish Church, to those who believe
in it, is a great institute which possesses and
administers all the resources of the divine grace.
Its power and influence in this character extend
not only to the seen but to the unseen world. The
hierarchy with the Pope at its head is able to bless
and relieve man, out of its treasury of merits, not
only while he is in this world, but in the world into
which he passes when he leaves this. There *are*
persons who, when they die, go to heaven, or at
least to blessedness ; these are they who have no

post-baptismal sins to make satisfaction for.   There
are persons also, who, dying in mortal sin, unshriven,
go to hell.   The first need no help from the
Church; the last are beyond the reach of help.
But the great mass of baptized persons, dying with
the Church's absolution, and in no danger of eternal
perdition, yet die without having made the *temporal*
satisfactions which they ought to have made for
their confessed and pardoned sins; and they find
their opportunity of making these, or of making up
for them, in purgatory.   Purgatory is their preparation for acquittal in the judgment; by means of
it they are made meet for the inheritance of the
saints in the light.   The souls in purgatory, however, are within reach of the Church's help.   They
can be benefited by the prayers of friends, just as
they could while they were in trouble in this life;
they can be benefited, especially, by the sacrifice of
the mass, offered, and paid for, on their behalf;
they can be benefited also by any penal works, or
works of satisfaction, performed in their name—such
as alms, fasting, and pilgrimages.   All this, I repeat,
is very intelligible, as part of a system, and it bulks
in Romish teaching and practice as we should
expect it to bulk; but I hardly need to argue
against it here.   The whole conception of purgatory
on which it depends—the whole conception of an
intermediate state in which our interposition can
be real and effective—is foreign to the New Testament; no scholar would think of defending it.   But
with this conception goes the whole conception of
intercession for the dead which is dependent upon
it, and with this it agrees that the New Testament

presents no unequivocal trace of any such thing.
The single expression appealed to in support of it
is the ejaculation of St. Paul in 2 Tim. ii. 18 : The
Lord grant to him to find mercy from the Lord in
that day. The person referred to is Onesiphorus, and
even granting that he was dead when St. Paul wrote
this, which is by no means beyond doubt, it seems
to me absurd to derive from such an ejaculation a
defence of anything that could seriously be called
' prayer for the dead.'   The most determined
opponent of any such practice might say of a good
man who had helped him, but who had gone beyond
the reach of *his* help, God reward him in that day,
and say it without compromising his opposition in
the least.   It is not this kind of thing which people
mean when they speak of prayers for the dead.
Neither is it the consciousness, when we pray for
the perfecting of Christ's Kingdom, that those who
have died in the Lord, the great cloud of witnesses
by whom we are encompassed, and who without us
are not to be made perfect, have an interest in the
consummation as well as we.   Christians have
always included the saints who are with the Lord
in their conception of the Church; they have
always understood that they, as well as we who are
alive and remain, are interested in the coming of
the Lord, and the manifestation of His glory ; but
when they pray for that coming and manifestation,
as the goal of the Church's hope, it is misdescribing
the exercise altogether, to call it, because departed
saints are also to be glorified, prayer for the dead.
I should think every one felt such a description
utterly misleading ; it uses, to point out *one*

thing, a name which suggests another totally different.

Those also, we cannot but remark, who justify prayer for the dead, although they limit it to prayer for the coming of the Kingdom, in which the dead and the living are equally interested, justify it by reasons which point directly to prayers of a different kind. Thus Dr. Plummer calls it 'a pious practice, full of comfort to affectionate souls'; Dr. Cooper says such prayers afford 'a legitimate relief to the Christian mourner, and supply an exercise wherewith to keep alive his love'; and Mr. Strong, a far abler man than either, says 'the use of it will probably depend very much upon individual feelings.'[1] I do not hesitate to say that all these expressions point to a kind of prayer for the dead which is unexampled in Scripture, and on spiritual grounds without justification. They point to the continued use for the dead of such intercessions as we made for them while they were yet alive. But such intercessions would virtually deny the absolute moral significance of this life, and would only be consistent with the idea that there was no real crisis marked by death, and that the spiritual conditions were the same after as before it. Further, they would introduce an unreal idea of intercession itself. Our prayer is not real unless it is the soul of effort: we do not truly intercede for a man when he is living unless we put ourselves at God's disposal for that man's service. We pledge ourselves to make common cause with him in his spiritual interests, to speak to him, to love him, to plead

[1] See Note B.

with him, perhaps to reprove him, to bring him under every spiritual constraint conceivable for his good. We have no right to pray for him at all unless we do this; and when death enters, and changes all the conditions, and puts him beyond our reach, as it does, then, with the readiness to minister, the time for prayer comes also to an end. It is not only a greater proof of trust in God—it is a greater proof of love to the departed—to say once for all, Father, into Thy hands we commend his spirit, than to indulge, under the name of prayers, affectionate wishes which may stand in no relation whatever to his actual condition, and which deprave the very idea of prayer. It is good for us to realise the tremendousness of death—which is only another way of saying the infinite value of this life; it is good for us to exercise that awful final act of faith. It does not deaden the tenderness of any natural affection : but it redeems it from all that is merely natural by lifting life up, in that last solemn crisis, out of nature, to eternity and God.

But to return again to the main subject. Whatever the conditions of existence in the intermediate state may be—whatever spiritual experiences or progress the saints may have in their time of blessedness awaiting perfect bliss—and of this we can say literally nothing—the New Testament teaches us to expect the consummation only after Resurrection and Judgment. Almost all theologians include in their interpretation of this a reference to the perfecting of nature. Here, at least, there is no room for dogmatism. That the environment of the blessed will match with their constitution we cannot doubt; creation itself will be delivered from the bondage of corruption into the liberty of the glory of the children of God. But what precisely is involved in this we cannot tell. If the universe is essentially spirit, sin must have disorganising and corruptive effects reaching to its utmost limits, and the New Testament suggests that redemption reaches equally far. There is a reconciliation to God not only of sinful men, but of all things, both on earth and in the heavens; a reconsecration of the universe, as of a temple that sin had profaned. That is of a piece with the whole Christian conception of God, man, nature, and sin; and in its place in the Christian system it is credible enough. But it is not intelligible if it be torn from its Christian context, and it can never be proved alone. Even in the New Testament it impresses one as grand poetry does; we dare not paraphrase it; to put it into any other than its original form is to lose its virtue altogether. The theologians who dispute whether the earth is to be transfigured only, or whether it is to be destroyed and replaced, or whether the change in us is to make the world new, seem to me to be engaged in a hopeless task. Let us put everything we can, except prose, into the great word of the Apocalypse: He that sitteth on the throne saith, Behold, I make all things new.

On the reverse side of the judgment it is not necessary to dwell. But we dare not conceal from ourselves, that according to the express teaching of Scripture, there *is* a reverse side. Dogmatic universalism is equally unscriptural and unethical; the very conception of human freedom involves the possibility of its permanent misuse, or of what our Lord Himself calls 'eternal sin.'[1] And we cannot overlook, what has often been pointed out, that the sternest and most inexorable language which the New Testament contains on this awful subject is to be found in our Lord's own lips. No one speaks so decisively as He of the broad way which leads to destruction, and of the narrow way which leads to life; of the outer darkness, and of the light of the banqueting hall; of the worm that dies not, and the fire that is not quenched; of the sheep and the goats; the everlasting punishment and the everlasting life. 'You seem, sir,' said Mrs. Adams to Dr. Johnson, in one of his despondent hours, when the fear of death and judgment lay heavy on him, 'to forget the merits of our Redeemer.' 'Madam,' said the honest old man, 'I do not forget the merits of my Redeemer; but my Redeemer has said that He will set some on His right hand and some on His left.' Imagination quails, if it seeks to give definiteness to the tremendous suggestions of these words, and perhaps the whole subject is one on which imagination should have nothing to say. The ideas which seem to me to comprehend all that is of faith on the subject are those of separation and of finality. There is such a thing as being excluded from fellowship with God and with good spirits; there is such a thing as final exclusion. It is not for us to say on whom this awful sentence falls, or whether they are many or few; we can trust the God and Father of our Lord

[1] Mark iii. 29.

Jesus Christ that it will not fall on any who do not freely and deliberately pronounce it themselves. The glory of heaven, rather than the privation of the lost, ought to fill our hearts and our imaginations as we look forward to the end : God has not appointed us to wrath, but to obtain salvation through our Lord Jesus Christ.

What has been already said will sufficiently indicate how I should regard the theory of conditional immortality. The religious truth and power of it lie in this—that it brings the positive Christian contents into the forefront of eschatology : it preaches life in Christ, and life in Christ only. So far I agree ; there is nothing worthy of the name of life outside of Him. But when this theory, right in its great affirmation, goes on to deny that man can exist after death, without being united to Christ by faith, I cannot confidently follow it. It seems to bring a relief to the feelings, but it does not permanently do so. The immortality of man cannot be something accidental, something appended to his nature, after he believes in Christ ; it must be something, at the very lowest, for which his nature is constituted, even if apart from Christ.it can never realise itself as it ought. The doctrine will always attract new minds from time to time, because of the truth embodied in its watchword ; it has done good service in helping to restore attention to, and to concentrate it on, the blessed consummation to be attained in Christ ; but it is, I fear, one of those half-way houses in which neither human intelligence nor Christian faith can consent permanently to dwell.

Gentlemen, here our conference ends. I count it a high honour and privilege that the authorities of this seminary have given me these opportunities of speaking to you on the great things of God. I am conscious of the imperfection with which it has been done; but I have spoken to you from my heart, telling you without ambiguity and without reserve how I have been led to think and feel about them. I cannot imagine that you have gone with me in every word; there may have been subjects on which our thoughts or our prepossessions were too far apart for us rightly to appreciate each other; but I have tried to be of service to you, and I thank you most heartily for the patience and constancy with which you have come to hear me.

NOTES

LECTURE I

Note A, p. 3.

There is a reference, through these Lectures as a whole, to that type of theologising which has its most conspicuous representative, and in some sense its source, in Ritschl. Of Ritschl's own works I have used principally his *Rechtfertigung und Versöhnung* and his *Unterricht in der christlichen Religion.* Bornemann's *Unterricht im Christenthum* is a luminous and interesting book of the same sympathies. Herrmann's *Der Verkehr des Christen mit Gott* is provokingly devoid of order and method, but gives a more vivid impression than any other production of the school of the real religious interest which animates most of its adherents. Harnack's *Dogmengeschichte* represents the same general conception of Christianity, and no more than this is meant, in some cases not even so much, by the occasional references to such writers as Wendt (*Die Lehre Jesu*), Schultz (*Grundriss der evangelischen Dogmatik*), F. A. B. Nitzsch (*Lehrbuch der evangelischen Dogmatik*). By far the fullest and most thorough-going discussion of all the questions involved is to be had in Professor Orr's *Christian View of God and the World*, and apart from special references I take this opportunity of expressing my great obligations to that work.

Note B, p. 8.

See Orr's *Christian View of God and the World*, p. 45 ff., where the passages from Ritschl and Herrmann are quoted.

Note C, p. 11.

Ritschl's views on miracle are given most plainly in his *Unterricht*, § 17. The positive part is clear. Die religiöse Betrachtung der Welt ist darauf gestellt, dass alle Naturereignisse zur Verfügung Gottes stehen, wenn er den Menschen helfen will. Demgemäss gelten als Wunder solche auffallende Naturerscheinungen mit welchen die Erfahrung besonderer Gnadenhilfe Gottes verbunden ist, welche also als besondere Zeichen seiner Gnadenbereitschaft für die Gläubigen zu betrachten sind. Deshalb steht die Vorstellung von Wundern in nothwendiger Wechselbeziehung zu dem besondern Glauben an Gottes Vorsehung, und ist ausserhalb dieser Beziehung gar nicht möglich.' After this he proceeds: 'Man begeht eine vollständige Verschiebung der religiösen Vorstellung vom Wunder, wenn man sie von vornherein an der wissenschaft-

lichen Annahme von dem gesetzlichen Zusammenhang aller Natur-
vorgänge misst.' The religious conception of miracle he holds
quite compatible with this assumption. But then comes the virtual
surrender of the Biblical facts. Wenn jedoch gewisse Erzählungen
von Wundern in den biblischen Büchern gegen diese Regel zu
verstossen scheinen [it is much more than 'scheinen'], so ist es
weder eine wissenschaftliche Aufgabe, diesen Schein zu lösen oder
ihn als Thatsache festzustellen, noch ist est eine religiöse Aufgabe,
jene erzählte Ereignisse als göttliche Wirkungen gegen die natur-
gesetze anzuerkennen. Man soll auch nicht seinen religiösen
Glauben an Gott und Christus aus einem vorausgehenden Urtheil
der Art schöpfen (John iv. 18; Isa. viii. 11, 12; 1 Cor. i. 22),
zumal da jede Wundererfahrung schon den Glauben voraussetzt.
*Aus dem religiösen Glauben aber wird jeder an sich selbst Wunder
erleben, und im Vergleich damit ist nichts weniger nothwendig, als
dass man über die Wunder grübele, welche Andere erfahren haben.*
Cf. the discussion in Bornemann's *Unterricht*, § 43, whose summary
is : Rechter Wunderglaube ist nichts anderes als der rechte leben-
dige Vorsehungsglaube unter bestimmten Umständen des Lebens
und der Geschichte. But the questions of fact which this leaves
open are not indifferent to the Christian religion (as *e.g.* the gospel
narratives of the miracles wrought by Jesus, and especially the
miracle of His resurrection), and faith requires us to meet and
answer them.

NOTE D, p. 12.

See Harnack's *Dogmengeschichte* i. 50, note 4 (first edition). Der
Historiker ist nicht im Stande, mit einem Wunder als einem sicher
gegebenen geschichtlichen Ereigniss zu *rechnen*; denn er hebt damit
die Betrachtungsweise auf, auf welcher alle geschichtliche Forschung
beruht. Jedes einzelne Wunder bleibt geschichtlich völlig zweifel-
haft, und die Summation des zweifelhaften führt niemals zu einer
Gewissheit. Ueberzeugt sich der Historiker trotzdem aber, dass
Jesus Christus Ausserordentliches, im strengen Sinn Wunderbares
gethan hat, so schliesst er von einem sittlich-religiösen Eindruck,
welchen er von dieser Person gewonnen hat, auf eine übernatürliche
Macht derselben. Dieser Schluss gehört selbst dem Gebiet des
religiösen Glaubens an. Es lässt sich aber ein starker religiöser
Glaube an die Herrschaft und Zwecksetzung des Göttlichen und
Guten in der Welt denken, welcher eines solchen Schlusses nicht
bedarf. The inference which is silently drawn, and acted upon,
is that to the Christian faith, in its proper strength, the supernatural power of Jesus, and His miracles, are matter of indifference.

NOTE E, p. 13.

The Godhead of Christ is fully discussed by Ritschl in *Rechtfertigung und Versöhnung*, vol. iii. pp. 364-455. Brief statements
are also given in his *Unterricht*, especially in §§ 22-24. In the
last he writes : Dieses Attribut (die Gottheit Christi) kann nämlich

nicht vollzogen werden, wenn nicht dieselben Thätigkeiten, durch welche Jesus Christus sich als Menschen bewährt, in derselben Beziehung und Zeit als eigenthümliche Prädicate Gottes und als die eigenthümlichen Mittel seiner Offenbarung durch Christus gedacht werden. Sind aber die Gnade und Treue, und die Herrschaft über die Welt, welche in der Handlungsweise wie in der Leidensgeduld Christi anschaulich sind, die wesentlichen, für die christliche Religion entscheidende Attribute Gottes, so wird eben die richtige Schätzung der Vollkommenheit der Offenbarung Gottes durch Christus in dem Prädicate seiner Gottheit sicher gestellt, unter welchem die Christen ihm wie Gott dem Vater zu vertrauen und Anbetung zu widmen haben. Bornemann apparently concedes more than Ritschl to the New Testament representations of Christ. Thus he writes : ' *Die Gewissheit der Auferstehung und göttlichen Erhöhung Jesu und der Mittheilung des göttlichen Geistes durch ihn vollendet sich in dem Glauben an die Gottheit Jesu.*'— *Unterricht*, p. 89. Yet what is said in the text applies to him also, for he peremptorily refuses to raise any questions as to what this 'godhead' presupposes or involves. Like Ritschl he quotes Melanchthon—*Scriptura sacra docet nos de filii divinitate non tantum speculative, sed practice, hoc est, jubet nos ut Christum invocemus, ut confidamus Christo ; sic enim vere tribuetur ei honos divinitatis*—but they both seem to disregard the *tantum*. The view of the subject given in Schultz is virtually the same. ' Christus ist uns Mensch, und nur Mensch, —wenn wir ihn mit uns zusammen Gott gegenüber anschauen (ethisch). Er ist uns Gott, wenn wir ihn als die Offenbarung Gottes für uns betrachten (religiös). Nur auf Grund seiner menschlichen sittlichen Persönlichkeit kann er uns Gott sein, —und *diese* sittliche Persönlichkeit ist nur als Selbst offenbarung Gottes zu begreifen.' And on the origin of Christ's personality he says : ' So muss sie (die Persönlichkeit Christi) für den Glauben ein Wunder aus dem Majestätsgeheimnisse des schaffenden Geistes Gottes sein. Dass sie aber auch ein Nature wunder nach Seite ihrer natürlichen Entstehung sein müsste, das folgt aus dem dogmatischen interesse in keiner Weise.' But this is only to say in explanation of Christ's personality what must be said of every human personality without exception.

NOTE F, p. 18.

See Harnack, *Dogmengeschichte* i. 57 f. *Glauben an die Person Jesu* war die entscheidende Grundforderung und, zunächst unter der Voraussetzung der Religion Abrahams und der Propheten, die sichere Gewahr der Seligkeit. So ist es nicht wunderbar dass uns in der ältesten christlichen Verkündigung ' Jesus Christus' eben so häufig entgegentritt, wie in der Verkündigung Jesu selbst das Gottesreich. Was man wirklich besass, war das Bild Jesu und die Kraft die von ihm ausgegangen war ; was man erwartete, erwartete man nur von Jesus, dem Erhöhten und Wiederkehrenden. *So musste die Predigt, dass das Himmelreich nahe herbeigekommen, zu der Predigt werden, dass Jesus der Christ sei, und dass alle Offen-*

barungen Gottes in ihm ihren Abschluss gefunden haben. Wer Jesum ergreift, ergreift in ihm die Gnade Gottes selbst und alles Heil. Man kann dies an sich noch nicht eine Verschiebung nennen ; aber sobald nicht mehr mit demselben Nachdruck verkündet wurde, was es im Sinne Jesu bedeute, dass er der Christ sei, und wie beschaffen die Güter seien, die er gebracht. *war nicht nur eine Verschiebung unvermeidlich, sondern auch eine Entleerung.* What this amounted to, he explains a little further on. Somit vereinigte sich alles um die ersten Gemeinden zu der Ueberzeugung zu bringen, dass die ihnen anvertraute Verkündigung des Evangeliums in der Verkündigung von Jesus als dem Christus aufgehe. Das ' διδάσκειν τηρεῖν πάντα ὅσα ἐνετείλατο ὁ Ἰησοῦς ' —eine Sache des Gemüths und Lebens—konnte nicht in demselben Masse zum Nachdenken anleiten wie das ' διδάσκειν ὅτι οὗτός ἐστιν ὁ Χριστὸς τοῦ Θεοῦ ; ' denn eine Gemeinde, die den Geist besitzt, reflectirt nicht darüber, ob ihr Verständniss ein zutreffendes ist, wohl aber—namentlich eine missionirende—darüber, worauf die Gewissheit ihres Glaubens beruhe. But surely reflection on this last point can never be out of date.

LECTURE II

Note A, p. 30.

The passage translated is from Didon's *Jésus Christ,* i. p. 452. Cf. an earlier passage, i. 418 f.: ' La dernière chose que l'homme accorde est la foi totale. Même en prodiguant l'admiration, le dévoument, les services, l'enthousiasme, et jusqu'à sa confiance, il garde ses idées, ses volontés, ses intérêts, et il se réserve, prêt à se reprendre, dès qu'il se sentira choqué dans ses idées, contrarié dans ses volontés et menacé dans ses intérêts. Personne, d'ailleurs, n'a le droit de démander la foi absolue. En la réclamant pour lui-même, Jésus s'est élevé au-dessus de l'humanité, il s'est placé plus haut que Moïse, il s'est fait l'égal de Dieu.'

LECTURE III

Note A, p. 49.

The merely negative relation to the Resurrection of Christ, assumed by the writers referred to in the text, is of decisive consequence in their theology. Thus Ritschl in his great work *Recht. und Versöhnung,* which covers the whole ground of dogmatics, has no eschatology, and refuses to connect Christ's Kingship with His exaltation after death. In his *Unterricht* he writes (§ 77) : Wie sich eine zusammenhängende Theorie von den letzten Dingen durch die Benutzung der Data des N. T. überhaupt nicht erreichen lässt, so *bleiben auch die Andeutungen im N. T., welche dem Zustande der Beseligten und Verdammten gelten, jenseits der Möglichkeit einer deutlichen*

Vorstellung. To admit Christ's resurrection as the New Testament teaches it would of course be inconsistent with his teaching on miracle (see Note C to Lecture I.). In much the same fashion Harnack says : In Bezug auf die Eschatologie vermag im Einzelnen Niemand zu sagen, was von Christus und was von den Jüngern herrührt. Gegen den Eindruck dass Jesus Tag und Stunde Gott vorbehalten und in Gottergebung und Geduld gewirkt hat, so lange es für ihn Tag gewesen, kommen einzelne Stellen der Evangelien, die in eine andere Richtung führen, nicht auf. (*Dogmengeschichte,* i. 51, *n.* 2). Wendt gives an elaborate discussion of the whole subject in his *Lehre Jesu,* ii. pp. 542-559 (*Die himmlische Zukunft des Messias*). He declines to accept in their traditional sense Jesus' words foretelling His resurrection, and he declines in the same way to accept the resurrection itself as the New Testament relates it. 'Jesus hat den Gedanken, dass auch er selbst durch den Tod in das Todtenreich hinabgeführt werde, nicht abgelehnt (Lc. xxiii. 43); aber wie er die allgemeine Gewissheit hatte, dass die Frommen, welche Gott als zu sich gehörige anerkannte, wegen dieses unzerreissbaren Verhältnisses trotz des Scheol zum himmlischen Auferstehungsleben bei Gott gelangen müssten (Mc. xii. 26 f.), so hat er auch geurtheilt, dass er selbst als der in der engsten Gemeinschaft mit Gott stehende Sohn nicht erst nach unabsehbaren Dauer, sondern in kürzester Frist aus dem Scheol zum himmlischen Leben aufsteigen werde. Drei Tage sind für ihn, auf Grund des herrschenden Spachgebrauchs (Hos. vi. 2 ; Lc. xiii. 32 ; John ii. 19), Bezeichnung für eine kürzeste Frist' (p. 545). Similarly he says further on (p. 556) 'that the certainty of Jesus that He would rise again from death to the heavenly life was not an expression of His specially Messianic consciousness, but only an inference from the fact that He regarded as good for Himself that hope of a blessed life in heaven which was good for all members of the Kingdom of God.' This seems to me an excellent example of how to make the New Testament unintelligible.

NOTE B, p. 51.

This antithesis is Grétillat's : ' Aujourd'hui, donc, le champ de la discussion ne laisse plus de place qu'à deux antithèses. L'une remplace le Dieu-Homme par l'Homme-Dieu, le Fils donné par le Père à l'humanité par le saint offert par l'humanité à son Dieu ; l'homme promu à la dignité divine par l'excellence de ses qualités humaines, mais dont l'existence glorieuse et éternelle dans l'avenir a commencé avec sa naissance humaine . . . L'autre opinion, rétenant l'élément fixe et incontesté du dogme christologique : la pré-existence personelle et éternelle de Christ, mais pour l'associer à une humanité non moins réelle, plus réelle même que la nôtre, a voulu prendre enfin au sérieux les déclarations de l'Écriture concernant le mystère insondable, mais non pas inintelligible, de l'anéantissement (κένωσις) du Fils de Dieu.'—*Exposé de Théologie Systématique,* vol. iv. p. 166 f.

Note C, p. 53.

The Pre-existence of Christ is discussed on the line here criticised by Bornemann in his *Unterricht im Christenthum* (§ 35. Die Voraussetzungen und Anlagen der Person Jesu Christi). Es handelt sich hier, he says (in reference to Paul's teaching) *um die selbstverständliche Anwendung eines bereits im Judenthum für den Messias feststehenden Attributs auf Jesum.* Apart from the criticism in the text, more is asserted here than can be proved. The only evidence for a Jewish belief in the pre-existence of the Messiah (if it *were* evidence) would be that which is found in the *Similitudes* in the Book of Enoch. But it is by no means certain that this part of the book is pre-Christian, and even if it were, the Messianic doctrine which it teaches is, as its latest editor, Mr. Charles, remarks, 'unique not only as regards the other sections of Enoch, but also in Jewish literature as a whole.' It is not 'selbstverständlich' that a conception so isolated should be immediately applied to Christ by His disciples. Bornemann, of course, like all writers of the same sympathies, minimises the importance of the question. 'Die Erörterung der Voraussetzungen der Person und des Werkes Jesu Christi ist mehr eine Sache der Theologie als der christlichen Religion. Jesus ist nicht dazu erschienen dass wir Menschen das Geheimniss seines Wesens wissenschaftlich lösen sollten, sondern dazu, dass er uns die Lösung des praktischen Räthsel des Menschenlebens darböte.' Cf. Schultz, *Grundriss der Evangelischen Dogmatik*, S. 95, who deliberately sets aside the apostolic interpretations of Christ's Person. 'An die besondere Art, wie sich die theologisch gebildeten Schriftsteller des N. T. dieses Geheimniss gemäss der gegebenen Art ihrer metaphysischen Vorstellungen zurechtgelegt haben, kann die christliche Dogmatik sich nicht gebunden fühlen.' The pre-existence is defended, with these considerations in view, in Grétillat's *Théologie Systématique*, ut supra.

Note D, p. 57.

One of the best and most accessible presentations of Kenotic Christology is to be found in Godet's Commentary on John, ch. i. vv. 1-18. A most valuable account and criticism of the principal writers and their views may be seen in Dr. Bruce's *Humiliation of Christ*, Lecture IV.

Note E, p. 57.

The sentences following the mention of Mr Gore's name are a summary of the pages in his Sixth Bampton Lecture, in which he discusses the *motive* of the Incarnation, and its *method* as conceived by St. Paul.

Note F, p. 58.

The last two sentences in this paragraph virtually reproduce expressions of Principal Rainy, in his exposition of Philippians. ('Expositor's Bible Series.')

NOTE G, p. 59.

See the fine characterisation of John's Christology by Principal Fairbairn,—*Christ in Modern Theology*, p. 345 f. The contrast he draws between Paul and John is striking and relatively true ; I am not so sure, when he contrasts John in the same way with the writer to the Hebrews, that the procedure is as sound. 'Christ is to him (*i.e.* to the author of Hebrews) the Archetype, the Antitype, the Son, the High Priest, the symbol of the most exalted idea ; but *He is not Jesus*, handled with the fondness of a love made tender by memory and sweet by hope.' Jesus, might not one rather say, is precisely what He is ; the writer even affects this name for Him more than is usual in the New Testament, employing it alone at least ten times. I only allude to this because I have often felt that, so far as its New Testament support is concerned, the theology of Ritschl, as opposed to historical Protestant theology, really amounts to an attempt to displace the *Christ* of the Pauline epistles in favour of the *Jesus* of the Epistle to the Hebrews—the object of the Christian's worship, by the religious subject whose perfect human life is our reconciliation to God. I believe it is a diffused sympathy with this which accounts for the unusual amount of study that has lately been bestowed on Hebrews.

NOTE H, p. 60.

The passage referred to in Harnack is one of the most striking that has ever been written on this subject. It is as follows (*Dogmengeschichte*, i. 66) : 'Die Entstehung der johanneischen Schriften ist übrigens, litterar- und dogmen-geschichtlich betrachtet, das wundervollste Räthsel, welches die älteste Geschichte des Christenthums darbietet. Die Verweisung auf Philo und den Hellenismus reicht hier gar nicht aus, sofern sie nicht einmal eine Aussenseite des Problems befriedigend erklärt. Nicht griechische Theologumena sind in der johanneischen Theologie wirksam gewesen— selbst der Logos hat mit dem Philonischen wenig mehr als den Namen gemein—sondern aus dem alten Glauben der Propheten und Psalmisten ist unter dem Eindruck der Person Jesu hier ein neuer Glaube geworden. Eben darum ist der Verfasser unzweifelhaft und trotz seines schroffen Antijudaismus für einen geborenen Juden, seine Theologie für eine christlich-palästinensische zu halten.'

NOTE I, p. 62.

Wendt admits the genuineness of the words in John xvii. 5, and John viii. 58. His interpretation of them may be seen in his *Lehre Jesu*, ii. 464-472. Das, was direct in diesen Worten (John xvii. 5) ausgedrückt wird, ist also das uranfängliche Vorhandengewesensein der himmlischen Herrlichkeit, welche Gott dem Messias zum Besitze bestimmt hat; Voraussetzung dieser Aussage ist aber allerdings der Gedanke, welcher am Schlusse des Gebetes in v. 24 einen bestimmten Ausdruck findet, dass Jesus selbst als der Messias von Uranfang her, *zwar nicht real* bei Gott existirt hat, wohl aber der Gegenstand der Liebe Gottes, seiner liebenden Vorstellungen, Pläne und Ordnungen gewesen ist. The other passage (viii. 58) he succeeds in explaining in the same way, and concludes : ' Den Unterschied, welchen wir Modernen machen zwischen ideellem Sein und Gelten und realem Sein, hat Jesus nicht *ausgedrückt,*—wie ihn überhaupt die Alten nicht bestimmt ausgedrückt haben. *Ob aber auch der deutliche Ausdruck fehlt und die Rede so gestaltet ist, als handele es sich um reales Sein, können wir doch aus dem Zusammenhange ersehen, dass an ein ideelles Sein gedacht ist,* und müssen zur Erklärung unsererseits jenen begrifflichen Unterschied deutlich hervorheben.'

NOTE K, p. 63.

Bornemann's opinion has been already referred to in Note C above. On the point in question here he writes (*Unterricht,* p. 92): ' Im N. T. finden sich besonders drei verschiedene Wege, das göttliche Wesen der menschlich geschichtlichen Person Jesu Christi schon aus ihrem Ursprung deutlich zu machen: die Gedanken (*a*) der übernatürlichen Geburt, (*b*) der Präexistenz, und (*c*) der Menschwerdung des ewigen göttlichen Offenbarungsworts (λόγος). Dabei ist zu beachten, dass diese Ideen unabhängig voneinander und nebeneinander dastehen, als selbständige, aber disparate Versuche, das Geheimniss des Lebens Jesu in seinem göttlichen Ursprunge zu ergründen.'

NOTE L, p. 66.

F. A. B. Nitzsch, whose *Lehrbuch der Evangelischen Dogmatik* was completed in 1892, belongs to what he himself calls the (positive) critical school, and on the doctrine of the Person of Christ, expresses himself as follows :—' An die Stelle zweier verschieden Naturen ist eine Doppelheit von Gesichtspunkten zu setzen, nach denen die ihrer psychologischen Form nach rein menschliche einheitliche Person des Heilsmittlers betrachtet werden muss. Nach der einen Richtung . . . ist Christus der heilige Mensch, nach der anderen wird er aus dem göttlichen Motive seiner *Sendung* angeschaut ; er ist nach diesem zweiten Gesichtspunkte der *Botschafter* im eminenten Sinne, der *Repräsentant* Gottes, durch welchen das Princip der göttlichen Gnade der Welt unmittelbar *offenbart* worden ist. Die erstere Benennung gilt der Persönlichkeit für sich, die andere dem Ganzen ihrer Erscheinung und Wirksamkeit als der Grossthat Gottes in der Menschheit. Das sind freilich keine zwei Naturen mehr, aber es sind doch zwei nothwendige Auffassungen, welche auf Einem Punkte zusammentreffen, und *sich in einem Grade einigen, wie dies an keiner anderen Stelle des religiosen Menschenlebens auch nur annähernd stattfindet.*' Why should Christ have a place in theology at all, if all you can say of him is, Look where you will among religious men, and you will not find one anywhere who is even approximately as good as He?

LECTURE IV

NOTE A, p. 79.

Ritschl's Doctrine of Sin is expounded in chap. v. of the third volume of his *Rechtfertigung und Versöhnung*, and in §§ 26-33 of his *Unterricht in der christ. Religion.* His main idea is expressed, positively and negatively, in these two sentences. Die Vorstellung von dem vollständigen gemeinschaftlichen Guten in dem Begriff des Reiches Gottes und die Vorstellung von der persönlichen Güte im Begriff Gottes und in der Anschauung von Christus begründen in der christlischen Gemeinde eine entsprechende Vorstellung vom Bösen und von der Sünde . . . Es ist unmöglich, die dem Christenthum entsprechende Einsicht in die Sünde vor der Erkenntniss dessen zu gewinnen, was im Sinne des Christenthums gut ist. This is quite true ; still the 'law' precedes the 'gospel,' and Christ *came* to save sinners, who were really sinners, and really needed salvation, though they did not know Him. Ritschl summarises his view (*R. u. V.* iii. p. 363) as follows :—*Sofern die Menschen als Sünder im Einzelnen wie in der Gesammtheit Objecte der aus der Liebe Gottes möglichen Erlösung und Versöhnung sind, wird die Sünde von Gott nicht als die endgiltige Absicht des Widerspruchs gegen den erkannten Willen Gottes, sondern als Unwissenheit betrachtet.*

NOTE B, p. 92.

The conceptions of righteousness, holiness, and wrath, in God, are treated by Ritschl in the manner here described. Righteousness is never vindicative, or distributive : it is God's fidelity to His purpose to bless His people. It is necessary, indeed, of a passage like Acts xvii. 31, to say, that though 'righteousness' evidently refers to the Gerichtsübung Gottes. the sense of this reference bleibt unbestimmt ! The holiness of God has as good as disappeared in the New Testament (*R. u. V.* ii. p. 100) ; the function which it performed in the old Covenant is performed in the new by God's love. As for the wrath of God, which has certainly a place in the scriptures of Old and New Testament alike, he sums up boldly thus : Ich habe kein Interesse daran zu wissen, dass Gott überhaupt gut ist, wenn ich nicht zugleich weiss, dass er es gegen mich und Andere ist. Ebensowenig Interesse kann es gewähren, im Allgemeinen den Zornaffect als Attribut Gottes zu denken, ohne dass man sich getrauen dürfte gewisse Erscheinungen in der christlichen Welt unter diesen Begriff zu subsumiren. Ist aber dieses verboten, so hat die Vorstellung vom Zornaffect Gottes für Christen keinen religiösen Werth, sondern ist nur ein ebenso heimathloses wie gestaltloses Theologumenon. (*R. u. V.* ii. p. 154.)

NOTE C, p. 98.

The whole of this discussion of the relation of sin and death follows that of Professor Orr in his *Christian View of God and the World*, p. 228 ff.

LECTURE V

NOTE A, p. 112.

See the passage from Galatians discussed in Fairbairn's *Christ in Modern Theology*, p. 480 f. Dr. Fairbairn writes: ' Christ hath redeemed us from the curse of the law ; ' certainly, but this was the law which the Jew loved, and which was thus for ever abolished, not the universal law of God. He became ' a curse for us '; certainly, but under the same law, for by it he was ' hanged upon a tree.' But the law that thus judged Him condemned itself; by cursing Him it became accursed. His death was not the vindication, but the condemnation of the law.' I confess myself quite unable to take this seriously. Paul could never have imagined a distinction between ' the law which the Jew loved,' and ' the universal law of God,' especially when the law to which he refers is expressly cited from the Old Testament, as in the present case it is. And in the third chapter of Romans he teaches in set terms, what Dr. Fairbairn in set terms denies, viz., that Christ's death *is* the vindication of the law. ' Do we then make void the law by faith (*i.e.* faith in Christ's atoning death, as the passage preceding explains it)? No : we establish the law.'

NOTE B, p. 120.

Many critics object to the historicity of the Baptist's testimony to Jesus in John i. 29, that the forerunner cannot have known the full Christian truth, or seen the end from the beginning. But (1) the Forerunner, according to Jesus' own word, was greater than the greatest of prophets, and at least in the moments when he was face to face with Jesus, may have been conscious that here was He of whom the prophet spoke (Isa. liii.), the sin-bearer, the Lamb that God had provided as a sacrifice for the world's sin. (2) A special illumination of the Baptist's mind in that crisis of his ministry when Jesus came to him to be baptized, acknowledged, and pointed out to the people, is not only natural, but is assured by what we are told of the circumstances accompanying our Lord's baptism. And

(3) the psychological preparation for such an understanding of Christ's vocation is given by John's own failure to overcome the sin of the world in other ways. Sin, experience taught him, was nót to be swept out of the world by sudden, violent assault ; it can only be overcome by being borne ; and in Jesus he saw that spirit, other than his own, and mightier, which should bear it.

LECTURE VI

NOTE A, p. 135.

Cf. Wendt, *Die Lehre Jesu* ii. p. 504 f. : 'Wie sich diese Erkenntniss der Nothwendigkeit und des Werthes seines Todes allmählich bei ihm entwickelt hat, können wir jetzt nicht wehr im Einzelnen feststellen, weil unsere Quellen nicht das Material dazu bieten. Aber wohl können wir auf Grund des Verständnisses, welches wir mittelst unserer evangelischen Quellenberichte im Allgemeinen von der Entwickelung Jesu und von dem inneren Zusammenhange seiner Anschauungen gewinnen, das Urtheil fällen, dass Jesus zwar keineswegs gleich am Anfange seines Berufswirkens die Nothwendigkeit des Todesleidens, welches er in Wirklichkeit erfuhr, so deutlich durchschaut hat, wie es uns von der Schlusszeit seines Wirkens bezeugt ist, dass andrerseits aber doch der allgemeine Gedanke der Nothwendigkeit seines Leidens nicht erst während des Verlaufes oder am Schlusse seines Wirkens, als ein ganz neues, fremdartiges Moment in den Inhalt seines Bewusstseins hineingetreten ist.

NOTE B, p. 135.

That death presented to Christ precisely the same problem which it presents to every man is an assumption with which many writers start, and which makes the New Testament incomprehensible *ab initio*. Thus Ritschl writes (*R. u. V.* iii. § 48) : 'Die Grundbedingung für die ethische Beurtheilung Jesu ist darin enthalten, dass er, was er überhaupt war und gewirkt hat, in erster Linie für sich ist' (p. 417). And on p. 423 : 'Also sind die Leiden, die er bis in den Tod durch seine Geduld sich sittlich angeeignet hat, Erscheinungen seiner Berufstreue, und kommen *für ihn selbst* nur unter diesem Gesichtspunkte in Betracht.' But, as is observed in the text, the fact that Christ's death can be subsumed under His ethical vocation by no means proves that this vocation is identical with ours. It is in the same line that Dr. E. Caird, in His Gifford Lectures on *The Evolution of Religion*, criticises the Christianity of St. Paul. It has two defects : (1) St. Paul admitted one transcendent miracle as the basis of his faith—namely, Christ's Resursurection. (2) 'While he taught in the most powerful way the lesson of Jesus, the lesson that self-sacrifice is the only way to self-realisation, he yet partly weakened its effect, as the simple exposition of the moral nature of man and the mode of his development, by *making the sacrifice of Jesus essentially different from that which is the ordinary trial of humanity.*' Oddly enough, these two mistakes of Paul—the belief in the resurrection, and in an atoning significance in Christ's death which belongs to it alone—are put forward by the apostle himself (1 Cor. xv. 1-4) as the sum and substance of the only gospel either preached or received in the early church. See *Evolution of Religion,* ii. p. 236.

NOTE C, p. 145.

See *Recht. und Versöhnung,* iii. § 39. Ritschl has great sympathy with an idea of Tieftrunk that pardon and law do not contradict each other when pardon takes place for the law's sake, *i.e.* when the realisation of the universal moral aim, especially love to the law, is impossible without previous forgiveness. God loves even sinners, in respect of their ideal destiny, and it is impossible to see why sin should make this relation inconceivable. It could only do so if sin were in all cases the final and conscious contradiction of God's end. *Unter dem theologischen Gesichtspunkte also findet auch der Zorn Gottes und sein Fluch über die zu versöhnende Sünder keine Geltung; um so weniger erscheint unter diesem Gesichtspunkte eine besondere Vermittelung zwischen dem Zorn und der Liebe Gottes als nothwendig und denkbar, um die Versöhnung der Sünder mit Gott zu erklären* (p. 306).

NOTE D, p. 148.

The two lines of reflection in the Atonement here referred to are stated in the words of Dr. Orr, *Christian View of God and the World,* p. 341.

LECTURE VII

NOTE A, p. 156.

Ritschl's own ideas on the Holy Spirit are to be found in § 61 of the third volume of *Recht. und Vers.* where he treats of Regeneration. It is difficult to find anything in it at once precise and positive, but one sentence may be quoted as fairly comprehensive: Dürfen wir es nun den Sectirern überlassen, sich nach diesen Vorbildern der alten Zeit zu beurtheilen [he is referring to the phenomena ascribed to the Holy Spirit in Romans viii. and 1 Cor. xiv.], so ist es rathsam, in der theologischen Lehre vom heiligen Geist sich auf die Feststellung zu beschränken, dass derselbe als die Kraft der vollständigen Erkenntniss Gottes das Zusammenwirken aller einzelnen in der Gemeinde in dem Vertrauen auf Gott als unsern Vater und in der Ausführung des Reiches Gottes begründet (p. 572).

LECTURE VIII

NOTE A, p. 187.

See Beyschlag's *Neutestamentliche Theologie*, i. 157 f.

NOTE B, p. 181.

The translation of Ritschl's sentence on this page is borrowed from Mr. F. H. Stead. The distinction drawn in it between Church and Kingdom pervades the whole of Ritschl's writings. Cf. in his *Unterricht*, § 81 : Indem die Christen Ecclesia, Kirche, heissen, so wird ihr identisches und gemeinschaftliches Gebet als das wesentliche Merkmal ihrer Einheit aufgefasst. Denn obgleich dieselbe Gemeinde zugleich zur sittlichen Ausführung des Reiches Gottes bestimmt ist, so tritt diese Thätigkeit nicht in directe, sinnenfällig merkbare Erscheinung. Hence 'the presence of the kingdom of God within the Christian Church is always invisible and an object of religious faith.' There is a charming simplicity and candour in Ritschl's Erastianism. He feels that the old defences are not quite sound : Jedoch ist die rechtliche Regierung der Kirche durch die Landesherren als ein selbständiges Annexum ihrer Souveränetät verständlich, weil der nationale Staat wegen der geistigen Wohlfahrt des Volkes die evangelische Kirche als Ganzes erhalten muss, und weil alles öffentliche Recht, welches mit Zwang verbunden ist, in den Bereich des Staates fällt. And a little further on : *Denn einerseits wird es durch die landesherrlichen Kirchenbehörden den Pastoren erspart, ihr Amt auch auf die Verwaltung und Regierung der Gesammtkirche auszudehnen, und dessen moralische Autorität dadurch zu verderben ; andererseits ist es den Landesherren zu zutrauen, dass sie die Eigenthümlichkeit der evangelischen Kirche in Gottesdienst und Lehre achten und ihr nichts aufdrängen, was wider das Evangelium verstösst* (*Unterricht*, § 88).

NOTE C, p. 182.

See Stearns' *Present Day Theology*, chap. vii. p. 121 ff : 'God has not only committed the work of the kingdom to individual Christians; he has also established certain great corporate agencies or institutions, in which individual Christians unite, and through which they accomplish their special tasks. These are what are sometimes called the great "teleological organs" of human society. First among them may be placed the Family and the Church. . . . The Church is often identified with the Kingdom of God. But this is wholly to misapprehend it. It is no more identical with the Kingdom than is the family. It is true that the members of what we not very happily call the invisible church are the same as the subjects of the Kingdom. But there the resemblance ends. The two stand teleologically connected. The Kingdom is the end, and the Church a means to that end ; and it is only one means, though in some respects the most important, alongside of a number of others.' But surely the Church as it appears in Ephesians and Colossians is not a means to another end distinct from itself; and if it were only one means among others, all alike related to the Kingdom as end, those others would figure in the New Testament in the character of such means ; which they certainly do not.

NOTE D, p. 186.

To those who are acquainted with the subject, it will not need to be stated that in its outline of the transformations which the Church, and the conception of the Church, have undergone, this lecture is much indebted to Harnack's *Dogmengeschichte*, vol. i. 243-371 (first edition).

LECTURE IX

NOTE A, p. 205.

A full and lucid account of Professor Robertson Smith's doctrine of Scripture can now be read in *The Expositor* for October 1894 (by Professor Lindsay, Free Church College, Glasgow).

NOTE B, p. 220.

Some of the writers meant are specified in Note A to Lecture I. But the general attitude to Scripture, to which reference is made in the text, prevails far beyond the limits of what could in any proper sense be called the Ritschlian School.

LECTURE X

NOTE A, p. 243.

The reference is to Dr. Orr, who discusses the subject of Future Probation in the last of his lectures on *The Christian View of God and the World*, p. 394 ff.

NOTE B, p. 252.

Dr. Cooper's opinion is given in the Sermon referred to on p. 249. Dr. Plummer's will be found in his work on *The Pastoral Epistles* (Expositor's Bible Series) pp. 325-330. He makes the most of 'the house of Onesiphorus,' but does not rest his whole case on it. 'Is the right, which is also the duty, of praying for the departed limited by the amount of sanction which it is possible to obtain from this solitary passage of Scripture? Assuredly not. Two other authorities have to be consulted,—reason and tradition.' Dr. Plummer finds that they both support his case. That reason does, I have given what seem to me convincing grounds for denying; that tradition does is true; but it is really tradition as part of a whole conception of the future (Purgatory, etc.) which we are bound to reject. Mr. Strong's opinion is given in his *Manual of Theology*, pp. 415-417, and shows a far truer sense of the difficulties of the practice, while conceding, I cannot but think, too much to a mood of feeling which reason and Scripture alike decline to approve.